Tears of the Desert

HALIMA BASHIR

Tears of the Desert

A Memoir of Survival in Darfur

with Damien Lewis

HARPER ● PERENNIAL

Tears of the Desert
Copyright © 2008 by Halima Bashir and Damien Lewis.
All rights reserved.

Published by Harper Perennial, an imprint of HarperCollins Publishers Ltd.

Originally published in Great Britain by
Hodder & Stoughton, an Hachette Livre UK company: 2008
First published in Canada by HarperCollins Publishers Ltd in a hardcover edition: 2008
This Harper Perennial trade paperback edition: 2009

HARPER ● PERENNIAL® is a registered trademark of HarperCollins Publishers.

HarperCollins books may be purchased for educational, business, or
sales promotional use through our Special Markets Department.

HarperCollins Publishers Ltd
2 Bloor Street East, 20th Floor
Toronto, Ontario, Canada
M4W 1A8

www.harpercollins.ca

Library and Archives Canada Cataloguing in Publication

Bashir, Halima, 1979–
Tears of the desert : a memoir of survival in Darfur / Halima Bashir
with Damien Lewis.

ISBN 978-1-55468-179-2

1. Bashir, Halima, 1979–. 2. Sudan—History—Darfur Conflict, 2003—
Personal narratives, Sudanese. 3. Women physicians—Sudan—Darfur—Biography.
4. Rape victims—Sudan—Darfur—Biography. 5. Darfur (Sudan)—Biography.
I. Title.

DT159.6.D27B38 2009   962.404´3092   C2008-908059-9

Printed and bound in the United States
RRD 9 8 7 6 5 4 3 2

For Mo and Raz

And for my beloved father
Rest in peace

Contents

PART ONE
CHILD OF THE DESERT

1. The Naming   3
2. Grandma's Trip to the Lost Valley   15
3. Moon-bone Madness   31
4. Mo, Omer and Me   46
5. The Cutting Time   62

PART TWO
SCHOOL OF THE DESERT

6. School Days   81
7. Fight School   97
8. Resistance for Grandma   111
9. The White Eyelash Attack   126
10. Cousins in Love   139
11. Dream to Be   152

PART THREE
DESERT OF FIRE

12. Medical School   161
13. University of Jihad   177

14. Rumours of War   189

15. Medicine Woman   200

16. Accident and Emergency   212

17. Mission to Mazkhabad   225

18. Rebel Doctor   238

19. Black Dogs and Slaves   249

20. They Come for Me   262

21. A Long-distance Wedding   273

22. The Devil Horsemen   280

23. A Time of Fear   291

PART FOUR
DESERT OF NO RETURN

24. Escape from Darfur   305

25. The Hostel of Despair   316

26. In London, in Love   328

27. Breaking the Silence   336

28. Will to Live   349

Epilogue   357

Glossary   366

ACKNOWLEDGEMENTS

Special thanks to my wonderfully supportive literary agent, Felicity Bryan, and all the staff at her agency. Special thanks to my British publisher, Judith Longman, and all the team at Hodder: from the very start you believed my story had to be told. Special thanks to my German publishers, Carolin Graehl and Hans-Peter Ubleis, and all at Droemer Knaur, for your commitment and boundless enthusiasm. Thanks also to my Italian publisher, Enrico Racca of Sperling & Kupfer, my Canadian publisher, Jennifer Lambert of HarperCollins, and my American publisher, Melody Guy of Random House. Special thanks also to Andrew Nurnberg of Andrew Nurnberg Associates, George Lucas of Inkwell, and Vanessa Matthews of Anne McDermid & Associates. Very special thanks to the following, for reading and commenting on early drafts of this book: Alan and Fran Trafford, Adrian Acres, Eva Lewis and Christine Major. Your words and thoughts were much appreciated. Very special thanks to David Brown, and all at the Aegis Trust, for your tireless work campaigning on behalf of the victims of genocide, regardless of race, colour or creed. Special thanks to Louise Roland-Gosselin, and all at Waging Peace, for your work in Darfur and for the use of the children's pictures. Special thanks to Baroness Caroline Cox, for supporting me in my fight to be recognised as a bona fide refugee. Special thanks to all at my lawyers, White Ryland and Co., for your fine work and support. And very special thanks to my husband, for standing by me in sickness and in health, forever and a day.

A donation from the money earned from this book will be made by the authors to the Aegis Trust (www.aegistrust.org).

AUTHOR'S NOTE

This is a true story. It takes place between the year of my birth, 1979, and the present day. Sudan has been at war for decades; my home, Darfur, has been particularly badly devastated. I have changed some names of people and places, to protect family, friends and communities. I am sure it requires no further explanation as to why such changes were required.

'Use a slave to kill a slave'
A Sudanese proverb

PART ONE

Child of the Desert

1

The Naming

Come here my love,
I have a song for you.
Come here my love,
I have a dream for you . . .

I sing-whisper this lullaby to my boy, my tiny child, as I rock him to sleep in my arms. Outside the window of our cell-like apartment the London traffic roars by. But here we are safe, he and I, this little sleepy miracle that I clutch to myself with a desperate joy in my heart. And as I sing, inside my head I am transported home, home to my beloved Africa.

Come here my love,
I have a kiss for you.
Come here my love . . .

This is the lullaby that my kind and gentle mother used to sing to me, of an evening by the fireside. This is the lullaby that my fierce Grandma Sumah would sing, on those warm African nights when she allowed herself to relax a little, letting her inner love shine through. And this is the lullaby that my wonderful, funny, clever father would murmur in my ear, as he rocked me on his lap and ran his fingers through my hair.

Come here my love,
I have a smile for you . . .

As I sing this song I am in Africa again, enveloped in the loving warmth and security of my family. As I sing this song I am with my tribe again, the Zaghawa, a fierce, warlike black African people who are the most generous and open when welcoming strangers. I am back in the hot, spicy, dry desert air of my village, a child dressed only in dust and happiness, and all in my life is wondrous and good.

I am in my home, with my family, with my people, in my village, in Darfur.

Darfur. I know to you this must be a word soaked in suffering and blood. A name that conjures up terrible images of a dark horror and an evil without end. Pain and cruelty on a magnitude inconceivable in most of the civilised world. But to me Darfur means something quite different: it was and is that irreplaceable, unfathomable joy that is home.

Come here my love,
I have a home for you . . .

I sing this song for my little boy who is not yet one year old, and reflect upon the miracle of his birth – for it gave me the spirit and the will to live. Without you, I tell his shining, sleepy eyes, I would have killed myself from the horror and shame of it all. The darkness would have overcome me, dragged me down into its eager drowning.

We Zaghawa are a fierce, warlike people, and death – violent and bloody and at one's own hand – is far preferable to dishonour and shame. It has always been thus for my tribe.

Come here my love,
I have a hug for you . . .

'You know what rape is?' The face is a mask of hatred – eyes close to mine, his soldier's breath stinking. 'You think because you are a doctor you really know what rape is?'

4

A second soldier lunges at me, pinning me to the floor. 'We'll show you what rape is, you black dog . . .'

'You think you can talk to the foreigners about rape!' a third screams. 'Let me tell you – you know nothing. But in rape we are expert teachers . . .'

'And when we are finished with you we might just let you live,' the first one spits out. '*Then* you can go and tell the world . . .'

I try to block out the memory of it all, but sometimes it is not possible and it comes crowding in on me, dark and suffocating, putrid and evil. I can still see their faces, even now, as if it were only yesterday. Bloodshot eyes, inflamed with hatred and lust. Greying stubble. Unclean breath, the reek of days'-old sweat and unwashed uniforms. A flashing blade as one tries to cut my trousers off me. I kick out, fiercely, aiming for his groin. He cries out in pain, recovers himself and stabs the knife into my thigh. The agony of that knife thrust, and a dead weight bearing down on my bound hands.

Come here my love,
I have a life for you . . .

I hug my little boy close to my pounding, fearful heart. You it is who gave me life, the will to live, the spirit to go on. And because of you – and the countless other women and children who never made it through the horror alive – I am going to sit at this desk in our tiny bed-sit while you peacefully sleep, and I am going to start to write my story.

Come here my love,
I have a story for you . . .

My name is Halima. It is an important name and you must remember it. It is important because my father gave it me seven days after I was born, in the village naming ceremony. In a sense my father saw into the future, for he named me after who and what I was to become.

I was my father's first-born child, and I was his favourite. I know all children say this, but I had an especially close bond with my father. For the first five years of my life I was an only child. I used to long for a brother or sister to play with. But I also knew that when one came along I'd have to share my parents with them, which was the last thing on earth that I wanted to do.

Whenever my father was home I would always be sitting at his side listening to his stories. He'd tell me about the legends of our tribe, the Zaghawa, or about the lineage of our family, which was descended from a long line of tribal chiefs. Or he'd tell me about his work buying and selling cattle, goats and camels, and about his travels across the deserts and mountains of Darfur.

One day when I was very young we were lying on some rugs by the fireside in the centre of our home. In each corner of our fenced compound there was a thatched, circular mud hut: one for the women, one for the men, one for my parents and one for visitors. And in the middle was a thatched wooden shelter with open sides. Here we gathered each evening, lounging around the hearth-fire and gazing up at the bright stars, talking, talking and laughing.

My father was playing a game with me. It is just like the 'This little piggy went to market' game that Westerners play with their children. He took my left hand in his, and traced a circle in my palm: 'The camel's home,' he announced, gazing into my eyes. Then he traced a similar pattern on my forearm: 'The cow's home.' Then higher up: 'The sheep's home . . .' Of course, we'd played this game many times before, and I knew what was coming. I was giggling and trying to pull my arm away and escape.

'The chicken's home . . .' he continued, tracing a hen coop at the top of my arm. And then, as I desperately tried to squidge myself up into a ball, he made a lunge for my armpit. 'And who is this home for?!'

We fell about laughing, as he tickled me and I tried to fight him off. When we tired of the game we leant back on the rugs, losing our thoughts in the dark night sky.

'You – you're my favourite little girl,' my father murmured, as he stroked my hair. 'You brought such luck to our family.'

'But why am I so lucky, Abba?' I asked him. *Abba* is 'Daddy' in our Zaghawa language. I was at that age when I always wanted to know 'why'.

My father went on to tell me the story of my naming ceremony. In our tribe each child's name must be announced within seven days of birth. My mother and father were so proud of their first-born that they invited everyone to the naming ceremony. My father was a relatively rich man in our village, as he owned many cattle, sheep and goats, and dozens of prized camels. My father slaughtered several animals and a feast was prepared for all.

My mother was resting after the birth, and would do so for forty days, as was our tradition. So my fearsome Grandma Sumah rounded up some of the village women to help cook. There were trays piled high with *kissra*, a flat sorghum pancake cooked on a metal plate over an open fire. There were cauldrons overflowing with *acidah*, a thick maize mash. There were bowls piled high with fresh salad, garnished with sesame oil and lemon juice. And there was lots of smoked cattle and goat meat, with hot, spicy sauces.

On the morning of my naming, people came bearing gifts of food or little presents. The women were dressed in *topes*, long robes of a fine chiffon material, decorated with all the colours of the rainbow. The unmarried girls wore the brightest, with flame-red, fire-orange and sunset-pink designs. And the men looked magnificent in their white robes that swathed the body from head to toe, topped off by a twisted white turban, an *immah*.

'You were lying inside the hut,' my father told me, 'a tiny baby at your mother's side. A stream of people came in to see you. But

Grandma Sumah was there, and you know what she's like . . . She had your face covered. "Please can we see the baby's face?" people kept asking. But Grandma just scowled at them and muttered something about protecting you from the Evil Eye.'

The Evil Eye is a curse that all Zaghawa – and many other Muslims – believe in with fervour. With my mother resting, Grandma Sumah was looking after me and she was very superstitious. She didn't want anyone looking at me too closely, just in case they had bad intentions and gave me the Evil Eye.

'She's so beautiful – what name have you chosen?' people kept asking. But Grandma just gave an even darker scowl, and refused to breathe a word.

My father had issued strict instructions. He wasn't prepared to announce my name until a very special person was present – the traditional medicine woman of our village. When she arrived, my father led her to the centre of our house. 'I'm calling my first-born child Halima, after *you*,' he announced. Then he took the medicine woman into the hut so she could bless me.

'But why did you name me after her, Abba?' I asked my father. The tradition in our tribe is to name your children after their grandparents. I'd always wondered where my name had come from.

'Ah, well, that's a long story,' my father replied, his eyes laughing in the warm glow of the firelight. 'And it's getting close to your bedtime . . .'

I knew he was teasing me, and I begged him to tell me the story. Eventually, as was nearly always the case, he relented.

'At first I thought about calling you Sumah, after Grandma,' my father continued. 'But she refused to let me . . .' My father rolled his eyes at me, and I giggled. We both knew what Grandma was like: she'd never agree to anything if she could help it. 'And then I remembered a promise that I had made when I was a young man. One day I was out on a camel rounding up cattle.

The camel stumbled in a dry riverbed and I fell. Some villagers found me lying unconscious, and they were convinced that I was near death . . .'

'But you couldn't die, Abba,' I objected. 'Surely you couldn't?'

My father chuckled. 'Well, nothing they could do would waken me. All the herbs and medicines failed to stir me. They cut me open here.' My father revealed a thick white scar running around his neck. 'They wanted to bleed me and let the infection run out, but it didn't work. Even the *hijabs* that the Fakirs prepared didn't help . . .'

I was amazed. *Hijabs* are potent spell-prayers that the village holy men – the Fakirs – would prepare to protect and heal people. We believe in their power absolutely. If even they had failed, my father must have been very ill.

'It was as if I was determined to die,' my father continued. 'Finally, they took me to Halima, the medicine woman. She treated me for months on end, and nursed me until I was well. She saved my life, of that I'm certain. Anyway, I promised her that I would name one of my children after her. And that's why I named you Halima.'

I felt so happy to learn how it was that I'd been named. The medicine woman was a kindly old lady who often visited our home. She'd search me out, calling to me: 'Come here, come here, little girl who has my name!' She'd give me a hug and pat me on the head. I'd always presumed that she was just happy that we shared the same name – but now I knew the true significance of what it meant for her, for my father and for me.

'But why does that make me *lucky*?' I persisted. He still hadn't explained that part of the story.

My father laughed, and his eyes twinkled like fiery coals. 'You don't miss a thing, do you, Rathebe?'

'Rathebe' was the nickname that my father had given me. There was a famous singer called Dolly Rathebe, and my father had seen her picture during a visit to one of the big towns. She had an unruly fuzz of hair just like mine, and she was a wild, spirited performer. She lived in a country called South Africa, and she sang about the suffering of black Africans at the hands of those who believed they were better than us. For some reason my father thought that I was going to grow up to be just like her.

'On the day of your naming, old Halima was brought into the hut,' my father continued. 'She was the guest of honour, so Grandma allowed her to see your face. She bent close to kiss you and spotted your white eyelash. She may have been old, but her beady little eyes missed nothing. She called me into the hut and pointed it out. She told me that it was a special blessing, and that you would bring luck to all the family. And so it proved . . .'

I put a hand to my face and touched my eyelash. Ever since I was old enough to listen, my parents had warned me that my white eyelash was precious, and that I should never cut it. In Zaghawa tradition a white eyelash signifies good fortune. My father was convinced that the year of my birth was the year that his livestock business had really started to flourish. He'd even managed to buy himself an old Land Rover – the first vehicle to be owned by anyone in our village.

The Land Rover was an old khaki-green thing, half-held together by string and bits of wire. But to us it was like a miraculous apparition from the modern world. When I was older we tried to get my father to sell it and buy a nicer, newer one. But he refused. He had a strong emotional attachment to that Land Rover, he said. He had so many memories bound up in it, and he feared that they would disappear with the car.

My father's name was Abdul, but everyone in our village called him Okiramaj – which means 'the man who has many camels'. It also has another sense – 'he who can do anything'; for the man who has many camels is rich, and capable of many things. He was tall and dark-skinned, with a long, ovoid face. He had a thick, glossy moustache, and I used to think that he was the most hand-some man in the world.

He had two vertical scars on either side of his head, at his temples. He had been cut when just a boy, to mark him out as being from the Zaghawa tribe. These two cuts were also believed to prevent eye infections, and so we called them 'the glasses cuts'.

If you didn't have them people would ask: 'You don't have glasses? Why not? Can you still see well?'

The more scarring a boy endured, the more of a brave warrior and fighter people believed he would be. Some Zaghawa men had clusters of scarring all over their neck and chest, but my father didn't. He came from a long line of tribal leaders, and education and skill at trading were highly valued. He was more a thinking man and a village philosopher. He was slow to anger and quick to forgive, and in all my years he never once raised a hand to me.

My father wore a traditional Zaghawa dagger strapped to his arm just below the shoulder. It had a wooden handle, a silver pommel and a leather scabbard decorated with snakeskin and fine geometric patterns. All Zaghawa men wore one, which meant they were ready to fight if need be. Around his waist was a string of *hijabs* – little leather pouches made by the Fakirs, each with a spell-prayer scribbled on a scrap of paper and sewn up inside.

My father was in his mid-thirties when he married my mother, Bokheta. She was just eighteen and a real beauty. One day he saw her walking through the village, and it was love at first sight. He sought out Grandma Sumah and asked if he might marry her daughter. Grandma was long estranged from her husband, and she and her children had had a hard life. My father was wealthy and Grandma knew him to be a good man. She felt he would make a fine husband for her eldest daughter, and she had readily agreed to the match.

My father and I lay around the fire talking long into the night. He explained to me what an extraordinary day my naming had turned out to be – quite apart from the discovery of my white eyelash. An old man on a camel had arrived at the gates of our home. Although he was a stranger he was invited in, for it was our culture to welcome visitors. But as soon as he clapped eyes on my mother and Grandma Sumah, he flew into a towering rage.

This was Grandma Sumah's long-estranged husband and he had ridden many days to find her. The Zaghawa are divided into three clans – the Towhir, the Coube and the Bidayat. Grandma and Grandpa came from different clans. When Grandma had run away from him, she'd returned to the heartland of her tribe, the Coube. Grandpa lived in the distant lands of the Bidayat, and for all these years he'd been unable to trace her.

Then he had heard of a beautiful young Coube girl in our village, Hadurah. He'd learned that she was marrying a rich and handsome man from the Towhir clan. He traced the family names and was convinced that it was his estranged wife who was involved. And so he had set out on his camel to discover if he had finally tracked down his long-lost family. Upon arrival he had realised that he had, and that his eldest daughter was already married. He'd flown into a rage against my father, drawing his dagger.

'How dare you marry my daughter?' he'd cried. 'Who gave you permission to do so? Certainly not me, and I am her father!'

Before my father could say anything, Grandma Sumah jumped to her feet and whipped out a dagger from her robes. Zaghawa women are not supposed to carry one, and everyone stared at her in open-mouthed amazement. It was fifteen years since Grandma had last seen her husband, but she had no problem recognising him.

'Just you try coming near me!' she yelled, her face like dark thunder. 'Leave me and my children be!'

Needless to say, Grandma's intervention didn't help very much. And when Grandpa discovered that I existed and that the feast was all in honour of my naming, it made matters even worse. Not only had his wife left him and his eldest daughter married without his permission, but his daughter had already given birth to a child. Grandpa demanded that he be allowed to take me back to his village. If my father wouldn't agree, then he would forever curse their marriage.

In Zaghawa tradition the worst one man can do to another is to dishonour him, so my father knew that he had to handle this carefully. He called together the village elders – men of Grandpa's age and older – and they tried to talk him down. They explained that however much everyone regretted it, what was done was done. My father and mother were married, the child was born, and it had been named that very morning.

My father left the elders to talk and returned with a pillowcase stuffed full of money. He handed it to Grandpa, explaining that it was a down payment on the dowry that he would be paying for his daughter's hand in marriage. Better late than never, Grandpa must have decided, for his mood suddenly brightened.

My father slaughtered another cow and announced that it was now a triple celebration: first, for my naming; second, for the discovery of my white eyelash; and third, for the reunification of a long-separated family. The only person who wasn't very happy with the turn of events was Grandma. She refused to say a word to Grandpa. She just stood and stared at him, gripping her knife and testing its edge on her arm.

Grandpa had stayed a day or two before he had to get back to his village. He told Grandma that now he knew where she lived and that she was happy, he could go home with a clear mind. But still Grandma brandished her knife at him and told him to be on his way.

The story of why Grandma had run away from Grandpa was an extraordinary one, my father added. Once he had heard it, it explained a lot about Grandma's fierce nature. But we should keep it for another day. Everyone else had retired to their huts to sleep, and it was time that we joined them.

My father ruffled my sleepy head. 'So, now you know the story of how you got your name,' he told me. 'And who knows, maybe one day you will be a healer – just like the village medicine woman, Halima.'

My father didn't know it, but his words were a prophecy of the future.

2

Grandma's Trip to the Lost Valley

My father was away early, spending the day out in the fields tending to his livestock. Over a breakfast of *acidah* I couldn't get the story of Grandpa and Grandma out of my mind. What had he done to her, I wondered, to provoke her to run away?

I peeked at the smoky hearth. Grandma was staring fiercely into a huge black cooking pot, stirring the *acidah* mash until it reached just the right consistency. For a moment I thought about asking her what had happened, but I dismissed the idea right away. I knew what Grandma was like, having been on the receiving end of countless tongue-lashings and worse. Deep inside her chest beat a heart of gold, but her manner was always stern and fearsome.

I called Grandma 'Abu' – Zaghawa for 'Grandmother'. She was tall and strong, and her round face was framed with plaited hair. In Zaghawa tradition a woman would plait her hair tight to her scalp, with one row running parallel to the forehead, and the rest running backwards to hang down her neck. Grandma had two deep diagonal scar marks on her temples, and the left side of her face was a mass of tiny cut marks. This was the scarring of the Coube clan, and each clan had its own distinctive markings.

We Zaghawa believe that scarring makes women look beautiful. One day Grandma had told me how her mother and grandmother had spent hours doing her cutting, when she was just a little girl. The two cuts to the temples had been made with a razor blade, but the tiny, shallow cuts to the cheek were made with a sliver of sharp stone. I thought it was wonderful, and I was dying to have it done to me when I was old enough.

Grandma loved to wear bright *topes* in all the shades of the rainbow, just as if she were still a young unmarried woman. She was over forty years old, but she was still regal and beautiful, and fit enough for hard work. She wore gold earrings, bracelets and necklaces, decorated with gems of a gleaming red. Some of the jewellery was handed down from her ancestors. Darfur is rich in gold, especially if you go searching deep in the mountains.

I couldn't risk asking Grandma to tell me the story of how she came to leave Grandpa. So I decided to corner my mum and force it out of her. My beautiful mother was considered a bit of a soft touch in our family. She had exactly the same scars as Grandma, and if someone saw them together they'd know from the scars alone that they were closely related. The style and shape of the scarring is specific to the family.

My mother was shorter than Grandma, and a little plump, which was just how Zaghawa men liked their women. Prior to getting married the bride is supposed to eat *damirgha* – a porridge made of durum wheat, milk and yoghurt. The idea is to fatten them up for the wedding day. After giving birth a mother has to lie on her bed for forty days and eat *damirgha*. Once again, the idea is to keep her plump, and to enable her to provide rich milk for the baby.

People used to say that Grandma could never get plump. She was too 'hot' and angry, and this would burn up any food that she had eaten. Even Grandma used to complain about it. 'You'll never be thin like me,' she'd grumble to my mother. 'Your life is too easy and comfortable.' As for me, I resolved to be just like my mother: plump enough to be beautiful, without being incapacitated in any way.

I went to ask my mother why Grandma had left Grandpa. I knew exactly where to find her. She had just given birth, but the baby had died during the prolonged labour. This wasn't uncommon in our part of Africa: like most villages in Darfur, ours had no proper midwife, doctor or nurses. Once the tiny baby had been buried it was quickly forgotten. But my mother still had to lie up for forty days, resting.

Inside her hut it was cool and dark, and it took a moment for my eyes to adjust to the light. I felt my way around the smoothness of the mud wall to my mother's low bed – a simple wooden frame, strung with a latticework of old sacking. The beds were light and easy to carry. During the hot season we would drag them outside and sleep under the stars in the soft breeze.

I shook my mother gently, and she opened her eyes. She'd only been dozing. She smiled. 'What is it, Rathebe?'

I perched on the edge of the bed. 'Why is Grandma so angry, Eya?' *Eya* is Zaghawa for 'Mummy'. 'She's always got a cross face.'

My mother sighed. 'What *has* she been up to this time?'

'Nothing, it's just she *looks* so angry. And you're stuck in here, Daddy's away, and I'm out there with her all the time . . .'

'She's had a hard life, Rathebe, long years spent all alone. She's not a bad person. She's kind within her heart.'

'Well, everyone *says* she's had a hard life, but no one ever tells me *why*. If I knew why, then at least I could feel sorry for her. It's all to do with what happened between her and Grandpa, isn't it?'

My mother gave a little shrug of resignation. 'Well, I suppose you had to know one day.' She pulled me closer, lowering her voice just in case Grandma might be nearby. 'When they were married Grandma and Grandpa went to live in his village, far, far away. They were happy for many years, but one day Grandma discovered that Grandpa had taken a second wife. He'd gone to a faraway place and married a younger woman. Everyone says he did it far away so he could keep his second wife secret from Grandma.'

I smiled to myself. Grandpa had every right to be fearful. No one in their right mind would want to cross Grandma.

'Just as soon as she learned of this Grandma decided to leave him. She told Grandpa's parents that she was going to pay a visit to her home village. She set off with me and my two brothers and just the clothes she stood up in. Grandpa is a rich man, but she left everything when she left him. Then she returned for my young sister, your Auntie Makka. She strapped baby Makka onto her back and was just setting off when Grandpa's relatives stopped her . . .'

'Why? What did they do?' I interrupted, all wide-eyed with curiosity.

'Well, they accused Grandma of spiriting the children away. There was a big fight, and eventually Grandma was forced to leave baby Makka behind. Grandpa's relatives soon realised their suspicions had been right and that Grandma had left for good. They were furious. They decided to keep baby Makka in the house, watching her like hawks. They knew that Grandma would return for her, and when she did they would capture her. But Grandma was too clever for that . . .'

'But what did she do?' I exclaimed.

'Sshhhh! Keep your voice down . . . Four years after she'd run away Grandma returned to the village in disguise. She went to the neighbours' house and gave them some gold. She told them to invite Makka over to play with their daughter. Grandma removed her disguise and your auntie recognised her mum. She spirited Makka away, warning the neighbours not to breathe a word.'

I shook my head in amazement. 'Wow . . . Grandma was tough, even back then.'

My mother nodded. 'She's been like that since the day she was born. When Grandpa's mother came to fetch Makka she was nowhere to be found. She searched everywhere, but finally she realised that Makka was gone. She knew then that Grandma had come in secret for her daughter. She cried and cried for a month . . . She'd lost her daughter-in-law and all of her grandchildren.'

Grandpa was a rich man, and Grandma could have had a very comfortable life with him. In Zaghawa culture it is normal for men to take more than one wife. What Grandma had objected to was *her* husband doing so, and in secret. Grandma was the daughter of a chief, and she had royal blood in her veins. It was the disrespect that she had found unacceptable. Grandma had been forced to bring up her four children alone. None of them had had more than a basic education, as she couldn't afford the school fees.

'Grandma did the right thing,' my mother added. 'She was right to run away – and don't you ever let people tell you otherwise. She did it for us, for the honour of our family.'

Grandma had agreed to my father marrying my mother in part because his father had only ever taken the one wife. He was a relatively rich man and could have had many. But his wife had told him: 'I will give you as many children as you want. I can even give birth to one a year. But you are not allowed to take another wife.' She had proven true to her word: my father had four brothers and eight sisters, so there were thirteen children in all.

By contrast, Grandma's father had taken nine wives. His family grew so large that he couldn't even remember the names of his children. Grandma used to have to join a queue of half-brothers and half-sisters whenever she went to see him. He would ask each the same question: 'Who is your mother?' That was the only way that he could place the child.

Grandma used to laugh and remark upon what a great job her father had done: 'He could raise an army from within his own family,' she boasted. But I think she was just putting a brave face on things. Her running away from Grandpa showed what she thought of men taking multiple wives.

When my father had married my mother he'd built a new house – a *baa* – for them to live in. There were four circular mud huts, each with a central pole supporting the beams and the grass thatch roof. Next to that central pole was a fire hearth. There was one hut for my parents, and a women's hut where Grandma and I used to sleep. Across the way was a men's house, and a hut for visitors.

Out at the back of the yard was a chicken coop. I used to love searching for the hens' eggs. The coop was on two levels. There was a lower roosting area for the hens, and wooden boxes hung from the rafters, which were for pigeons. Most Zaghawa families keep pigeons: they are given as gifts at weddings and births. Grandma used to collect the pigeon droppings and mix the dry powder with oil to make a paste. She'd dab this onto our skin if we had allergies or bad cuts, and often it did seem to help.

The whole of our *bah* – huts, central living area and chicken coop – was enclosed by a fence made of tree branches driven into the ground. The fence was so high that I couldn't see over it. But it was just the right height for a fully grown adult to peer over, and call out a greeting as he or she was passing. When I grew older I was to learn that the fence was mainly for defensive purposes, as there was forever the threat of conflict in our region.

While I was young and still an only child I was never lonely, because the village children were my playmates. Every day I would be out running, jumping and laughing with them. But in the evening I'd be back with my family, listening to my father's stories. In the background I'd hear the cattle lowing, dogs barking and the camels calling to each other. Sometimes I'd catch the distant noise of animals in the forest – the roar of the leopard, the *hjar*, or the ghostly howl of the hyena, which sent shivers up my spine.

Come bedtime I was meant to sleep with Grandma, as an elder should never be left alone. But if my father was away in his fields I'd sneak into my mother's hut. My mother would have found time during the day to cook my father a special dish, which we nicknamed the 'bed-leg'. It was usually a spicy chicken stew, and it was supposed to give the man special power so that he could make fine, strong children.

Each evening it was left at the foot of the bed – hence the nickname. I'd be lying on my little bed, pretending to sleep but peeping across at the clay bowl that contained the bed-leg. I'd savour the delicious spicy smell in the still air of the hut. Eventually, once it really was too late for my father to be coming home, my mother would pass the bowl across to me. I had to pretend that I didn't know what it was.

My mother would tell me it was just some food left over from lunch, and to eat it quietly. I'd open the pot and peep inside. If it was the cold season a fire would be burning in the centre of the hut, to keep us warm. I'd tilt the pot towards the firelight, so I could see to eat. If it was the hot season I'd be sleeping outside, so I could see by the faint light of the stars. Getting to eat the bed-leg was a very good reason to sleep in my mother's hut.

When my father came home from his work travels he'd bring a gift for Grandma – usually a little meat from the village market. Grandma would never eat with my father, or any other men. But she would often prepare him a special homecoming treat: perhaps chicken, boiled and then deep-fried in oil, or lamb smoked over the fire. If I caught Grandma cooking his treat I'd beg her to give it to me instead. But she'd scowl and tell me it wasn't for a lazy, good-for-nothing girl. It was for someone special – my father.

My best friend in the village was called Kadiga. She lived in the house next door and we were the same age. We wore simple clothes – a plain cotton dress, which fell straight from the shoulders to the ankles – and we'd run around barefoot and bareheaded the whole time. We had our hair braided in the same style as Grandma, which we called *beeri*. Grandma used to try to braid my hair, but I much preferred my mum doing it. She was far gentler, and the end result always seemed to be more beautiful.

I actually preferred the *gumbhor* hairstyle of the Fur tribe, a black African people whose lands border those of the Zaghawa. The Fur girls would wear their braids done up in a stiff ponytail. But Grandma told me that all Zaghawa girls had to have their hair done *beeri* style. She referred to the Fur style dismissively as being for *nasarra* – foreigners. But the ultimate sin in hairstyles was the 'Bob Marley', as far as Grandma was concerned, where girls wore their hair in a mass of loose braids.

Whenever Kadiga came round to ask me out to play, Grandma would scold us to cover our heads or else the Evil Eye would get us. But usually we scampered off and ignored her. Kadiga was strong and a good fighter. She and I would stand back to back, whenever we were having a play fight with the other village kids. Her nickname was Sundha, 'the lady with the bright face'. Her complexion was more a golden-red, as opposed to smoky-black like mine, and people used to say that she was the more beautiful.

The men of our tribe preferred lighter, more reddish-skinned women. In fact, they went crazy over anything red. They painted the leather scabbards of their daggers with a bright red dye. They ate meat cooked in a spicy tomato sauce. They even liked to drink Fanta whenever they could, simply because it was red. And people always got married in red. The bride would wear a red *tope*, a red headscarf, red shoes and jewellery encrusted with red gems, and her hands and feet would be painted with red henna.

But I used to tell myself that my black skin was better: it couldn't be damaged by the strong sun and it was the original colour of us Africans. I was far more robust and suited to being here than was Kadiga. I'd tease her that she looked like an Arab, telling her to paint her skin with some black paint. Kadiga would retort that black girls like me had to wear lots of makeup in order to look pretty, whereas her light skin made her naturally beautiful.

Above all else Zaghawa men prized a woman's long hair. Grandma had the longest of any woman I knew, but she'd rarely if ever let it be seen. One day she told me proudly how it took three women five days to prepare it for her wedding. My mother had inherited Grandma's long tresses, but my hair was bushy and uncontrollable, like my father's. Of course, Kadiga had lovely long hair to go with her light skin. Sometimes, I'd jump on her, grab a handful and threaten to cut it all off.

Each week Grandma would take me to the forest to collect firewood. I'd ask if Kadiga could come, for then I'd have someone to play with. Our village was set in the centre of a dry plain, and the only trees around were thorny bushes and spiny acacia. The rivers only flowed in the rainy season, and our drinking water came from a well in the village centre. But two hours' walk away were the foothills of the Jebel Marra – the One Mountain – a range of rocky peaks that are thickly forested and full of wild animals. For us, two hours' walk away was just nearby: Grandma made sure that we were used to travelling such distances on foot.

One day Grandma heard about a place where there was an abundance of firewood. Few people had been there, as it was far away in an isolated spot. Kadiga's family had found the place, and they had nicknamed it the Lost Valley. They spread the word, and that's how Grandma heard about it. This was the way things worked in our village. Life was hard and you'd do all you could to help your neighbours, knowing that they in turn would help you.

As soon as she heard about the Lost Valley Grandma decided to head off on a firewood-gathering expedition. In the early morning Grandma, Kadiga and I loaded up with some peanuts and a couple of old cooking oil bottles filled with water. As we set off on our adventure I knew in the back of my mind that we didn't have to be doing this. We could buy all the firewood we needed from the village market. But Grandma insisted that we should do our chores, just as she had as a child. It hadn't done her any harm and neither would it us.

On the outskirts of the village she stopped to collect the leaves of a weedy plant. Kadiga and I recognised it immediately. Grandma would make *molletah* out of it – mixing the raw leaves with onions, peanuts and lemon juice. It was horrible and bitter, but Grandma insisted that it was very good for you. 'It makes your tummy all clean,' she'd tell us. She had a special bag for gathering *molletah*, one made of old sacking. Whenever I saw her returning with that bag bulging full of leaves I would run to hide in Kadiga's house.

For Grandma, every trip to the forest doubled as a medicine-gathering expedition. She would stop at a certain tree, grab some leaves, crush and sniff them and smile knowingly. 'Good for malaria,' she'd mutter, as she stuffed it into her bag. Sometimes it might be the bark of a tree, or sometimes the roots of a shrub. With one plant, the *birgi*, she'd pull up the whole thing, leaves, roots and all. She'd dry the plant and burn it, mixing the ash with cooking oil to make a kind of paste. For cuts or wounds it did seem to have strong healing properties.

We walked for three hours on a path that wound into the foothills of the Jebel Marra. Finally, we were following tiny tracks made by wild animals, and I was worried that we would lose our way. I was tired and hot and hungry. I kept asking Grandma if we were there yet. Eventually, Kadiga pointed out a cleft in some rocks. On the far side lay a high-walled valley, which was cast into dark shadow. It had a forbidding and ghostly feel to it, and I was hardly surprised that no one had been there collecting firewood. If it wasn't for Grandma's fierce temper, I would have insisted that we turn back.

We passed through the rocky cleft, the forest closing in all around us, thick and black and mysterious. There was no doubting that this was the place: fallen branches were scattered on the ground. Normally, you'd have to search for any wood that others might have missed. Here, you couldn't help but stumble over it. As we gathered up the branches, I kept glancing around myself anxiously. There was an eerie silence and stillness to the place, broken only by the sharp snap of breaking wood and our laboured breathing.

Grandma being Grandma, she lashed together three enormous bundles. It was almost as if she couldn't bear to leave a single branch behind. She told Kadiga and me to roll up our carry-cloths into a thick doughnut shape. The circle of cloth would sit on top of our heads, so cushioning the load. I glanced at Kadiga, and I could see she was thinking the same thing. We had four hours' walk ahead of us with little water remaining, and how on earth did Grandma expect us to carry such enormous loads?

I bent at my knees until I was in a squatting position, holding the cloth doughnut on my head, my fingers raised to receive the heavy load. I heard Grandma grunt as she lifted and lowered it, and then I gripped the rough branches with the tips of my fingers. I tried to straighten my legs and rise, but the load was just too much for me.

'I can't manage it!' I blurted out. 'I can't do it! And neither can Kadiga . . .'

Grandma snorted. 'Rubbish, girl! You think we came all this way for nothing? There's no way we're leaving empty-handed. Either you carry the firewood, or you can stay here!'

Grandma was an expert at scolding us. She'd realised from our worried expressions that we didn't like the Lost Valley very much, hence the threat to abandon us.

'Abba will never leave me in this horrid place!' I retorted. 'You just wait, he'll come and find me . . .'

Grandma threw up her hands in horror. 'Your father! He spoils you! You just listen to me: you're carrying that bundle whether you like it or not. Or do I have to get one of those sticks and beat you?'

Grandma was far too smart to leave it at threatening us. Instead, she took my bundle down, removed two of the smaller branches and then tried telling me that it was far lighter than before. She grabbed some dry grass and wove it into two doughnut shapes, so that Kadiga and I had extra padding for our heads. And finally, she made us a promise. Once we reached home she would cook us our favourite food. That could mean only one thing – *libah*. I was hungry and thirsty already, and my mouth watered at the very thought of it.

Libah is made from the milk that a nanny goat gives to a newborn calf – the colostrum. It is boiled for several minutes until it becomes like thick rice pudding, and it has a taste like sweet cottage cheese. Facing a mixture of Grandma's threats and her promises of *libah*, Kadiga and I were convinced to take up our bundles and walk.

I'd been taught to carry things – pots of water, firewood, bowls of fruit – on my head from the earliest age, so it was like second nature to me. But retracing my steps on the winding path while carrying that enormous load took all of my skill and strength. I had one hand steadying the bundle, another steadying myself, and my eyes flickered from the ground to the wall of branches up ahead, searching for a way through.

All of a sudden there was an ear-piercing screech to one side of me, and the branches erupted in a blur of something dark moving fast and powerfully towards me. I let out a cry of terror, dropped my bundle and fled. It wasn't unusual for us girls to be out collecting firewood, but we knew that if we were attacked by wild animals, or worse, then we should run for our lives back to the village. That's what my parents had always drilled into me.

My terrified feet flashed along the path, sharp branches and thorns tearing at my clothes and my flesh. I flailed with my arms to clear the way. My heart pounded in my head as I ran. I became aware of Kadiga's presence just behind me. I stole a glance over my shoulder: there was my best friend running for her life and equally wide-eyed with fear. Behind her I caught a fleeting glimpse of something dark and shadowy flitting through the trees. I turned back to the path and ran and ran.

I was petrified. I was convinced that the dreaded *agadim* was after us. According to Grandma the *agadim* was the size of a large dog, was covered with coarse black hair, and would jump on your neck and bite you. It was the threat of the *agadim* that Grandma would use to frighten me if ever I wanted to go out at night. I'd never seen an *agadim*, and I wasn't even sure they really existed – but if they did then the Lost Valley was sure to be the place to find them.

As I ran and ran I heard a cry from behind me. It was Grandma, and she was yelling for us to stop. She sounded very angry indeed. We'd just reached the narrow rocky opening that led out of the Lost Valley. As we raced towards it Kadiga and I glanced at each other, the same thought going through our minds. Which was more terrifying – the Thing back there in the forest or an enraged Grandma Sumah? We must both have reached the same conclusion, for we stopped running and collapsed, panting, against the cold of the rock walls.

Behind us, Grandma came labouring up the path, one enormous bundle of wood perched on her head and another tucked under each arm. She threw down the bundles in front of us and proceeded to give us a severe tongue-lashing. Had it not been for the fact that she needed us in good physical shape to carry the wood, I'm sure she would have beaten us too. The Thing turned out to have been a large owl – completely harmless, but terrifying when seen out of the corner of one's eye racing out of the shadows.

Humbled by the owl incident, Kadiga and I took up our bundles once more. Two hours later we emerged from the forest and found ourselves on the edge of some farmland. We were exhausted and parched. The sun beat down from a merciless sky, and still we were barely halfway home. With each step my head-load felt heavier and heavier, my body increasingly drained. Inwardly I was cursing Grandma. She had overloaded us and starved us of food and water. Why did she make us do such things?

Just when I felt I couldn't go another step Grandma brought us to a halt. 'There,' she announced. 'What are you complaining for – I told you I'd find water.'

I looked where she was pointing. A shallow irrigation ditch ran down the nearside of the field, and it was half-full of stagnant water. Normally, I would never have dreamed of drinking it. The water from the village well was sparkling clear. But in my present state I barely hesitated. I stumbled down the bank and knelt at the water's edge. With one hand I brushed aside the slimy scum, and with the other I scooped and drank greedily. The water was warm and brownish, and it tasted of dust and earth. Even so, it was delicious relief.

Before long Grandma was scolding us to be on our way again. I wasn't sure if she'd bothered to drink herself, and it struck me then that she seemed totally indestructible. Was there nothing that could tire or frighten her? When we finally stumbled into our yard – hot, dusty, covered in scratches and with torn clothing – I was too tired to notice my father's Land Rover parked outside the gate. He had just got home from the fields.

We dropped our bundles with a resounding crack. The relief of doing so made me feel as if I was weightless and floating several inches above the ground. Kadiga and I went and collapsed onto the rugs in the living area, while Grandma bustled off to her hut to prepare our treat. She'd promised us some *libah* and we were going to get some, with extra sugar to replace our lost energy. Whether we'd actually stay awake long enough to eat it was quite another matter.

I felt my eyelids drooping, but just then I heard my father's raised voice. He was clearly angry, which in itself was a rare thing.

'You sent them all that way *to collect firewood?* Why? Look at them, the state of them. They're finished. You know how far it is? Anything could've happened . . .'

My father was complaining to my mother. He would never tackle Grandma directly, as she was the elder of the family and to be respected. He pointed out that there were men who made a living from fetching firewood with a donkey and cart. Each morning they would pass by calling out, '*Orwa! Orwa!* – Firewood! Firewood!' Why hadn't my mother got one of them to bring her a cartload?

I'd heard my father making the same argument before, about water. Grandma was forever dragging me off to the village well. We'd queue for hours, most of which time I'd spend playing in the mud with the other children. Grandma would fill up two big pots. While mine was smaller than hers, it didn't bear any relation to our relative size. But when I pointed this out, Grandma told me that I had young bones and muscles, so I should stop complaining.

There was a man in our village who had an old oil tank mounted on a creaky donkey cart. He'd fill up with water at night, when the well was deserted, and come around in the morning, banging a stick on the metal drum. When you heard that noise you knew the water-seller was passing, and you could cry out for him to stop. There was a hole in the back of the oil drum sealed with a length of inner tube. From there he'd use his standard water container, a *koii*, to measure out the amount of water you wanted.

My father just couldn't understand why we didn't buy our water from the water-seller. It was almost as foolhardy as Grandma dragging us off to the forest to collect firewood. Once he'd finished telling my mum off, she went to have a word with Grandma. Grandma had just handed Kadiga and me our *libah*. It was hot and sweet and delicious. In fact it was so nice that I almost forgave Grandma for taking us on such a horrid journey. That was

Grandma's great gift, of course: in the space of a few hours she had shown us the harshness of life, before treating us to its kinder side. In that way, I learned to better appreciate our family's good fortune.

'Abba Abdul isn't very happy . . .' my mother began, but Grandma held up her hand to silence her.

'You think I don't know? Let me tell you something: my father was a wealthy man, but still we had to work hard and do the chores. He used to say to us: "One day, all of this may be gone, and then you will have to know how to survive." You think our fortunes won't ever change? You think we will always be blessed with peace and prosperity?'

'No, but all that way to this Lost Valley . . .' my mother began, before Grandma cut her off again.

'Where we went is none of your business. But if your daughter doesn't learn to work, how will she ever get a husband? And when she does miraculously find one, you want her to be divorced because she's never learnt the meaning of hard work?'

With that my mother fell silent. In Zaghawa culture, there was nothing worse than the thought that your daughter might fail to find, or keep, her own Zaghawa man.

3

Moon-bone Madness

The Zaghawa tribe is renowned for its independent warrior spirit and its strong sense of identity. Our people are spread across the Sudan–Tchad border region, in what is present-day Darfur. But for centuries this area was the ancient African kingdom of Kanam, a vast land ruled by Zaghawa chiefs. The kingdom lasted for hundreds of years, during which time our language remained a purely verbal form of communication.

The first attempt to write it down wasn't made until 1986, when a scholar used the symbols with which the Zaghawa brand their cattle to form a basic alphabet. Today, each of the Zaghawa clans – the Towhir, the Coube and the Bidayat – has its own dialect. The dialect I spoke as a little girl was closest to Coube, because Grandma came from that clan line.

My father was proud of our Zaghawa history, and especially our resistance against the British. He was forever telling me about how we had never been conquered by the *khawajat* – the white men. There were fierce battles between the Zaghawa warriors and the British soldiers. One day, the British commander decided it was time to crush the Zaghawa once and for all. He set out in a fleet of armoured cars, carrying guns. En route other tribes fled from these terrifying mechanical monsters, as they saw them.

The Zaghawa chief called together his finest warriors and rode out on horseback to meet the enemy. The British commander was impressed by the Zaghawa chief's warrior spirit and his arrogant bearing. The Zaghawa chief pointed at the armoured car. 'What is this?' he demanded. 'Does it need food? Does it eat? Does it drink? Does it die?' The translator relayed the Zaghawa chief's words. The British commander smiled. 'No,' he replied. 'It is like an iron horse. It doesn't need any of these things, and it will live forever.'

The Zaghawa chief proposed an exchange: they should swap his horse for the armoured car. The British commander replied that he would need a whole army of horses of the flesh to swap for his iron one. Now it was the turn of the Zaghawa chief to laugh. The Zaghawa chief and the British commander sat down to negotiate a deal, and in the process of doing so they settled upon an historic peace accord. In this the Zaghawa retained control over their lands, but they agreed to support the British in their battles against other rebellious tribes.

Our fiercely independent nature didn't mean that we Zaghawa were hostile to other tribes or races. If they came in peace, we would welcome strangers as honoured guests. It was inconceivable for a Zaghawa to refuse hospitality, just as it was inconceivable to eat alone. Eating alone was considered a sin, and it was as bad if not worse than living alone. And it was better to be dead than to be bereft of one's family.

At meal times we would call out to the neighbours in our *gini* – our little hamlet – 'Have you eaten yet? Come, come and eat with us! You can't eat alone!'

We believe that the bigger the group that is eating, the bigger your appetite will be. We eat off one big tray set in the centre, each person taking food with their right hand and throwing it into their mouth. We'd sit outside in the fresh air, eating milk fresh from the cow, meat fresh from the animals and vegetables fresh from the gardens. In our village eating was a celebration of good food, good company, good conversation and good health.

My favourite food was *acidah*, the thick maize-flour mash. It was delicious with *mullah*, a spicy meat stew. But it was best when mixed with a dark powder called *kawal*. Grandma used to make this using the leaves of a particular tree. She'd place them in a clay bowl along with some water and spices, and leave the mixture in a hole in the ground for several days. When she took out the gooey mush it smelled horrible. But once it was dried and ground into a powder, it had a rich, meaty aroma.

For breakfast I loved *acidah* with fresh yoghurt. Yoghurt-making was another of my chores. Each evening Grandma would take me to the fields to milk the cows. I'd perch on a low stool and grab the back leg of the nearest animal, holding it tight between my knees. I'd place a clay bowl under the cow, take two of the teats and start pulling and squeezing at the same time. If my hands got tired I'd ask Grandma to take over.

I'd pour the warm, frothy-fresh milk into a *tagro*, a gourd with a hole cut in it. I'd pop a cork into the top, and hang the *tagro* from the rafters of Grandma's hut. Three or four days later I'd take it down and start to shake, shake, shake. Eventually, the milk would separate into a thick layer of butter, with the thinner yoghurt beneath. The longer I shook, the more butter we'd have.

In the same field as the cows we kept our goats and a donkey. Grandma was very proud of her herd of goats, and she'd get so excited if one of the nannies was about to give birth. She would sell off the young kids to earn herself a little private income, or keep them to fatten for the pot. I loved the goats when they were alive, but I hated having to eat them. They were so cute and so cuddlesome, and the meat seemed to me to be hairy, somehow, even after the goat had been skinned.

One day Grandma became so angry that she wanted to cry. Three of her goats had fallen ill, and she had to get a man to slaughter them. They must have been poisoned by something, but we had no idea what it might be. Grandma argued that they had probably eaten some plastic bags, which had bunged up their insides. Goats would eat just about anything. But I was worried that they'd been poisoned by something really dangerous, and if Grandma made us eat them then we'd all die.

Of course, Grandma was having none of it. She gutted the animals and each turned out to have a horribly twisted intestinal tract. Normally, we'd eat the liver, kidneys and parts of the intestines fried with spices, as a delicacy. But even Grandma relented when she saw the state of the goats' innards. She threw them out for the village dogs.

She skinned the animals and jointed up the meat. There was too much for our family alone, so she gave some to the neighbours – but she didn't breathe a word about how the goats had died. The remainder of the meat she soaked in fermented sorghum flour, which has a strongly bitter flavour. She argued that this would kill off any poisons that might remain. Grandma fried the goat meat and added lemon juice, watching over me with a big stick as I ate my share.

I survived eating Grandma's poisoned goat meat with no obvious ill effects, and shortly thereafter my baby brother was born. I was five years old at the time, and the first I saw of him was a tiny wrinkled face all wrapped up in a white bundle. Like all firstborn Zaghawa males he was named Mohammed, after the Holy Prophet of Islam.

Baby Mohammed grew up shockingly fast, and in no time at all his true nature began to show. He had inherited my father's generosity and calmness and my mother's gentle softness – and none of Grandma's warlike spirit and argumentative ways. As a toddler he spent his time making shapes from clay and playing quietly in the yard. He was open-hearted and kind. If my father gave him some sweets, Mohammed would share them. If my father gave him some money, he would pass it to Grandma to look after.

My little brother quickly became my mother's favourite. As night settled over the village and oil lamps were lit in people's homes, I knew the competition for the best sleeping place was about to begin. Especially during the cold season, we both wanted to sleep with our mother but Mohammed was always the one invited into her bed. As a consolation Grandma would stoke up the fire in her hut and allow me to sleep by her feet – which was hardly the same as cuddling up to my mother.

Once he was old enough Mohammed started to venture outside to play, but it almost always ended in tears. He'd come crawling back in, wailing: 'That boy, that boy, he beat me!' One day he was out playing when he was set upon by some boys from the Fur tribe. They stole his toy aeroplane, ripped his clothes to shreds and beat him soundly. He came home with his face streaked in mud, and covered from head to toe in dust and scratch marks. He stumbled through the gate, half-blinded by his tears.

Grandma Sumah was the first to spot him. 'Mohammed! Mohammed! What happened? And where's your plane?'

'The Fur boys . . .' he wailed. 'They beat me . . .'

'WHAT? You let the Fur boys beat you? But you are Zaghawa – why didn't you fight them?'

'I tried to,' Mohammed sobbed. 'But there were four . . .'

Grandma knew just where those Fur boys lived. Their family had a house on the outskirts of the village. With barely a moment's hesitation she scooped up Mohammed, grabbed me by the hand, and we set off to seek our revenge. The Fur boys saw us coming and they scampered inside their house, slamming shut the gate. But that didn't stop Grandma. She hammered on the gate with her fist, demanding that they open up. When they refused, she flew into a burning rage.

'Come out!' she screamed. 'Come out and fight! Come and fight like men, you Fur cowards!'

Still the Fur boys refused to open up. The fence was over a metre and a half tall, but Grandma wasn't going to let that stop us. She lifted me up and dropped me on the far side. I was around six years old at the time, so I was considerably bigger than the

Fur boys. Even so, I was outnumbered, and as soon as they saw me they came running. Quick as a flash I unhooked the gate, just as the first of the Fur boys tried to slam it shut. By then it was too late, as Grandma set her shoulder against it and forced it open.

She burst into the yard, her eyes blazing like angry coals. The Fur boys fled to a distant corner, where their mother was preparing some food. Grandma marched up to them in a towering fury. The Fur lady tried asking what her sons might have done, and to apologise, but Grandma simply ignored her. She grabbed three of the Fur boys and started to beat them, while I jumped on the fourth. I can't remember if we managed to get Mo's toys back – but it was a good fight and Grandma won the day.

My father was reluctant to buy us any new toys, especially if they were just going to get stolen from Mo. As a result, we had to make our own entertainment. My favourite game was chasing my father's Land Rover. When it chugged away in the morning it would take a while to pick up speed, which meant we could jump onto the rear bumper. Kadiga, Mo and I would hold onto the canvas-covered back for dear life, while trying to stifle our giggles.

Eventually, someone would call out to my father that he had a bunch of unwanted passengers. He would slow to a stop and come round to check, only to discover us kids hanging there. My father always found it too funny to get angry or to punish us properly. We'd run back home, and on the way we'd stop to play the shadow game. I'd stand in the sun and make my body into an animal shape, or the shape of a teapot, and Kadiga and Mo had to guess what I was simply by looking at my shadow.

We'd make rag dolls from old clothes stuffed with straw. We'd roll up a sausage of straw and sew it into a length of cotton, tying it into leg and arm shapes. Then we'd sew those into the shape of a human body. If it was a man we were making, we'd use our own hair to give him a short head of fuzzy hair. But if it was a woman, then we'd try to find something longer and softer, like some sheep's wool.

There was always a bag of our hair hidden in the rafters of Grandma's hut. Each evening, she would comb and oil my hair, to keep it shiny and healthy. She would collect all the combings, and when the bag was full she would bury the hair in the yard. Grandma was forever warning me of the danger of letting others get hold of my hair. If you wanted to curse someone there were evil Fakirs who could do this for you, but they would first ask for some of the person's hair to 'work' the curse onto.

Once we'd made our rag dolls, we'd need cars for them to drive and houses for them to live in. We made them out of clay. We'd mould a car, complete with a roof, windows and wheels, and leave it in the rafters of the hut directly over the fire until it was baked hard as iron. Or sometimes we'd made *herdih* – horses – for the rag dolls to ride. We'd place a man on the horse's back, and a spear in his hand made out of a fine sliver of wood.

I'd make a warhorse for Mohammed, one for Kadiga and one for me, and then we'd ride forth to fight the other children. We'd have one row of clay horses with rag doll warriors facing another, and on the order to attack the ranks would advance. 'To War! To War!' we'd shout, although little Mo never sounded quite as enthusiastic as we girls did. Each side's horseman would pick an opposing horseman to fight. Of course, the clay horses would eventually break, and the last one left standing would be declared the winner.

Often, it would take us several days to make replacement horses. Water was in limited supply, and Grandma used to grumble that it was for drinking, not for making playthings. I'd have to wait until no one was around and then scoop up a bowlful, hoping that Grandma wasn't watching. If that failed, we'd head down to the village well to see if we could scrape up enough mud from around there. But there were usually several other children with the same idea, so the competition was fierce.

My favourite game of all was the 'moon-bone' game. I used to keep one of Grandma's goat's thighbones hidden in the rafters of the hut. Of an evening when the moon was full I'd run out into the yard and cry out: '*Keyoh adum jaghi gogo keyh!* – Come and play the moon-bone game!' It was as if all the neighbourhood kids had been just waiting to hear those words. At the centre of our hamlet was an open area similar to an English village green. Crowds of children would rush down there, their parents bringing tea and milk and hot snacks.

It was so nice to be out under the bright moon, enjoying the cool of the night without needing oil lamps to lighten our way. The children would line up in a row, with their backs towards me, and I'd throw the goat's thighbone as far as I could. Then I'd yell out, 'Start!' Everyone would go racing off searching for the bone. It would be lying in the grass somewhere, glistening blue-white in the silvery moonlight. Whoever found it would cry out: 'I've found the treasure! I've found the treasure!' and then race back to the starting point.

Of course, all the other children would be trying to snatch the bone out of their hands, so this is when the game became really fun. Sometimes there'd be a huge pile-up, as one child dived on whoever had found it and everyone else jumped on top of them. Parents would be watching and laughing and yelling out excitedly. I could hear my father calling out his support for me, and that always spurred me on to win.

What I loved most about the moon-bone game was its total unpredictability. The main advantages you might have over the others were speed, and skill at fighting. And for some reason – most likely Grandma's influence – I seemed to excel at both. Once the others realised what a tough, merciless fighter I was, they seemed to hold back from tackling me. Whenever I won, my mother would cook me some *fangasso* – sweet doughnuts, deep-fried in oil. I'd eat them finger-scalding hot and dipped in milk.

But, of course, life could never be one long episode of fun and games. Shortly after our fight with the four Fur boys I landed myself in some real trouble. As ours was a Muslim village there was supposed to be no alcohol, but there were always people who broke the rules. A handful of women specialised in making sorghum beer – *goro*. They couldn't do so openly, but they had private drinking dens in their homes. We could always tell which men were their best customers, because drinking *goro* made them have big, bulbous stomachs.

The location of the beer dens was communicated by word of mouth. Some of the beer women had the reputation for making good strong brews, but others would water it down. The drinkers would gather together, sitting on a rug on the floor or on little stools. The beer women would serve big trays of smoked lamb, and *goro* by the half-gourd. Often the men would drink too much and it would end in a big fight. The beer women made certain that they only ever had cheap furnishings, as everything would get smashed up.

Everyone knew who the beer women were. The only people they could really socialise with were other beer women. Sometimes the village Imam would speak with the men who drank, warning them that they were terrible sinners. The Imam tried arguing that both the beer and the money earned from selling it were *haram* – forbidden. But more often than not the beer women were single mothers or widows. They would argue that they had no way to survive other than by selling their beer.

One evening I went around to Kadiga's house to ask her out to play. I noticed a group of men sitting around laughing and drinking. They were Kadiga's uncles and cousins. We knew that some of Kadiga's family were drunkards, and Grandma had warned me to avoid them. The men believed that beer made you fat, healthy and strong, and so they were not averse to slipping the odd bowlful to their children.

One of Kadiga's uncles held out a bowl to me. 'Come! Come! Try some,' he called. 'It's good for you. It'll make you grow into a big strong girl.'

Of course, I'd never had any and I was curious. After a moment's hesitation I took the bowl. I raised it to my lips, but the sweet fermented smell made me gag. I steeled myself, as all the men were watching me now. I took a gulp. It had a lumpy consistency and a bittersweet taste. It wasn't very nice, but it wasn't totally disgusting, either. I knew that I'd never get the chance to drink any at home. I'd watched people drinking, and they seemed happy – chatting and laughing together – so I thought that maybe it was a good thing.

I drained the whole bowl. The first sensation that came over me was drowsiness. I forgot all about playing with Kadiga and made my way unsteadily home. With barely a word to anyone I went to bed and fell into a deep sleep. I awoke late the following morning feeling totally awful. I had a terrible headache, I couldn't open my eyes and I felt nauseous. At first my mum was worried, but once she got close enough to smell my breath she became suspicious.

'You were at Kadiga's house, weren't you?' she demanded. 'Did you drink any beer?'

I felt so bad that I didn't even have the energy to lie. I nodded. 'I did. But please don't be angry. I feel so horrible.'

My mother's faced clouded over. She disappeared, and a second later she was back with a big stick. Suddenly she was beating me on my legs and crying out – how many times had I been warned that I was never, ever to drink any beer? It wasn't the pain of the blows that shocked me, it was the very fact that my mother was beating me. I was used to that from Grandma, but not from my gentle mother.

In an instant my hangover was forgotten, and I ran towards Grandma to escape.

'What? What is it?' she cried, jumping to her feet. 'What's happened?'

Before I could answer, my mother cried out that I'd been to Kadiga's house and that I'd been drinking beer. In an instant Grandma had me caught in her iron grip.

'What? You went there, to that drunkard house? *To drink beer?*'

Grandma proceeded to give me my second, and much more fierce, beating of the morning. So rarely did my mother hit me that just as soon as she'd raised that stick to me I knew I'd committed a big wrong. But Grandma's beating was only to be expected. Grandma used to beat us regularly, and mostly we used to think that we were getting what we deserved.

As with many things in our culture, the taboo on drinking was enforced much more strictly against the women than the men. I knew that my father occasionally drank sorghum beer. He had a group of friends who would call and take him away to one of the secret drinking dens. One day I overheard my mother quarrelling with him about it.

'Why d'you go drinking with those people?' she demanded. 'They're no good. They just use you for your car and money. Shame on you – you should be thinking first of your family.'

'But they're my friends and I like being with them,' my father objected. 'And anyway, we don't go *drinking* . . .'

My mother snorted in derision and turned her back on him.

Whenever those friends came to call, she would tell them that my father wasn't in. But then they'd point out that they'd seen his car outside. My mum would roll her eyes and give them the silent treatment. Finally my dad would come strolling out of his hut, welcoming his friends with smiles – and they'd head off to have a nice time drinking sorghum beer together.

Most Zaghawa women objected to their men drinking. They

41

would go out with a pocketful of money and come back broke. In our culture men didn't worry much about the cost of living. Nearly everything was freely available: meat, sorghum, milk, salad, vegetables, fuel, water – none of these things had to be paid for. So they didn't see what the problem was if they spent their money on beer.

The women did most of the work, and the men believed that the more wives they had, the easier life would be. A man with only one wife might be laughed at by his friends: they'd say he was like a man with only one eye. If a woman's husband died, one of his brothers was duty bound to marry her – so as to keep the children in the one extended family. Such customs might seem barbaric to outsiders, but to us that was the way things had always been. Our identity as Zaghawa was defined by such traditions.

One day Grandma decided that it was time Mo and I had our traditional Zaghawa scarring done. She had everything ready in her hut – a bowl of hot water, a razor blade and some paste made from *birgi* ash mixed with oil. She told my mother to go and fetch Mo and me, as she had 'a treat' in store for us. But as soon as I was in her hut I took one look at the shiny razor blade, the ash paste and the bowl of water, and I just knew that I didn't want this scarring done to me. I turned and ran.

'Don't let her escape!' Grandma yelled. 'Catch her! Catch her!'

My mother grabbed me and tried to hold me down, but I was struggling and fighting like a wild animal. I could sense that her heart wasn't really in it, so I twisted and broke free and darted out of the hut. I made a run for the gate, as Grandma cried out for someone to close it. But I was through in a flash. I ran and ran as fast as my legs would carry me, and I didn't stop until I was on the far side of the village.

I made my way to a friend's house.

'Why've you come alone?' her mother asked, in surprise. 'What happened?'

'Nothing,' I lied. 'It's just my mum said that I could. Where's Shadia? Can she come out to play?'

I spent all day playing with Shadia. When the sun went down I told her mother that I was scared of the dark, so I didn't really want to go home. Could I stay there for the night instead? Of course, Shadia's mum knew then that something was wrong, and she insisted on taking me home. As soon as we walked in through the gate Grandma started scolding me, and she told Shadia's mother exactly what I had done.

When I caught sight of little Mo I knew that I'd been right to run away. He had angry red cut marks on his face, and they were packed out with the grey ash paste. He was tearful and confused, and he kept trying to touch the wounds. He had a sad and bewildered expression, as if he was wondering why on earth they had hurt him. He was barely two years old, and he was far too weak and gentle to run away.

I knew that from then on I had to give Grandma's hut a very wide berth, or else she would get me. But Grandma was much too clever to make a big deal out of it, and she quickly pretended that it was all forgotten. She kept on trying to entice me into her hut, but that only served to make me more suspicious.

'Why don't you come to my hut, my darling?' she'd say. 'I've got a lovely treat for you.'

I'd scowl at her. 'No! No way! I know what you're up to – you're trying to cut me!'

A few months later Bakhita, one of Grandma's best friends, came to visit. Grandma called me over, telling me that Bakhita had a present for me. I went to her hut all smiles, as I had forgotten what had happened previously. But as soon as I stepped inside Grandma grabbed me, and instantly I knew what they were up to.

Grandma imprisoned me on her lap in a vice-like grip. I was screaming and fighting like a wild cat as Bakhita came at me with the razor blade. She tried to make the first cut to my left temple, but I kicked her away with my legs. As she fell backwards the razor blade sliced into my cheek, right next to my nose. I felt the warm blood trickling down my face. I sank my teeth into Grandma's arm, biting down as hard as I could, while thrashing around with my legs so that Bakhita couldn't get near me.

'I can't do this!' Bakhita cried. 'She's like a madwoman!'

'You have to do it!' Grandma yelled back at her. 'You have to do it!'

'Look, how can I, with her going crazy like this? It's impossible. I'll end up hurting her.'

I still had my teeth sunk deep into Grandma's arm, as the two of them proceeded to argue it out. Grandma hadn't so much as flinched: to do so would have been to acknowledge that I was hurting her. Eventually, once I had landed a few more good kicks on her, Bakhita threw down the razor blade and refused to go on.

Grandma turned on me. 'Cowardly girl!' she spat out. 'Where is your bravery? *Your bravery!* Don't you know you are a Zaghawa? A Zaghawa! Coward!'

I ran to my mum's hut in tears, although secretly I was happy that I'd escaped.

'Why is Grandma so horrible?' I sobbed. 'She's always beating us and trying to hurt us. Look what she's done now!'

My mum took me in her arms, and tended to my cut face. Then she went to have words with Grandma.

'Look, she's got a very hard head, has this one. She won't listen and she won't obey. Don't try to cut her again. There's no point, and you really might hurt her.'

Grandma didn't object. As far as she was concerned she'd washed her hands of me. But when my father came home that evening and saw what they'd done, he became so angry. I told my father not to get too upset: I'd fought them off and escaped once more

– they'd hardly managed to cut me at all. And now Grandma appeared to have given up trying to do so once and for all.

That seemed to improve his temper no end. He held out his arms to me, singing softly:

> *Come here my child,*
> *I have a hug for you . . .*

He took me on his lap, ruffled my hair and gave me a kiss on the top of my head. 'While I'm here no one can do anything to hurt you. You're safe here with me.'

Of course, my father meant every word that he said.

But no man is invincible, no matter how much a little girl might wish him to be so.

4

Mo, Omer and Me

One day my mother awoke with a terrible pain in her ear. We were worried that an insect might have crawled inside during the night. Grandma inspected the ear and concluded that we had to pour in some hot sesame oil to force the insect to crawl out. My mother lay down on Grandma's bed. Grandma heated up the oil, tested it with her finger, and when it was just right she poured a little inside. She asked how it felt, and my mother said it was quite nice, sort of warm and soothing.

Grandma proceeded to pour in enough oil to fill up my mum's ear, and then we sat and waited. And we waited and waited and waited. Finally, Grandma had to concede that no insect had come crawling out. There was only one thing stronger than sesame oil, Grandma said, and that was petrol. I'd never heard of anyone having petrol poured into their ear, but Grandma insisted it would do the job.

She went to fetch the can of petrol that my father used for his Land Rover. My father had warned me about that petrol can – it was dangerous, and I wasn't allowed to touch it. I wondered if it really was the right thing to be pouring into my mother's ear. It was meant for the Land Rover, a machine, not for people. Grandma returned with the heavy metal can. She unscrewed the lid and poured a little of the liquid into a clay bowl. As she did so, my nose caught the rich, heady fumes.

'D'you really think it's good for Mummy's ear?' I ventured.

Grandma glared at me. 'It's strong enough to move that big

46

car, isn't it? So it must be better than sesame oil. Or do you have a better idea?'

I shook my head. 'No.'

'Well then, keep quiet. Who's the medicine person around here, anyway? If you had your way we'd leave your poor mother to die . . .'

Grandma warmed the bowl of petrol over the fire, and poured a goodly dose into my mother's ear. We stood back, holding our breath as we watched. For a second or so nothing happened, and then my mother started to splutter and cough horribly. An instant later she was heaving and clutching at her throat, her face a vivid red colour. She kept trying to choke out some words, but her voice came out as a breathless, strangled croak.

I grabbed my mum's arms, which were shaking violently, and put my ear close to her. 'Water! Water!' she rasped.

I rushed out of the hut and grabbed a bowl of water. I watched in mounting panic as my poor mother gulped it down, and an instant later it all came up again. My mother clutched at her stomach and her throat in agony. All that day she lay on the bed getting steadily weaker. Her breath came out in short, wheezing gasps, and nothing would stay down. I was worried that she was going to die. It was terrifying.

When my father came home that evening he was beside himself with anger. He kept marching up and down the yard, cursing under his breath. 'Stupid woman! Stupid woman! That stupid, stupid woman.' He meant Grandma, of course, but I couldn't understand a word of what he was saying. He was cursing Grandma in English so that she wouldn't understand and be offended. It was only years later, when I started learning English at school, that I realised what he had been saying.

All night long my mother was retching and struggling to breathe. At the crack of dawn my father was up and about, preparing to drive her to hospital. He carried her out of the yard and laid her across the two front seats of the Land Rover. I was sick with worry and I wanted to go with him. But he told me that I had to stay behind and look after little Mohammed. With barely a wave goodbye he set off on the long drive to the nearest large town.

The following evening my father returned. He was grim-faced and exhausted, anxiety etched across his features. My mother was very sick, he explained. The petrol had gone down the narrow tube that connects the ear to the throat, and from there it had got into her stomach and her lungs. She would be many weeks in hospital, although the doctors hoped she would make a full recovery.

Later that night my father took me on his knee. He stared into the firelight, worry in his eyes. 'That Grandma of yours, Rathebe . . . You know, she believes in some stupid things. Some of them are so wrong, yet can anyone tell her? Of course not. She'll never listen, so she'll never change her mind.'

I told my father that we needed a doctor in our village, a proper one like they had at the big hospital. Otherwise, Grandma might end up killing someone. That made my father laugh. There was nothing he could think of that the village needed more, he said. It would be a real blessing. The next day I told Grandma what my father and I had decided.

'What rubbish!' Grandma snorted. 'A doctor! What do we need a doctor for? What use are people who just read books? *I* can cure most things, and with the help of the Fakirs . . .'

Three months passed before my mother was well enough to come home. Even then she had to rest in her hut, and wasn't allowed to expose her damaged chest to the smoky cooking fire. This was the time that I taught myself to make *kissra* – the flat sorghum pancakes that we all loved to eat. Grandma was useless at making them and my mother was too ill. The best *kissra* has to be light and thin, like a crisp crepe. The secret lies in three things: getting the mixture just right; allowing it to ferment a little before cooking it; and handling the *garagaribah* – the special *kissra*-making spatula – correctly.

The *garagaribah* is a thin woody spatula, made from the pithy insides of a date palm leaf. Once the batter is poured onto the hot cooking iron, the *garagaribah* is used to spread it out in a series of sweeping circular motions. I quickly learned that a good *garagaribah* would last for many months without drying or splitting if left in a cup of batter to keep it moist. I would add the cup of batter to the next batch, as a culture to aid in its fermentation. It was that which gave the *kissra* a slightly sour, fermented flavour.

Some six months after the petrol incident my mother fell pregnant again. The day my second brother was born it was as if a tiny version of Grandma had entered the world. He came out kicking and screaming and demanding to be at the very centre of attention. Grandma must have sensed that she was no longer alone in the world, for she was instantly inseparable from her angry, warlike grandchild. She and gentle Mohammed had never really hit it off, but now she had her tough little Zaghawa grandson with whom to go to war.

In keeping with Zaghawa tradition my father gave his second-born son his own surname – Omer. On the day of little Omer's naming, Grandma was so proud of her tiny warrior grandchild. She held the little bundle of energy and fight in her arms, beaming with happiness. Halfway through the day's ceremonies, who should turn up but Grandma's estranged husband. Yet nothing, it seemed, could put a damper on her good spirits. Soon she and he were chatting and laughing away as if they were long-lost friends.

'You're such a hot woman,' Grandpa remarked, with a fond

smile. 'No other woman could have escaped like that, and stolen my children away . . .'

Grandma gave a fierce grin. 'And don't you forget it! I'm warning you – you try and cross me again and there'll be hell to pay!'

Grandpa turned to my father. 'How can you live in the same house as this hot woman – this fierce, runaway wife of mine?'

My father shrugged. 'Well, she has her own place and we have ours. It works for us, doesn't it, Abu?'

Grandma smiled happily and tickled little Omer. She had a real liking for my father, in spite of their differences on how to bring up the children. He had given her a home and respect, and he never openly crossed her. Whenever she did something truly outrageous, my father was usually the first person to defend her. She was the elder of the family and we had to respect her, he'd argue. Even if she was wrong, we should learn to live with it.

Well, I could learn to live with most things, but right now I was having real problems with Grandma's newfound fondness for Grandpa. I watched in amazement as she bounced little Omer on her lap and fed Grandpa choice titbits from the feast. It was almost as if they were being *intimate* together, and Grandma was . . . well . . . she was *Grandma*, and far too old and wizened for that sort of thing.

That evening I went and found my mother. I plonked myself down beside her. 'What *is* Grandma up to now? I mean, have you *seen* her and Grandpa . . .?'

My mother smiled. 'What's wrong, Rathebe? They're just making friends again, that's all.'

'But why? I mean, are they divorced or married or falling in love again or *what*?'

My mum laughed. 'I don't know. And you shouldn't really ask . . . All I do know is that no one's ever been able to tame her. That's just Grandma: she always gets her own way.'

This wasn't the first time that Grandpa had been back to visit us, my mother explained. Ever since his surprise appearance at my naming ceremony he'd been back each year, but I had been too young to remember. It was almost as if he admired Grandma, as if he felt proud to have such a rebellious, renegade bride. And they were definitely starting to get close again.

Grandpa didn't stay for long, and once he was gone I was relieved to see that things went back to normal – or at least as normal as they could be now that Omer was around. Omer was basically Grandma reborn as a tough little fighter boy. Already he was the spitting image of her. He was going to grow up tall and strong, like her, and built for fighting. Of course, Grandma thought Omer was just perfect – even though he was off making trouble with the neighbours' children almost before he could walk.

'Ah, now, this – *this* is a man!' Grandma would announce, whenever he returned from making the other boys cry.

Omer was the exact opposite of Mohammed, who loved getting hugs. Whenever my mother called him for a cuddle he would refuse to come. If Mo had sweets he would share them, but Omer would keep them all to himself. If Mo were given some money by my father, he would immediately hand it to Grandma for safekeeping, but Omer would hoard his. Sometimes, he would have saved up so much money that my mother would ask to borrow some, and pay him back when our father came home.

I didn't mind handing over my pocket money to Grandma, rather than have it fall through a hole in my clothes when I was out playing. But I would keep a careful eye on it. From time to time I'd ask Grandma: 'How much do I have now?' Grandma would scowl at us before retreating into her hut. We all knew what she was doing in there: she was checking on her special hiding place. She kept her valuables buried in a hole by the central post of the hut – and that's where she hid our pocket money.

Grandma used to tell us that once we had saved up enough

money we should buy gold. She called gold *tibrih* – the money-saver – and *tibrih* was to be cherished.

'Sell anything, *anything*, but not your gold,' she'd tell us. 'If gold is gone it will never return.'

Once Omer was old enough he got a tiny wooden 'sword' strapped to his waist, and a little wooden 'dagger' strapped to his back. He was ready to fight anyone, regardless of their age or size. If there was a quarrel between them, Omer would attack Mohammed with his sword. He would even attack me, although I was so much older than him. The rest of the time he spent climbing onto the roofs of the huts, clambering over the trees, escaping from our yard, and getting lost and causing trouble.

Mo was always good to me, but in a way it was Omer who was my favourite brother. Whenever I wanted to go on an adventure to the forest or climbing trees, Omer was always up for it. And he was the one I could rely on whenever the going got tough. He was like a little protector by my side.

I wasn't alone in relishing Omer's fighting spirit. Whenever Grandma went to the village market to sell some chickens or goats, she'd take Omer with her. From the earliest age Mo had started to follow Omer's lead, so he would invariably tag along behind. If Grandma got into an argument or a fight, Omer would join in right alongside her, but Mo would come rushing home.

'Quick, quick! Come! Come!' he'd cry. 'Grandma and Omer – they're causing trouble! Come quick – come and help!'

Whenever we were out and about play-fighting I'd pick Omer first to be on my team. We might be wrestling or using impro-vised wooden swords. There was only one rule: you could do anything you wanted to win, apart from hitting people in the face. You could grab someone in a headlock, throw them to the ground, box them in the tummy or twist their arm behind their back. Usually it would be boy against boy or girl on girl. But sometimes we girls would fight the boys, just to prove that we were as tough as they were.

Omer had scars all over his legs and arms, which marked him out as a real toughie. Invariably, someone would end up hurt and crying whenever they fought him, and then there'd be trouble. Their parents would come round to our house to complain. My mother would rush to apologise, but Grandma would tell her to keep quiet. Saying sorry was cowardly, she'd argue. My mum would counter that she had to apologise or the neighbours might beat Omer. But Grandma would point out that if the other kids didn't want to get hurt, they shouldn't join in the play-fighting.

I knew in a way that fighting wasn't ladylike, but I still felt that a girl should be able to stand up for herself. In any case, as the oldest child I often had to fight Mo's battles for him. But my father wasn't happy whenever he heard that I'd been fighting. I think he feared that there was too much of Grandma in me, and that I would end up hot and angry like her.

'Why d'you fight so much, Rathebe?' he'd ask me. 'Let your brothers fight the battles. If you keep fighting, people will say you're a fierce, troublesome girl.'

'I'm not fighting because I *like* it, Abba,' I'd reply. 'I'm just defending myself against the others . . .'

In truth I actually enjoyed fighting and I knew that I'd inherited enough of Grandma's hot spirit to be reasonably good at it. I was only saying this to cheer up my father. I wanted him to continue believing that I was a good, well-behaved daddy's girl.

By contrast, Omer quite openly courted trouble. Close by the village were some fields where we grew our crops of sorghum, maize and sesame. My father employed several young men to help with his livestock, but Grandma insisted that we should grow our own food. We'd have to wait until the rains came before we could start planting, but each of us children was expected to plant three or four rows of sorghum and of maize.

The day after the first rains we'd head down to the fields. Grandma would count out the same number of seeds for each of us. First, we'd make a row of holes in the damp earth with a sharp digging stick. Then we'd each go along our row, dropping two or three seeds into the holes and stamping down the earth with our bare feet. At the end of the planting our feet would be hot and swollen and in need of a clean and a rest.

Before leaving the fields, we'd have to make a *jahoub kadai* – a scary man. We'd cut two sticks, one slightly shorter than the other, and tie them together in a cross shape, driving the longer stick into the ground. We'd dress the sticks in some raggedy clothes and tie an old turban around the scary man's head. When the wind blew, the *jahoub kadai* looked just like a person running across the fields, and it would scare the birds away.

As is the case in most families, there was a great deal of competition between me and my brothers. The first time that Omer came with us to the fields, I realised that I could play a trick on them. If I cheated and put twice as many seeds into my holes as I was supposed to, I reckoned I could finish my rows in double-quick time. Grandma was astonished when I completed my work so quickly. Better still, I could see how it annoyed Omer.

But a week later we returned to check on the fields, and my trick was found out. The young plants in my rows were far too dense, and would soon strangle each other.

'Who did this?' Grandma demanded.

No one answered.

'I said, *who did this?* Who was it? Who cheated?'

'It was him!' I blurted out, pointing an accusing finger at Mohammed.

'Mohammed!' Grandma snorted. 'I should have known!'

Mohammed burst into tears. 'It wasn't me! It wasn't me! She's lying, she's lying.'

I turned to Omer. 'Well, it must have been him, then. He's too young to know any better.'

I saw Omer puff out his chest in defiance. 'What if it *was* me? What if I *did* do it? *So what?*'

'*Which one of you was it?*' Grandma demanded.

'I did it,' Omer repeated. '*I did it*. And what are you going to do about it?'

For a second Grandma stood there in astonishment. Then she grabbed Omer, threw him over her knee and gave him a beating. But her heart wasn't in it, of course. And even if she had beaten Omer to within an inch of his life, he would never have cried. It just wasn't in his nature to do so. After that, I often wondered if Omer really believed the cheating rows were his. But I just think that he was a natural-born bad boy and he liked getting into trouble.

Grandma used to hang a raffia net in the roof beams of her hut, in which she'd keep little treats. Omer realised he could stand on a wooden stool and use a cleft stick to unhook it. He'd pull it down, and Mo and I would gather around to peep inside. As soon as we saw that there was something delicious we'd not be able to resist having a nibble. A nibble quickly became a bite and in no time it was all gone.

Later that day Grandma might have guests coming, and she'd go to fetch her bag of treats only to discover that it was empty. She'd fly into one of her rages, and we three would flee the compound as fast as we could. If Grandma caught me or Mo, we'd each try to blame the others. But if Omer was caught he'd announce proudly that he was the thief, and what was Grandma going to do about it?

Grandma could never be angry with Omer for long; she was too fond of him for that. She was forever telling him stories of the old times – of heroic Zaghawa exploits. One day an old man and his wife came calling. They stayed for ages, drinking hot, sweet mint tea and chatting. Just as they were leaving, Grandma grabbed us children.

'See that old man?' she announced. 'One day, long before you were born, he was a great Zaghawa hunter. He went to the forest and single-handedly killed an *hjar* . . .'

We stared at him in astonishment. The *hjar* – the leopard – is one of the most fearsome wild animals in our area.

'He killed an *hjar* – but how?' I asked.

'He was very brave,' Grandma continued, in a grand fashion. 'And like all great Zaghawa warriors, he was very clever. He tricked the *hjar*, and that's how he killed it.'

'I'm going to do the same,' Omer announced proudly. 'When I'm bigger, I'm going to kill an *hjar*.'

I prodded him in the tummy. 'In your dreams, fat boy!'

Grandma silenced me with a clip around the ear. 'Can you guess how he tricked the *hjar*?'

We shook our heads. 'Then I'll tell you. First, he killed a goat. He took the goat and rode into the forest. He checked until he found fresh leopard footprints. Then he got down from his donkey and he started to dig a hole. Once the hole was big enough, he covered it with branches and grass, old leaves and mud – until it was impossible to know it was there.'

Grandma paused. Her eyes were gleaming with excitement.

'But what happened next?' I blurted out, unable to keep quiet.

'Well, that man was very, very clever,' Grandma continued. 'He climbed a tree and tied the goat to one of the branches. Then he hid himself as best he could, and settled down to wait. Late that night the *hjar* came along the path, sniffing in the darkness as it went. It could smell the dead goat, and taste its blood on the air.'

The leopard had bounded forward to seize the goat, but the ground suddenly gave way. As the magnificent animal had fallen into the hole, the hunter had dropped from the tree, spear in hand. The *hjar* had clawed and snarled at its attacker, but it was unable to escape the trap. As Grandma told us about the death of the *hjar*, I felt somehow sorry for it.

'Was it very beautiful?' I asked. 'The *hjar*, I mean.'

Grandma fixed me with a baleful eye. 'Beautiful? *Beautiful*? It was big and fierce with savage teeth and sharp claws – is that what you mean by *beautiful*? It had eaten half the cows in the village – perhaps that's what you mean by *beautiful*? And it had killed lots of little children as they scampered through the forest, and eaten them all up . . . Maybe in a way you're right: anything that kills and eats little children *has to be all right*.'

With Grandma's fierce comments about sharp claws and little children being eaten, Mo was close to tears. His bottom lip was quivering, which was always the first sign. As for Omer, he was loving it. I took hold of Mo's hand and tried to move the subject along a little.

'So what did he do with the *hjar*?' I asked.

'He skinned it, of course,' Grandma replied. 'The *hjar* has a beautiful, bright yellow coat, with brown spots. He rode back to the village with the skin slung over the donkey's back. All the children came running and crying out in excitement: "Look! Look! The hunter has killed an *hjar*! The hunter has killed an *hjar*!" He made his way to the market place and sold the skin for a lot of money. They used to make fine shoes out of the skin of the *hjar*, you know.'

I wondered why it was that they didn't still make *hjar*-skin shoes. Was it because most of the *hjar* had been killed? We knew there were a few leopards left, because occasionally we'd hear their calls. But they were deep in the forests of the Jebel Marra, and as far away from people as they could possibly get.

The next time the three of us were out as a group, Omer made a special point of tracking down the grandchildren of that old man, the village leopard-killer. He challenged them to a fight.

'Ha!' Omer exclaimed, once he'd beaten them. 'Ha! Your grand-father may have killed an *hjar*, but you can't beat me! I'm going to be the greatest leopard-killer there ever was!'

While Grandma's stories were always about the family, the clan or the tribe, my father would try to inform us about the wider world – about the history of Sudan, about foreign cultures and distant countries. Omer had no time for such things and Mohammed was indifferent, but for some reason I had a thirst for such knowledge. As for Grandma, she thought it positively dangerous to turn our minds away from the timeless certainties of the village. Their battle for control of our minds was at its fiercest when concerning the radio set.

One day my father came home with a tiny battered radio that he'd bought in the nearest big town. It had a wonky aerial that had been half-repaired by sticky tape. Each evening he would try to tune it to the news, and he was a particular fan of the BBC World Service. He used to tell me that he didn't believe a word of the Sudanese news until it was first confirmed by the BBC. This was one of the earliest inklings I had that there were dark powers at work in our country, and that little they said could be trusted.

We were one of the few houses in our village to have a radio. Oddly enough, bearing in mind that it was 'new-fangled technology from the outside world', Grandma became its greatest fan. This was largely because it was such a status symbol. Every morning she would fetch it and place it outside her hut. Grandma didn't care what she listened to, as long as it *wasn't* the news. She would twiddle the dial until she ended up on some foreign music programme, and then she'd leave it on that all day, at full volume. She couldn't understand a word, of course. She just seemed to love the noise.

When my father came home in the evening he'd retrieve the radio, place it back in the living area and start trying to retune it to the BBC. I knew he found this hugely frustrating, but he never complained. He just came up with a way to deal with it. On his next trip to town he purchased a much bigger radio set. This one was bright purple and shiny-new. When he presented it to Grandma she was overjoyed. As status symbols went this really was it.

My father quietly repossessed his little battered radio. He replaced it in the living area, where it remained permanently tuned to the BBC. What he had neglected to tell Grandma was that the new radio had a very limited range, and could only pick up broadcasts within Sudan. His tiny old thing was a long-wave set, which could pick up programmes from all over the world. It made no difference to Grandma: as long as her radio was big and impressive, and noise came booming out of it, then she was happy.

<hr />

But however insular Grandma might have wished our life to be, the outside world had a way on impacting upon us, and often in the most unwelcome of ways. To the east and south of our lands lived several semi-nomadic Arab tribes – the Rizeiqat, the Hamar, the Ta-aisha and others. We called these people the Ahrao – a word that for us signifies 'the Arab enemy'. Traditionally, there was little love lost between the Ahrao and us black African tribes. If trouble was to come, it came invariably from the Ahrao.

My father employed a *hiry carda*, a cowboy, to look after our cows and our herd of goats. He was around eight years old, and he came from a neighbouring black African tribe called the Birgid. I didn't look down on him because he was poorer than us and my father's worker. In fact, Mo, Omer and I admired him, because he was older than us and he had a job. We'd always want to help look after the animals, and often he would take us along.

Each morning he'd fetch the animals from their *gory* – the house of the animals. This was a circular enclosure made of cut thorn trees driven into the ground. He'd gather up the animals and drive them into the bush to find good pasture. While doing so he had to prevent them from eating any farmer's crops, and he had to chase any wild animals away. The best pasture was in the foothills of the Jebel Marra, and he'd have to make sure that none of the animals wandered off and got lost in the mountains.

At the end of each day he'd return the animals to the *gory*. It served two purposes: the thick barrier of acacia thorns would keep out wild animals, and it also deterred anyone who might be tempted to steal our livestock. Before leaving them for the night, the cowboy would drag across a rough gate made of thorn scrub to seal off the entrance. Finally, he would place one of our dogs at the gateway to warn us of any trouble.

One afternoon he came running into the yard. His face was bloody, his shirt was torn and he was terrified. He had been driving the animals to some new pasture when the Ahrao had attacked. He was only a small boy, and he had run for his life and hidden in the bush. In no time, all our goats were gone. The Ahrao had left the cattle and our donkey, but the goats were small and fast and relatively easy to herd eastwards into their flat desert lands.

Just as soon as Grandma heard this she flew into a towering rage. She had branded her goats on the ears with three vertical marks, using a dagger heated over the fire. She tried to raise a war party to go after the Ahrao and recover her animals. Omer strutted about with his wooden sword and was all for going with her, but my father told her not to be so hot-headed. The Ahrao would be long gone by now, he argued. And even if we did catch them, there would be a big fight and people might get killed.

My father promised that the very next day he would go and buy Grandma a replacement herd of goats. He would make sure they were the finest animals – the strongest, healthiest specimens in the market-place. He had the money to do so, and in that way no one risked getting hurt. In the long run Grandma would end up better off, he argued. Grandma agreed to my father's suggestion, but still she couldn't bear it that the Ahrao had got one over on her.

The Ahrao were drawn to our lands, and especially the foothills of the Jebel Marra, by the rich grazing. During the dry season they would drive their livestock westwards, searching for water and forage. They would travel through our area, herding their animals before them. It was at times like these that most of the rustling would take place. The Ahrao men were armed with knives and swords and ancient guns, and it was they who led the risky, animal-stealing raids.

Whenever I saw the Ahrao approaching I would recognise them by their light skins, their pointed features and their beards. The very sight of them made everyone fearful, and in the months of the dry season no one went out alone. After the theft of Grandma's goats my father sat me down and told me all about the Ahrao. We Zaghawa, together with the other black African tribes, had to resist them, he said. Otherwise, they would push and push and push until we had lost our villages, our fields and our very identity.

'Never trust the Ahrao,' he warned me. 'They smile on one side of their faces, but behind that smile they hide another face.'

How horribly prophetic my father's words would prove.

5

The Cutting Time

Shortly after the Ahrao's raid on our goats, my luck almost ran out. Mo, Omer and I were playing a game of chase in the market. An old man stopped me, and I presumed he was going to complain about all the noise we were making. Instead, he bent down to inspect my face.

'You've something caught in your eye, little one. It must be a piece of grass . . .'

In an instant his hand shot out and grabbed hold of my white eyelash. As he tugged I felt a searing pain in my eye socket, and my vision went blurry with tears. Omer launched himself at the old man and started to beat him around the legs. I tore myself away from his grasp and raced home to my parents. But the whole of the side of my face was in agony, and I felt the muscles around my eye going into a series of spasms.

By the time I reached home my left eye had closed over completely, and my father practically had a heart attack. He got my mother to bandage me up, and then all three of us set off for the hospital. I was in so much pain that all I could think of was how a tiny white eyelash could cause me such agony. It was only a little hair, after all.

As soon as we reached the hospital my father rushed me in to see the white-coated eye specialist. He prized apart the swollen mess, shone a little light into it and announced that I would have to undergo surgery. The only solution was to have the white eyelash removed, he said. But my father refused. Instead, we drove across town to see a Chinese doctor. My father hoped that he could help save my white eyelash and our family's good fortune.

Of course, I had never seen anyone looking even remotely like Dr Hing, the Chinese physician. He was a little wizened man with yellowish skin, wispy hair and odd, slanting eyes. He took me into his examination room and listened intently as my father explained what had happened. Every now and then he peered at me with his bright beady eyes.

When my father had finished speaking he asked if he could take a look at my eye. I told him that he could, but it was very painful so would he please be careful. Dr Hing nodded and smiled and said that he wouldn't hurt me at all. Strangely enough, I felt quite at ease with him. Gently, he prised apart my swollen eyelids and peered inside. He took a good look and then he straightened up, a faint smile creasing his oddly serene features.

'Ah, this is a very lucky one,' he announced softly. 'Very, very lucky.'

Did he mean that I was lucky in that my eye wasn't too badly damaged, I wondered. I hoped that he did. I allowed myself to relax a little. I had been worried for my sight in my left eye, as much as for the survival of my white eyelash.

'What exactly d'you mean, Doctor?' my father asked.

'Your daughter – she is very lucky,' Dr Hing repeated. 'You know, she has the *white eyelash*. In Chinese culture white eyelash very lucky. Very, very lucky . . .'

Dr Hing busied himself at his desk, preparing some powders and some potions. He asked me to stick out my tongue, so he could examine it. He studied it for a few seconds, making some notes on a chart, and then he turned to speak with my father again.

'White eyelash very special,' he pronounced, in his soft voice. He held up a cardboard packet full of a brownish power. 'This is crushed Chinese herbs. Dilute one part to ten parts with clean water – for shock. Big shock to the system when white eyelash pulled so roughly.' Next he held up a paper envelope with some crumbly yellow pills inside. 'And this is to boost immune system, to help fight off infection. And this,' he added, holding up a packet of dark green powder, 'very special Chinese medicine to give strength to eye.'

He glanced from me to my father. 'White eyelash so very, very lucky,' he repeated, beaming at us.

'So is that it?' my father asked. 'It doesn't need to be . . . cut out? No need for surgery?'

'Surgery?' Dr Hing asked quizzically. 'Surgery? Why would you want to hurt white eyelash? White eyelash very lucky . . .'

Dr Hing went on to explain that my white eyelash had its own distinct blood supply. This accounted for the way it kept growing at a quicker rate than the others. If anyone tried to operate, it might damage the whole eye. And in any case, why take the risk? A white eyelash signified good fortune. And with the help of his herbs it would heal itself.

Dr Hing proved to be right. A week later I was back at home with the swelling almost gone. The Chinese medicines tasted disgusting, but they really did seem to be doing the trick. Even so my father was very angry with the old man who had tried to pull out my white eyelash.

'We'd better get Rathebe off to school,' he remarked to my mother. 'Otherwise someone's going to pull it out for real – and take away all our good luck and her wisdom!'

From then on, every time my white eyelash grew too long my father would sit me down, take out a pair of tiny scissors and carefully trim it back to size. In that way he hoped I would avoid anyone else trying to rip it out of my eye socket.

I was approaching eight years old by now, and my father had always said that this was the age when I would be sent away to school. There was no school in our village, and the sum total of my education to date had been learning the Koran. Every Friday morning we were supposed to go to the Imam to memorise verses of the Koran. If we didn't learn fast enough, the Imam would beat us with a big stick. So when it came to Friday morning and a toss-up between a morning with the Imam or one climbing trees, fighting with our friends and causing mayhem, there was really no competition.

But it was now time for me to start my proper learning in the big school in Hashma, the nearest town to our village. Yet before I could do so there was one thing I had to go through: my circumcision. All girls in our tribe were circumcised, most when they were ten or eleven years old. Grandma insisted that I couldn't go away to school without first going through my cutting time. After my experience of the facial scarring, I was more than a little apprehensive. But I had been to the celebrations for other village girls – and their circumcision always seemed such a time of happiness, brightness and laughter.

The night before I was to be cut there was a party for the women and girls. My mother, Grandma, Kadiga and lots of my female relatives were there, and I had the place of honour. In our tradition circumcision is supposed to mark the passage from girl-hood to womanhood, and so I was treated almost as if I was getting married. I had beautiful new clothes and shoes, all in red.

Grandma and my mother spent hours painting my hands and feet with beautiful red henna designs, just as if I were a bride. My skin was rubbed with oil, so that when the henna powder was applied it would take on a more intense colour. The soles of my feet were painted in a layer of rich, dark red. Fancy whorls and flower patterns were painted from my ankles to just below my knees. The tips of my fingers were painted a splash of bright orange, with intricate circle and spiral designs running up my arms to my elbows.

By the end of the preparations all my misgivings over the cutting were gone. I felt so beautiful, so grown up and so special that I positively wanted to go through with my circumcision. Early the next morning the *taihree* arrived – the traditional circumcision woman of our village. She had no formal training, but she did all the womanly things. I was taken into Grandma's hut and perched nervously on the edge of her bed.

I watched as the *taihree* prepared her instruments – her razor blade, bowls of water and cloths. I felt a stab of panic. It was so like my scarring time, when I had managed to run and escape. For a second I considered doing the same, but I knew that my family and friends were gathered outside. I couldn't run. If I did, I would never live it down.

A huge, grotesquely fat woman came to join us. I recognised her immediately, for all the village children knew her. If we saw her out on the street we'd point and tell each other that that was the woman who held you down during your circumcision time.

'Let me have the child on my lap,' she offered Grandma. 'I can hold her, while you help the *taihree*.'

Grandma nodded. The fat lady sat down next to me, and I felt the bed all but buckle under her weight. She patted her lap, smiled at me and lifted me onto it. I realised that there was no escaping now. I was enveloped in her embrace, and she was hugely heavy and strong. The *taihree* turned to me with the razor blade gripped in her hand. As she did so, I saw my mother's face turn pale.

She glanced at Grandma. 'You don't need me . . . I'll go and help prepare the food.'

Grandma nodded, and with a quick kiss to the top of my head my mother was gone. Grandma took one of the cloths from the *taihree* and handed it to me.

'Put this in your mouth. Bite down hard. And remember, you mustn't scream or cry – it's shameful. Be brave.'

I did as Grandma instructed. Part of me still wanted to go

through with this, to prove that I was a big, strong girl. I felt the
fat woman move my legs apart, forcing me onto my back until
all I could see was the roof of Grandma's hut. There was a twitch
at the door, as a curious child peeped inside. I heard Grandma
yell for him or her to get out. For a second my fearful mind
wondered if it might have been crazy Omer. It was just the sort
of thing he would do. And then the *taihree* reached down between
my legs.

With the first slash of the razor blade, a bolt of agony shot
through me like nothing I had ever experienced. I let out a blood-
curdling scream, and as I did so I started kicking and fighting to
get free. But all that happened was the huge woman bore down
on me, clamping my legs in her vice-like grip. I cried for them
to stop, but as I did so I heard the women outside start making
the *illil*. 'Aye-aye-aye-aye-aye-aye-aye!' they cried. It was supposed
to be a celebratory chant, but in truth they were doing it to hide
the noise of my screaming.

The *taihree* pawed at me again, and I felt Grandma grab me
by the arm. She put her finger in her mouth and bit on it, to try
to show me to bite the cloth and to shut me up. But as the blade
cut into me again I screamed, wide-eyed with terror and pain.

'No! No! Mummy! Mummy! Make them stop! Make them stop!'

I felt Grandma hissing angrily in my ear. 'Be brave, girl! You
are Zaghawa! Cry and the children will laugh at you! *Be brave!*'

I didn't give a damn for Grandma's words. I was a terrified
child with all the adults in the world that I trusted causing me
unspeakable pain. The shock of the betrayal was beyond imag-
ining. I tried, desperately, to fight and to get away, but the huge
lady was crushing me into her vast bulk. I twisted my head and
bit into her flesh, as hard and as viciously as I could. My hatred
for this woman who had imprisoned me in pain knew no bounds.
I wanted to wound and to kill her. But she hardly seemed to
notice what I was doing.

I felt a gush of warm blood as the *taihree* took hold of me again, slicing deeper and deeper. Through a mouthful of the fat woman's flesh I screamed and screamed, hot tears rushing down my face, but the cutting and the cutting and the cutting just went on and on and on.

The *taihree* reached down one last time, grabbed something, sawed for a second, twisted and dropped it into the bowl on the floor. The pain was so unbearable that it had taken over my whole head, driving me to the borders of sanity. I felt as if I was dying, and even death would have been preferable to where I was now. Through a state of half-consciousness I heard my own, pathetic whimpering filtering through to me.

Finally, with her arms covered in blood, the *taihree* straightened up. She turned to Grandma. 'Almost there,' she announced.

'*Alhamdu lillah* – Praise be to God,' Grandma replied.

'*Alhamdu lillah*,' the *taihree* confirmed. 'Is there boiling water?'

Grandma reached for a bowl on the fire. As she did so, her eyes met mine and she scowled, shaking her head despairingly – as if I was the one who had done something wrong. *As if I was the one who had done something wrong.*

The *taihree* readied a needle and thick cotton thread. As she turned back to me, I felt myself withdraw into some inner world where the pain and the horror of whatever was coming next could never reach me.

With a sickening sound of tugging rawness she began to sew up my flesh. With each tug of the needle I felt a bolt of pain surge through me, but I was now in a place where I was insulated from the physical suffering. I knew that somewhere deep in my lost womanhood there was a burning heart of agony, but I had removed my mind to a place where it couldn't be hurt any more.

By the time the *taihree* had finished I had been sewn up, leaving just a tiny little hole. Everything else was gone. I was half-delirious.

I barely noticed as Grandma went to the door of the hut and announced that it was done – that I had been circumcised.

A series of cheers went up from outside, and the women made the *illil* again: 'Aye-aye-aye-aye-aye-aye-aye! Aye-aye-aye-aye-aye-aye-aye!'

While my family and friends celebrated, I was sobbing my heart out. Only now did my mother come in to see me. She sat down on the bed and tried to soothe me, stroking my hair and whispering comforting words. She had tears in her eyes, but it didn't make up for the fact that she had left me at the mercy of Grandma and the circumcision women. She had made some pigeon soup, she told me, a rich broth that would help me recover.

'Every day, Rathebe, I'll kill two pigeons for you,' my mother promised. 'Every day. And the soup will make you well again.'

Grandma and the *taihree* did what they could to dress my wounds. Grandma had collected some seedpods, and the freshest leaves of the *pirgi* tree. She proceeded to boil the leaves and bathe me with the warm water. The dry pods she ground into a powder, which she mixed with oil to produce a paste. This she applied to my raw flesh. As for the *taihree*, she took some capsules of antibiotics, broke them in two and poured the powder over my wounds. She finished off with a sprinkling of baby powder.

The *taihree* bandaged up my groin area in the cloths she had laid out ready. When she was done I was wearing something akin to a large nappy. Then she and Grandma took a thick rope and wrapped it around my thighs until they were locked tightly together. There was no way in which I could move now, even had I wanted to. I would have to stay like this for two weeks, Grandma warned me, to give my wounds time to heal.

Grandma and the *taihree* went off to join the crowd. At last I was left alone in the hut. I drifted off into a pained, troubled sleep, wondering why on earth they had done this to me. Grandma had warned me that if I went off to school uncircumcised, the girls would laugh at me. 'Oh, you still have your stuff? Those big bits?' they'd remark, mockingly. But why would they? Why would they say such things? What was wrong with the way we were born? What could possibly be so wrong that would justify what I had been through?

~

Day after day I lay on that bed, unable to walk or go outside and play with the other children. Whenever I needed to pee it was such agony, and I needed the help of my mother. The first time I couldn't crouch down properly, because of the pain and the ropes, so my mother had to hold me as I tried to pee half-standing up. As soon as I started there was a blinding, stinging sensation down between my legs.

'I can't do it,' I cried, as I held onto my mum and shuddered with pain. 'It hurts too much.'

With my mother's help I hobbled back inside. Every now and then I would have a visitor. The children would sit with me and tell me all about the adventures they'd been having, which did cheer me up a little. But the adults just wanted to congratulate me on my cutting, as if it was something to be proud of.

'Ah, clever girl, brave girl,' they'd tell me. 'Here. Take this small gift . . .'

It was as much as I could do not to spit in their eye. After a week of this I was beside myself with boredom. One morning I decided to try to take a few steps. Maybe I was well enough to walk and to go out and play. I eased my legs over the edge of the bed and got to my feet unsteadily. But I had barely taken a step when I went crashing down. The ropes bound me too tightly and the pain in my groin was terrible.

I heard my mum let out a cry of alarm, as she caught the noise of my falling. She came rushing in, took one look at me sprawled on the floor and burst into floods of tears. What was I doing, she wailed. It was too early! I would break my stitches and then I would be ruined. She helped me back to the bed, and took an anxious look at me. Everything was still as it should be, she told me. But she made me promise that I wouldn't try to move again.

As I lay back down on the bed I felt sick of everything – sick of the stupid visitors, sick of the hut, sick of pigeon soup and sick of the inactivity. But most of all I was sick at the way these people had brutalised and crippled me. My mother's worries were well founded, of course. We all knew of girls who had died during their cutting time. Sometimes, a vein was cut during the butchery, and no one could stop the bleeding. At other times, a girl's wounds would become infected and she would die a long, lingering death. Still more died years later, during childbirth, because they couldn't give birth properly. The cutting left terrible scarring, and without surgery childbirth remained horribly risky.

Two weeks after my cutting time my ropes were unbound. I was allowed out and I took my first faltering steps – but there was to be no running, jumping or play-fighting for some time. When I first ventured into the village one of the girls tried to tease me for crying during my cutting time. In an instant I had forgotten that I was forbidden to fight: I rounded on that girl and beat her so soundly that she never dared tease me again.

As I had lain in Grandma's hut recovering, I'd had ample time to think about what had happened. I was angry with my mother, with Grandma, and even with my father for what had been done to me. While Grandma had played the lead role, neither of my parents had told me the truth about my cutting time. Had they done so I would have refused to go through with it, just as I had done before with the scarring.

But what I couldn't for the life of me understand was the role the women played in all of this. My mother and Grandma must have gone through the same torment during their cutting time, and suffered the same sense of shock and betrayal. Yet it was they who had charmed and praised me and convinced me that it was a good and proper thing. They had lulled me into a false sense of security, and then played their part as that huge evil woman had held me down and the *taihree* had done her butchery.

It took me weeks to forgive my father for the role that he had played. It may have been a passive one, but he it was who was educated and enlightened, and surely he could have seen another way. It took me months to forgive my mother, because out of weakness she had abandoned me in that hut and left others to do their worst. And I think that perhaps I never really forgave Grandma. She it was who had insisted that if I was going away to school then I would have to be cut, and proceeded to orchestrate the whole thing.

I was the only child from my village being sent away to the big school. The other children would go to a school in a neighbouring village, or not at all. That school had no proper classrooms, and lessons were held under a tree. There was no school uniform, and most pupils didn't even have shoes. My father had promised me something very different. All of my childhood friends – Kadiga included – were envious of my good fortune.

Like most families in our village, Kadiga's parents couldn't afford to send her away to the big school. I knew that it was costly, but my father had said that I was more than worth it. As it was too far for me to travel back and forth each day, he had arranged for me to lodge with his brother's family. They lived in a house in town that my father owned, so I would be staying with my extended family in a place that was still our own. It softened the blow of separation somewhat.

I would stay in Hashma town for the school term, and return to my village for the holidays. It was too expensive for me to come home at weekends, or even for half-terms. In any case, I was being sent away to be educated, my father told me, and during term times I should dedicate myself to my studies. I was keen to do so. I was keen to prove to him that his trust in me, and his faith in my intellectual curiosity, was well founded.

As for my mother and Grandma, they were far from happy that I was leaving the family home. Grandma went into a long and dramatic sulk. This going away to school lark had never happened in her day, she grumbled, so why now? Such nonsense, she complained. My mother was worried about me being sent away from home at such an early age. Mo and Omer did little to hide their disquiet, either. They were deeply jealous that I was going away on a big adventure while they had to stay in the village. But my father was resolute: he had made up his mind and I would be going away to school.

A week before I was due to go, my father returned from town with a bulging bag of school kit. He proudly presented me with my brand new beige-and-white school uniform. There was a *fustan* – a long, loose dress, but with two ribbons to tie it at the waist. There was a snow-white Muslim headscarf and black leather shoes. And there was a bright red plastic rucksack, which was full of pens and pencils and pristine white exercise books.

I tried the uniform on, and I could tell that my father was so proud. I was dancing around the yard showing off, but then my mum made me take it off again. Mo and Omer were trying not to show it but they were green with envy. My father must have noticed, for he promised that when they were old enough he would send them away to the big school.

The day of my departure dawned, and early that morning I loaded my bags into the Land Rover. I knew that I was going away for three months – the whole of my first term – so I had to take everything with me that I might need. My father and I were just about to depart when my mother came rushing up to the car. She had changed her mind, she declared. She had decided that she wanted to come with us, after all.

'I want to see where you're taking her,' she announced, as she squeezed into the front. 'I want to see where she will live and eat and sleep. I need to see it for myself.'

My father shrugged his shoulders and chuckled. 'You're welcome . . . Glad you're taking an interest in Rathebe's education at last.'

He was just about to pull away when Omer cannoned into the canvas rear of the Land Rover and leaped inside. Grandma was at the gate, holding Mohammed by the scruff of his neck as he too tried to join us.

'Out!' she bellowed at Omer. 'Get back here now! NOW!'

Omer was just about to reply with something cheeky and defiant when my father silenced him.

'Get out, Omer,' he commanded. 'Do as your grandma says, before you make her angry.'

The one person in the world that Omer would never defy was my father. Behind his calm, quiet exterior there was a huge authority and firmness about him. Omer got down from the vehicle and returned to Grandma, his feet dragging and his head held low.

'And Omer, be good to your grandma while we're away,' my father called after him. 'You make sure you do what she says, you hear me?'

'Yes, Abba,' Omer replied.

As we pulled away I could hear Grandma scolding him. 'You just calm yourself down. So much fuss over nothing! Driving all that distance, and just to read a few books. No good will come of it . . .'

The Land Rover had a single bench seat running across the cab, which meant that my father, my mother and I could sit there in relative comfort. In the rear there were only our bags, which left plenty of spare room. As we weaved our way between the houses, my father stopped and picked up some passengers. There was an old woman who needed to go to the hospital, and men who had business in town. It was a rare occasion when his car would leave without a full load. If he had the room, my father would take people.

I pushed my face towards the window, jeering and making faces at the children. I didn't want anyone to miss the fact that I was in a vehicle being driven away to the big school, while they were stuck in the village.

The road ahead was really a series of rough tracks that criss-crossed the bush and desert. As I watched the scenery go past, I couldn't for the life of me understand how my father could find his way. It all looked the same to me. Luckily, he had driven the route countless times before and he knew it like the back of his hand. As we chugged along I couldn't hide my excitement.

And I couldn't stop talking. 'Where are we now? Are we nearly there yet? When will we get there?'

All of a sudden I heard a loud hissing through the open window. I looked at my father. He glanced at me and frowned, bringing the car to a halt in a cloud of dust.

'I think, Rathebe, we have a puncture,' he announced.

Sure enough, a sharp stone had blown out one of the inner tubes. We dismounted, and before my father could say a word the male passengers had started to change the wheel. One fetched the big jack from the rear, while another unscrewed the spare tyre from the bonnet. My father went to undo the wheel nuts, but they stopped him with insistent gestures and firm words. He was the esteemed owner of the vehicle, and the least they could do in exchange for the free lift was to fix the car.

When we reached town the first thing my father would do was get the puncture repaired. He hated driving without a spare, for if the car had another puncture then we would be stuck in the desert. Even though it was fast and powerful, a car was not as reliable as a camel, he explained. If a camel went lame, still it would hobble on until it got its rider to safety. But if a car ran out of petrol, or broke down, then that was it – it was finished. As for me, my biggest worry was arriving late and missing my first day at school.

With the spare tyre fitted we continued on our journey. My father stopped at the next village to buy some fruit, which we shared with the passengers. It had been hot, dusty work changing the wheel, and the fruit was deliciously refreshing. As always, I saved the bananas to last. Mo, Omer and I would have a competition to see who could throw the banana skins out of the car the furthest. But I was feeling far too grown up for such things now.

Late in the afternoon we reached the town. My father headed directly for a garage to fix the tyre, and then on to his brother's house. I had been to town once before, when I had ended up being treated by the Chinese doctor. Now I was back again, hoping that my white eyelash had brought me wisdom, as well as good fortune.

My uncle's house turned out to be very similar to our own. There were four buildings arranged around a central living area. Each building was about the same size as our mud huts, but made from cement and bricks instead. Each had a flat roof, with a thick layer of mud at the edges to weigh down the thatch. Out at the front of each was a wooden veranda, and as most of the neighbourhood was Zaghawa it was similar to the set-up in our village.

Several years back my father had built this house, with a view to moving our family to the town. He was drawn to the more educated, cosmopolitan lifestyle. But Grandma and my mother had refused to leave the village. My father had suggested a compromise:

half the year we would live in the village, half of the year in the town. But Grandma had argued that if we lived like that we would be lost, never knowing which part of our life was home.

My mother liked the house as soon as she saw it, and she declared that I would be happy here. My Uncle Ahmed and his wife, Samiah, welcomed us in. They took me to the hut that I would be sharing with their two daughters, Salma and Fatma. The girls were a little older than me, but they were friendly and I warmed to them immediately. I had a bed next to theirs, and there were rugs on the floor for us to sit on and do our homework.

I had a day settling in with my parents, and then it was time to go to the big school. Early in the morning I dressed in my pristine uniform, my mother fussing over me, and then my father drove us to the school. He'd been there before to reserve my place and to pay my fees. As we drove in through the big gates my heart was in my mouth. I gazed around me, my eyes drinking in the wondrous place to which my father had brought me.

There was a posh sign in Arabic and English announcing the school's name – *The Hashma Junior Academy for Girls*. Then there was a large dusty playing field, and beyond that a dozen low oblong buildings, each with fine walls and a gleaming iron roof. These were the classrooms. We peeped inside the nearest. The floor was of earth, there was a blackboard at one end, and there were ranks of wooden desks, each of which would seat three pupils. There was no glass in the windows, and the doorways had no doors. But to me this was still the smartest place that I had ever set foot in.

On the far side of the playing field was the teachers' staff room and the headmistress's office. These buildings even had fine wooden doors and glass windows. In Sudan, teachers were held in great respect, because they were educated people with status. These were just the sort of grand buildings that I had imagined them working in.

My father took me to the staff room. He signed some papers to hand me over to the care of the school. Then one of the teachers, a Miss Shadhia, took charge of me. Miss Shadhia was my form tutor, and she was friendly and looked kind. I was shy and self-conscious as my father said a rather stiff goodbye and my mother did some last-minute fussing, and then he turned her away by the shoulders and they stepped out of the door.

I watched through the window as he led her back to the Land Rover. They went to wave a last farewell, and I could see that my mother was crying. I waved back, but I couldn't raise a tear. I was too excited about all the adventures that now lay ahead of me.

Of course, I had no inkling of the darker side of my school-days to come.

PART TWO

School of the Desert

6

School Days

There was a mixture of Arab and black African teachers at the school, just as there was with the pupils. Miss Shadhia was a black African, although I wasn't sure from which tribe she came. She was both my tutor and my maths teacher. I warmed to her immediately, and I felt that she did to me. In a stroke of good fortune I was to prove gifted at maths, which would cement the friendship between us.

That first morning Miss Shadhia sorted out where we would sit. The smallest pupils went at the front and the tallest at the back, so that everyone could see the teacher and she them, in case anyone was misbehaving. My desk of three seats was halfway back and tucked in against the wall. I rather liked it. I could see the blackboard clearly, yet I wasn't in the limelight.

I took the seat against the wall. The seat next to me was filled by a little black girl. I took a peek at her face and my heart skipped with joy: she had scars that just had to be Zaghawa. I reached out and gave her hand a friendly squeeze. She smiled at me and gave me a squeeze in return. The last seat was taken by an Arab-looking girl. She had her hair done up in long glossy pigtails, complete with bright red ribbons. I gave her a shy smile of welcome, and she half-smiled back at me. And with that our row of three was complete.

As the sun climbed into the sky the iron roof above our heads made the room like an oven. To make matters worse the lessons were all in Arabic. My father had given me a crash course in basic

Arabic, but as we broke for lunch I found that my head was spinning. It was partly from the heat, and partly from the mental effort of trying to comprehend a language that was alien to my tribe. I went and sat on the grass, and delved into my school bag for my packed lunch. The girl who sat next to me in class came and joined me.

'Hello. What's your name?' I ventured.

'It's Mona,' she replied. 'What's yours?'

I told her that it was Halima but everyone called me Rathebe. 'You're Zaghawa, aren't you?'

Mona nodded. 'What about you? You look Zaghawa, but where are your glasses?'

She meant my 'glasses' scars, the two deep cuts to my temples. I giggled. 'Well, my nasty old grandma tried to cut me, but I ran away. See,' I added, pointing to the faint scar running down my cheek. 'That's where they cut me when I escaped.'

Mona grinned. 'You're crazy . . . But you *are* Zaghawa, aren't you?'

I nodded. 'So that makes two of us.' I looked around at the other girls. 'I wonder how many more we are.'

Before Mona could answer, I felt a sharp crack on my head. I turned around to see a figure towering over us, a big stick in her hand. An instant later she cracked Mona around the head too.

'No speaking Zaghawa!' she snapped, her face like dark thunder. 'You speak only Arabic at my school. If I hear you doing so again, it's in my office with you!'

Before we could answer she stalked off, searching for other offenders. It turned out that this fearsome lady was our headmistress. She and I were soon to become the best of enemies.

I turned back to Mona. 'Nasty old bag,' I muttered. 'Can you speak any Arabic?'

'*Shweah-shweah* – A little,' Mona replied.

'Me too. Well, we're just going to have to learn quickly, otherwise that old bag will have a perfect reason for beating us . . .'

Our lessons that first term included science, maths, Islamic studies and Arabic. I found myself enjoying maths most of all, especially with Miss Shadhia as teacher. It was also the only subject in which speaking Arabic wasn't an advantage: numbers are universal, crossing all language barriers. But in the other subjects the girls who spoke good Arabic were soon poking fun at us. The worst was our Arabic lessons. As we struggled to write, or to make ourselves understood in our bush Arabic, they would titter and tease.

Miss Jelibah, our Arabic teacher, tried her best to be fair. No matter that she was an Arab herself, she scolded the Arab girls and warned them to stop being nasty. They did quieten down a little when she was facing class. But as soon as she turned her back to write on the backboard, the teasing resumed. As I struggled to answer a question in the Arabic words that my father had taught me, I noticed that the Arab girl with pigtails who sat next to Mona was laughing at me. I felt a burning resentment growing inside me.

The start of our school week was Saturday, with lessons through to Thursday. Friday – the Muslim holy day – was our one day off. I'd spend it with my uncle's daughters, washing and ironing our school uniforms, and rebraiding our hair. Salma and Fatma went to the same school as me, but they were in senior classes. While my school day was finished by one o'clock, they would have to stay long into the hot afternoon.

First thing each morning there was an assembly on the school playing field. The assembly bell rang at eight o'clock sharp, and woe betide anyone who was late. A teacher would be standing by the gate to catch any stragglers. Sometimes I was late, because I had such a long walk to school. Punishment would be to clean the toilets – a series of wooden shacks at one end of the playing field. Inside each was a wooden platform with a hole cut in it, and a bucket down below. Cleaning them was the very worst.

As soon as you opened the door a thick cloud of flies would come buzzing up from the depths, and you would be hit by the sickening smell. You had to fight your way inside, unhinge the wooden platform, lift the bucket and carry it over to a wooden cart, from which, each week, a man would haul the stinking slops off to the local dump. After emptying the bucket you had to return to scrub down the toilet with a mop and rags.

Some mornings when I was late I would skulk outside the gates, waiting for the eleven o'clock break. I would try to mingle with the girls who came out to play, and sneak into the classroom. But half the time I got caught and punished with a beating. The only alternative was to go home, but then my uncle and aunt would be upset, and they might tell my father. The only option really was to be on time for that dreaded assembly bell.

The assembly itself was still a trial. Pupils had to stand in rows, the youngest at the front and the oldest at the back. We had to hold out our hands as the headmistress inspected our nails, our clothes, our faces and our hair. If you had a speck of dirt on you from walking to school, then she'd give you a crack with her stick. And we had to keep totally silent. Everyone had been beaten and no one wanted to be next.

But the worst was if you'd forgotten your socks, or if your nails were too long. Then she'd order you into her office. She had several different diameters of garden hose, and she would choose the size best suited to the crime. It was bad enough getting beaten on the bum. Over time I learned to wear extra knickers, to cushion the blows. But the headmistress soon got wise to that, and so she started beating us on the bare soles of our feet. The worst was the large hosepipe across the feet. That was truly agony.

After the first two lessons we'd break for brunch, at eleven o'clock. By that time a jumble of stalls would have been set up at the school gates. Mona and I would race to be first at the stall of the lady from the Felatta tribe, a black African people who originated in Nigeria. She sold the finest falafel, with aubergine salad and chilli sauce, in a fresh bread sandwich. We'd follow that with an 'ice-lolly' – fruit juice frozen in a poly bag. My favourite was made from the sap of a tree that tastes like the juice of fresh peas.

Whenever we tired of falafel we'd order *foul* – a bean stew mixed with tomato and sesame oil. It was delicious with fresh yoghurt salad. If we were really lucky the Felatta lady would have some diluted yoghurt blended with cucumber and spices. She'd give us a cupful to wash down our falafel sandwich or our bean stew.

After we'd eaten we'd head for the playground. We'd draw a hopscotch course, marking out a series of staggered squares in the dusty earth. While standing on the first square you had to throw a stone to land in the second, and then advance to that one. If your stone fell outside the square, you'd have to start all over again. Others would be playing with skipping ropes, with two holding and one jumping in the middle.

But my favourite game was sock-ball, using an old sock stuffed full of rags and bound tightly into a ball. One girl would stand in the middle while the two on either side had to try to hit her with the sock-ball. If the girl in the middle was 'got' then she would become one of the throwers, and whoever had hit her would be piggy-in-the-middle. Sock-ball was the nearest we ever got to a rough and tumble at school, because fighting was totally banned.

After school Mona and I would walk most of the way home together. Her family had lived in town ever since she was little, and so she was street-wise and worldly. I felt secure and confident in her company. Our route took us through the bustling market-place and past the central mosque, where she would head for her house and I to my uncle's.

One afternoon we were just leaving the market when she grabbed me by the arm. 'Look! Look! *Khawajat! Khawajat!* Bet you've never seen anything like that before!'

I caught sight of two white people – *khawajat* – strolling through the market-place. I knew that white people existed, of course, because my father had told me all about them, but I'd never actually seen any before. There was a woman with long hair like liquid gold, and a man with an enormous beard like red fire. I stared and stared and stared. I didn't need to worry about being rude, because just about everyone else was staring.

I watched the *khawajat* wander through the market-place. Their skin was so white it looked like butter, and I wondered if it melted in the sun. They were both wearing wide-brimmed hats, so perhaps they were frightened of the sun's rays. But the man was wearing a pair of strange trousers that ended above the knees, so perhaps their skin didn't melt after all.

They were desperately trying to ignore the fact that they had a straggly gaggle of street kids running and skipping after them. The kids kept yelling out: '*Khawajat! Khawajat! Khawajat!*' at the tops of their voices. Every now and then an adult would grab one of the cheeky kids and box them around the ears, in an effort to make them stop their teasing. But it didn't work for long. Teasing the *khawajat* was clearly too much fun.

The *khawajat* came from a far-off country called Germany, Mona explained. They were said to be good people. They lived out in the bush where they dug wells and built schools for the Zaghawa villagers. They came into town once a month to stock up on supplies. As we left the market-place I told Mona some of Grandma's funny stories about the time when the British ruled Sudan. Soon we were laughing fit to burst.

'You know what Grandma used to say? She'd say: "Those *khawajat* – they don't know the meaning of stopping work, or of resting and taking it easy . . . If you work with one of those *khawajat* they will drive you to death, and one day you will simply die."'

Being a real townie, Mona had her hair done in a different style each week. Today she had it braided Bob Marley style – the one that Grandma truly hated. I really liked it, and I decided to have my hair done the same way. When I got back to my uncle's house I would ask Salma and Fatma to do it for me. I didn't care what Grandma thought: I wanted to do it as my rebellion against her controlling ways.

Salma and Fatma didn't mind braiding my hair Bob Marley style one little bit. Once it was done, I spent the rest of the evening on my homework. I lay on the rug on the floor and read my books and practised my Arabic. Now and again I asked Salma or Fatma for help. They had become like the big sisters that I'd never had. But of course, no one could take the place of my real family.

Within days of going to school I had realised that I was missing home – my mother, father, Mo, Omer and even Grandma. Other pupils were brought to school by their parents, and I missed having them around to do the same for me. Other children got packed lunches with special treats, but I bought my lunch at the Felatta woman's stall. Of course, every evening I'd eat with my uncle and aunt and my cousins. They tried to treat me just like their daughter, but it wasn't the same.

With few distractions I studied hard and soon I started to do well. I was determined that none of the Arab girls were going to laugh at me any more. I practised and practised my Arabic until it was almost as good as theirs. In no time at all my marks in all subjects were better than Mona's, and then in everything but Arabic I started overtaking the others.

Two Arab girls, Najhad and Samijah, were always competing to be top of the class. But barely a month into term I was beating them in my favourite subject, maths. Shortly after I was threatening to overtake them in Islamic studies and science. Neither of them seemed very happy about it, but I had Mona and the other black girls egging me on.

I imagined how pleased my father would be if he could see me now. The thought filled me with a warm glow of pride. But just when things were going so well, a dark shadow fell over these first, happy days.

One morning at assembly I was standing on the playing field, the headmistress stepping down the line. As she drew level with me I felt a savage blow to the side of my head. An instant later I found myself sprawled on the ground. I struggled to get up, but none of the girls could help me, for then they were sure to get beaten. I stumbled to my knees, and I found myself staring into a face contorted with rage. I tried to focus on the words, but the whole side of my face was stinging horribly and my ear had gone quite numb.

'Stand in line, you stupid girl!' the headmistress yelled. 'Stand in line! If I find you out of line again . . .'

As I held that cruel woman's gaze, I felt hot tears of rage running down my face. She had three scars running down each of her cheeks, and I knew these to be the traditional marks of the Ahrao. I felt certain that had I been one of the Arab girls, she would have simply ordered me to stand back in line, not lashed out so viciously. I hated that woman more than anyone else in the world. I fixed in my mind that I was going to get my own back. No way was I going to be treated like this, just because I was a little black Zaghawa girl.

A week later I was called to the staff room by Miss Ursah, one of the science teachers. It was her job to organise the cleaning rota. Each week pupils would be tasked with picking up leaves and waste paper from the playing field, sweeping the classrooms or scrubbing the dreaded toilets. Each pupil was paired up with another from her class. Miss Ursah announced that I had been teamed up with Sairah, the Arab girl who shared the desk with Mona and me. Sairah would clean the back half of our classroom while I did the front.

The following morning I arrived an extra twenty minutes early, so I could complete my cleaning duties. I found myself a broom and started on my half of the classroom. It was tiresome to have to get up so early. I had an hour's walk to school and back as it was. But I didn't mind doing the cleaning, as we all had to do our share. In any case, it was nothing compared to the chores that I was used to back in the village. Time passed quickly as I swept and scrubbed and dusted down the desks and cleaned the blackboard.

But with eight o'clock assembly fast approaching there was still no sign of Sairah. My half was pretty much finished by now, and I was just wondering whether to start on hers when Miss Ursah arrived. I stood with my broom in hand, proud of my half of the classroom. Miss Ursah swept her eyes from end to end, her face darkening as she did so.

'Why is this end so dirty?' she demanded, pointing to Sairah's part. 'And where's that other girl – Sairah?'

'I don't know, Miss,' I answered. 'She must be late, Miss.'

'Obviously she's late. But why haven't you done that half?'

I looked around myself, in confusion. 'But isn't that Sairah's side . . .?'

'Don't argue with me, girl,' Miss Ursah interrupted. 'Clean that part – and quickly, before it's time for class.'

'But Miss, it's not . . .'

'I said, "Don't argue with me"! Or didn't you hear me? Now, get your broom and start sweeping!'

If only she'd spoken a kind word to me about what a nice job I'd done, then I would have gladly done Sairah's side. If only she'd asked me to do it, rather than ordering me to. It was the unfairness and bullying that I found so unacceptable. I gulped, as I felt the fear rising within me at what I was about to do. But I knew that I had to do it. I had to make a stand.

'No,' I muttered, my eyes cast down at the floor. 'I'm not doing it.'

Miss Ursah stared at me. 'What did you say? *What?!* I hope I didn't hear you properly!'

I plonked my brush down defiantly. 'I'm not doing it.'

'You're not . . .?' she repeated, incredulously. 'Listen, girl, you do as I say, you hear me? *You do as I say!*'

'I'm not doing it. It isn't fair.'

'Isn't fair! *Isn't fair!*' Miss Ursah's face was glowing red with anger. 'I'm the one around here who decides what's fair! So start cleaning – now! Now! *Now!*'

For a moment there was a horrible stand-off. And for an instant I felt my resolve waver. But then a thought came flashing into my head. My father had nicknamed me Rathebe, after a black African woman who had stood up to those of other races – *and I was going to do the same*. Whatever happened to me, I was going to make a stand. I felt certain that my father would stand by me, even if I was banished forever from the school.

'No,' I repeated, more stubbornly than ever. 'I'm *not* doing it.'

I flinched as Miss Ursah took two quick strides across the room, grabbing me by the scruff of the neck.

'This is your last chance,' she hissed, her face close to mine. 'I'm ordering you to clean this room. *Ordering you.* If you don't I'll . . .'

'I said I'm not doing it,' I cried. 'It's not fair . . .'

'I order you to obey me!' she thundered. 'Now – obey. *OBEY!* Get cleaning!'

She shoved me roughly towards the rear of the classroom and I caught myself awkwardly on a desk. I turned to face her. We all knew by now that Sairah's mother was a teacher at the school. She had tried to keep it quiet, but the word was out. I couldn't bear the thought that I was being ordered to do Sairah's cleaning all because she was a spoilt teacher's daughter. The last thing on earth that I could stomach was being treated as anyone's slave.

I shook my head at her. 'No! No way! I've cleaned my side. And I'm not doing Sairah's dirty work . . .'

Miss Ursah let out a yelp of rage and lunged for me, grabbing my hair with the one hand and the broom with the other. As she dragged at my roots to stop me escaping, she beat me on my bare legs. Each stroke of the broom was agony, but I refused to cry out or to show that it hurt. I wasn't going to give this cruel bully the satisfaction of feeling my pain. Finally, she shoved me again and I hit the edge of a desk with my thigh.

A bolt of pain shot through me, and with it came a surge of fiery rage. There was no way that I was taking any more from her. If she came for me again, I would fight and bite and scratch like a wild thing, and I knew that I would win. I had learned my skill at fighting as a tough little child in the village. And deep inside I was like Omer – as fearless as a lion. By contrast, Miss Ursah's violent exterior masked the fact that she was a coward.

I darted out of her reach, placing a desk between us. My face was fixed in a mask of bitter defiance as I stared her down. For a few seconds we circled each other. I wasn't afraid of her any more, and I knew that she could see it. In fact, what I read in her face was surprise and fear. Surprise because I was a young village girl and I had chosen to disobey her command. And fear because I was a black African, and like many Arabs in my country she believed that she was my natural-born master.

'*One last chance,*' Miss Ursah hissed. 'I'm ordering you to get cleaning. One last chance – you hear me? Or I'm reporting you to the headmistress.'

'Then report me,' I retorted. 'Report me. I'm not afraid of you, or her, or anyone. My only fear is for my God.'

Miss Ursah turned on her heel and was gone. For a second I stared after her, a wave of relief washing over me. And then my fear and anxiety returned with a vengeance. What on earth had I done, I wondered. And what were they going to do to me now? I didn't have long to wait to find out.

Once assembly was over I was marched to the headmistress's office. She sat down behind her desk, her cold dark eyes boring into me. I stood there in front of her, trying not to reveal my fear. In a hard, flat voice she related what Miss Ursah had told her. Was it true? Was it true that I had refused to do the cleaning? Was it true that I had defied and insulted Miss Ursah, a teacher at her school? If so, I was a rude, impolite girl and I would be punished very severely.

I began to relate the story from my side. As I did so I told myself to hold my nerve. They could beat me to within an inch of my life, but better that than let Miss Ursah, or any of them, tyrannise me. I admitted that I had defied Miss Ursah, but only because she was being unfair. I had cleaned my side of the class-room. The other side was the duty of Sairah, and I shouldn't be punished for her failings. I told her that I was not going to be abused by anyone unfairly. For that, God was the only one that I would answer to.

'Well, I've never heard such impudence!' the headmistress scolded. 'Never! It may be your God that you answer to outside these walls, but not in my school. Here you answer to me. Now go! Just get out of my sight! I need some time to decide what to do with you . . .'

I went back and rejoined my class, wondering all the time what was coming next. In a way I wished that the headmistress had beaten me there and then, and got it over and done with. Now I had my punishment hanging over me like a death sentence. But in spite of my worries, nothing more happened to me that day. As I walked home I reflected on what my father had done by sending me away to get a proper education.

My father had convinced me that coming away to the big school would be a wonderful fairytale adventure. I had believed every word. But had he really known what was in store for me? Maybe I would have been better off staying in the village and going to the local school. At least there I would have been with my family and my people, and no one would have treated me badly. I missed my family with an ache deep within my heart. And I missed the friendly hustle and bustle and the easy, simple freedoms of the village.

My uncle had sent news to my father of my successes at school, but not a word would have reached him of my troubles. The only person I had talked to about it was Mona. She had advised me not to make trouble for myself, and to do what the teachers said. But for some reason I just couldn't find it in myself to do so. If I was to stay at this school I would have to fight for what I felt was right. I just wanted to be treated fairly, and as an equal.

A week went by, and it was as if an uneasy truce existed between Miss Ursah, the headmistress and me. But I knew that it couldn't last. Whenever I saw them together they scowled at me, their faces dark with an evil intent. I did my best to avoid them and I waited in fear for whatever was coming. Of one thing I was certain – they were not going to let this pass.

I hadn't breathed a word of what had happened to Sairah, my absent cleaning mate. In spite of this, she started acting strangely towards me. Whenever I went to take my place by the wall I had to squeeze past her. Each time that I did so she would sigh and harrumph, as if it was a real pain to let me pass. It was almost as if she was deliberately provoking me.

I tried to concentrate on the end-of-term tests, which were less than two weeks away. The days flew past with study, and I did my best to stay out of trouble. When the results were posted on the school notice board I was dumbfounded: I had come top of the class in everything save Arabic. Mona and the other black African girls were overjoyed. But as for Sairah and the other Arab girls, I didn't get a sense that they were best pleased.

The following day my father arrived to take me home. I threw my bags into the back of his beloved Land Rover, and with barely a wave goodbye we were on our way. As we headed into the bush my father passed me a bag of biscuits. I munched away happily, and he brought me up to date on all the news. Then he told me how proud he was of my achievements. Of course, as soon as he mentioned school I was reminded of all my troubles.

'How were the exams?' he asked me eagerly.

'I came top of the class,' I answered.

'Wow! Rathebe!' My father let out a cry of delight, and banged his hands on the steering wheel. 'Just like I said – that white eyelash brought real genius, as well as good fortune!'

I nodded, and stared out of the window. I had just spent three months in a foreign place where the adults had bullied me horribly. I wanted to unburden myself of my troubles, and my father was the only person in the world with whom I wanted to do so.

'Top of the class in everything?' he asked.

I sniffed, trying to hold back my tears. 'Everything but Arabic.'

My father glanced across at me, and slowed the vehicle. I kept staring out the window, trying to hide my emotions from him.

'Rathebe, is everything all right?' he asked me, gently. 'Are *you* all right?'

'I'm fine,' I lied. My bottom lip had started to quiver, just as Mohammed's did when he was about to cry.

'It doesn't matter about Arabic,' my father said, as he eased the car to a stop. 'You'll soon improve . . .'

'It's not that,' I blurted out, bursting into tears. 'It's all your fault . . .'

My father killed the engine and reached over to give me a hug. I resisted stiffly for a second or so, and then I melted into his embrace. He told me over and over how much he loved me, and how much everyone had missed me at home – until I had all but cried myself out.

'You lied to me, Abba,' I told him then, my words tumbling over each other as they rushed to come out. 'You said that school was wonderful but it isn't and the teachers hate me and beat me and the Arab girls are horrid and you nicknamed me Rathebe so I think I've got to stand up to them but really I just want to come home and live with you and Eya and Grandma and go to a school where people are nice . . .'

My father took my hand in his, gently but firmly. 'Look, Rathebe, did I ever say that it was going to be easy?'

'No, but you still tricked me, Abba. You said that school was a nice place, but they just don't like us there. Or they don't like me, anyway . . .'

I told my father all about the horrid headmistress, about my fight with Miss Ursah and about my troubles with Sairah. Once I'd finished doing so I felt a little better. I wiped my nose and tried to smile.

My father smiled back at me encouragingly. 'Rathebe, there's one thing you have to understand. The Arabs won't make anything easy for us in this country . . .'

I nodded. I knew now that my father was right, for I'd experienced it myself at school.

'I'm glad you stood up to them,' he continued. 'I'm proud of you, Rathebe, more proud of you for doing that than for anything. But if you want to get a proper education and challenge the Arabs in this country, it's the only way. The village school just isn't good enough. They won't like it. They'll try to stop you. But that's all the more reason to go on. You've already proven that you're better than them – so don't give up. It'll get easier, you'll see.'

I nodded. 'I *did* come top of the class, Abba. I beat all those Arab girls . . .'

My father grinned. 'That you did! So will you do what I said? Will you persevere? Will you do that just for me?'

I nodded again. 'I'll try, Abba.'

For my father I'd do just about anything.

7

Fight School

By the time we reached the village my worries felt as if they were a million miles away. It was as if a great weight had been lifted off me. My mother fussed around, pinching my flesh to make sure I was healthy and well fed. My brothers rushed around firing question after question at me. It was so good to be home. I went to dump my bags in Grandma's hut. She bade me welcome – all smiles, as she held out her arms for a hug.

'Come, come, come, my sweetheart,' she mouthed at me.

I buried my face in the warm, spicy smell of her. I realised just how much I had missed Grandma's proud, fearless ways: if only she had been with me at school, no one would have dared bully me. She hugged me tight, then held me at arm's length to have a good look at me. I had rarely seen Grandma looking so happy, and it just showed how much she really loved me.

'You – you haven't changed one bit,' she announced. 'At least this going away to school lark hasn't ruined you.'

'Abu,' I murmured. 'I've missed you. I've missed you all so much . . .'

'Hold on a minute,' Grandma exclaimed, her face darkening. 'Hold on! What's this?'

Her hand shot out and tugged my headscarf to one side. As she did so I suddenly remembered that my hair was still braided in the Bob Marley style. For a second Grandma stared at me in horror, her eyes practically popping out of her head. Then she grabbed hold of my ear, twisting it until the flesh burned, and marched me across to my mother's hut.

'What's this?' she shrieked. 'What's this? What's this girl done to her hair? A Bob Marley! *A Bob Marley! Beeri* not good enough for the big city girl now, is it?'

Grandma shoved me in front of my mother. I tried to explain that my best friend at school, Mona, had a Bob Marley, and she was Zaghawa, so what harm could there be in it? And my cousins had done the braiding for me, so my uncle hadn't minded . . . But Grandma stopped me in mid-sentence, twisting a pinch of flesh on my tummy until it really hurt.

'Arabic! Arabic! Arabic!' she scolded. 'Speaking that rubbish Arabic! Blah, blah, blah, blah – so Grandma can't understand a word . . . Arabic – pah! You think your mother and I want to hear that croaking, rubbish language of frogs? Well, do you?'

I caught myself. Grandma was right – I *had* been speaking Arabic. On the journey home I had been doing so with my father, and I had continued with my mother. That was the result of three months away at the big school where we were beaten for speaking anything else.

'Language of frogs!' Grandma continued. 'We don't want to hear it, and neither does the rest of the village. And we'll finish that Bob Marley style right now. *Right now!*'

Grandma plonked me down on a little stool in the middle of our living area. I felt certain that she wanted everyone to witness my humiliation.

'Sit there and don't move,' she ordered, as she stomped off to get some scissors. She returned and started working on the braids, muttering away as she did so. 'A Bob Marley . . . You go and mix with strangers and immediately you want to be like them . . .'

Being careful to speak in Zaghawa, I tried explaining to Grandma that I just wanted to be like my Zaghawa school friend, Mona. I liked the style, as it made me look different. But Grandma was having none of it. The more I protested, the harder she yanked out my braids. I told myself that I would have to be more careful in future. Next time, I would have my hair redone in the *beeri* style just before returning to the village.

'Three months in that place and you've forgotten your roots,' Grandma grumbled. 'I said no good would come of it. And if you're so keen to speak Arabic, well – you can go and live with the Arabs . . .'

An hour later my hair was back in the boring *beeri* style, braided into hard rows tight against my scalp. After eating supper with my mother and a grumpy Grandma, I went to relax with my father on the rugs in the living area. My mother, Mo and Omer joined us, and I began telling them about life in the big town. But Grandma went and locked herself in her hut: she wanted nothing to do with such talk of foreign places and strangers.

I told them about the two *khawajat* that I'd seen in the market. I described their skin like creamy butter, and how we marvelled that it didn't melt in the sun. I described the woman's hair, like fine threads of spun gold, and the man's bushy beard, flame-red like the setting sun.

People in our village knew that white people existed, of course. On the rare occasions that an airliner flew high above the village, children would run out and gaze up at it, shouting and waving as if the passengers could hear and see.

'*Khawajat! Khawajat! Khawajat!*' we'd cry. Then we'd sing: 'Plane Number 3! Plane Number 3! This is Plane Number 3!'

I've no idea why we used to sing 'Plane Number 3'. Maybe someone had once seen that number written on an aircraft, and that's where the song had come from.

I explained how the *khawajat* from Hashma market actually lived in the remote bush. They'd been in town stocking up on supplies, so they could return to their work building wells and schools. My school friend, Mona, had told me that they were good people, because they came from far, far away to help the Zaghawa.

My father chuckled. 'Yes, Rathebe, the *khawajat* do come to do good things – *now*. But it wasn't always thus. Hundreds of years ago the British came as invaders, to divide the tribes and make them fight each other. They called this policy "divide and rule".'

Omer snorted. 'Are you two just going to talk boring politics stuff now? You always do when Rathebe's around. I'm off to bed.'

My father ignored Omer as he stomped off into the shadows. I glanced at the others. Mohammed was lying half-asleep by the fire, my mother equally sleepy beside him.

'Back then the British came to our country for one reason,' my father continued. 'They came to take what they could for themselves. They took the land to grow their crops; they took the mountains to mine gold; and they tried to take the people to work for them. But we Zaghawa resisted, and we were never truly conquered.'

My father glanced at me, his eyes glinting. 'But you know the worst thing the British did? The very worst? When they left they gave all the power to the Arab tribes. They handed power to the Arabs. Now that's the sort of things you should be learning at school.'

'So maybe they're coming back now to try to make up for it,' I suggested. 'Maybe they're feeling guilty.'

My father laughed. 'Maybe they are, Rathebe, maybe they are. They certainly should be. They owe us . . .'

We lapsed into silence, gazing into the heart of the fire. I had missed all this so much, this feeling of family closeness and love; of the cool, velvety night air caressing my skin; of the flickering glow of the firelight; of the ebb and flow of easy talk and laughter.

'I'll tell you something else,' my father added. 'There is one country now that leads the world – America. And if America wasn't doing so then it would be China. Both are huge countries. But when the British ruled Sudan they ruled most of the world, and Britain is just a tiny island. You have to admire the British: with nothing they managed to conquer the world.'

'How did they do it, Abba?' I asked.

'I don't really know. But you know how if someone turns up bang on time we joke that they're running on *khawajat* time? You know why we say that? It's because the British were always on time. Always. And another thing, they knew the meaning of hard work. They never stopped. So maybe it was that. Maybe with hard work and good time-keeping they managed to conquer the world.'

'Did you ever work with the *khawajat*?'

'It was before my time . . .' My father was silent for a moment. Then he said: 'But you know, Rathebe, I've been thinking. I've been thinking that if you continue to do well at school, and if I can ever afford it, maybe we should send you away to Britain, so you can study there. That's where you'll get the best education possible . . .'

That night I went to sleep wondering whether my father could possibly be serious. Just going away to Hashma had been daunting enough. The very thought of travelling far, far away to study in the land of the *khawajat* was both thrilling and terrifying, in equal measure.

The following morning I awoke early to a deep roaring-chugging reverberating through the air. I glanced across at Grandma's bed, but it was empty. I heard the noise grow louder and then fainter, as whatever it was moved closer and further away. Curiosity finally got the better of me, and I went to have a look. It turned out that a tiny aeroplane was flying over the fields to the east of the village, trailing a cloud of white dust.

A swarm of locusts had arrived in the night, my father explained, and the aircraft was spraying the fields to kill them. For many years we wouldn't see any *gubhor*, as we called them, and then the first of these giant flying insects would arrive. In the past there had been swarms so large that they had eaten everything. Gardens, crops of maize and sorghum, bushes and trees in the forest – all had been stripped bare. This had never happened in my lifetime, and my father reckoned we were about due a big swarm.

After a hurried breakfast I rushed off with Mo and Omer on a locust-gathering expedition. We headed into the bush, and soon we spotted a tree shimmering with a heavy load of insects. Omer couldn't wait. He shinned up the trunk and started shaking them free.

Meanwhile, Mo and I set about preparing a fire. I'd brought a glowing branch from the hearth at home. I covered it in dry leaves and grass, blew hard, and shortly I had a strong blaze crackling away. I grabbed a burning stick and thrust it where the locusts were thickest. As the smoke got in among them they tumbled off the branches, some having their wings burned in a pop of fire and plummeting to earth. Omer came down from the tree to collect the fallen locusts as Mo and I worked our way around it with fire sticks.

Soon we had a sack stuffed half-full of *gubhor*. We headed off to find some more, and discovered a carpet of locusts feasting on some low plants. We could hear the eerie snap-rustle-snap of a thousand tiny jaws chomping away. We pounced and captured as many as we could in the cup of our hands. The insects rose as a carpet and flew off, but they quickly settled again nearby. We advanced and began our second capture operation.

When the sack was full to bursting we hurried home to Grandma. Grandma loved eating locusts. She believed they were a wonder food that would prevent most illnesses. She grabbed the sack excitedly and emptied out the live insects into a big clay pot, slamming shut the wooden lid.

'Now, go!' she urged, handing me back the empty sack. 'Go and get some more!'

By the end of the day we were covered in dirt and dust and completely exhausted. But we were happy, and I felt more at peace than I had done for many a day at school. Grandma had our reward waiting for us at home: plate after plate of deep-fried locusts. All you had to do was grab one, pull off the head and wings, pop it into your mouth and chew. The result was an explosion of sweet, fatty juices, and an urgent desire to eat more.

Because water was in short supply in our village we would only ever wash on a Friday – the Muslim holy day. Most nights my mother would rub sesame oil over our bodies, to moisturise and cleanse. Before we went to bed Mum gave us an extra thorough oiling, to try to get rid of the worst of the day's grime from the locust hunting. As she did so she sang softly to us, and I told her all about the day's adventures.

My mother used a special type of oil for my hair, called *zit karkar*. This consists of sesame oil scented with sandalwood and mixed with beeswax until it becomes a thick gel. I sat between her knees as she massaged the *zit karkar* into my hair, the sensation soothing and relaxing. By the time she had finished I had fallen asleep. I woke to her tying a scarf tightly around my head. If she didn't do this I'd end up with dirt all over my hair, as it would stick to the waxy oil.

━━◆━━

That first week home from school I spent every waking hour collecting locusts. At the end the swarm just seemed to disappear, and it had never reached truly plague-like proportions. Of course, we were sick to death of eating *gubhor* by now. But still Grandma served them up for breakfast, lunch and supper, and woe betide anyone who didn't eat their share.

'You kids – you're spoilt,' she grumbled. 'You don't know the value of food. One day there will be hunger in the village and people will die. And then you'll understand.'

Grandma proceeded to tell us the story of the last big hunger. First the rains had failed and then the locusts had come – a swarm so large that it had blocked out the sun. This had happened during the time when Ronald Reagan was president of America. American aid workers had come to the village in a convoy of shiny trucks, bringing emergency food aid. Then American aircraft had dropped sacks of corn flour. The children had danced around, pointing at the sky and chanting: 'Reagan! Reagan! Reagan! Reagan coming!'

One of the villagers had composed a song during the time of hunger. It went like this:

> *Reagan came,*
> *Reagan came,*
> *Flying in the air,*
> *High in the sky,*
> *Helping the poor,*
> *Bringing the food,*
> *God bless him,*
> *God help him,*
> *God sent him,*
> *To the Zaghawa.*

Grandma warned us that we could never know when the next big hunger might come. That's why we should never waste any food.

~

My holiday flew past and soon it was time to return to the big school. My days in the village with my loving family had healed much of the hurt of my first term. I felt a renewed thirst to study and learn – and I hoped that everything would be all right this time. Catching locusts and avoiding Grandma's beatings was all well and good, but I was hungry for some education once more.

My father decided to come with me to the school. It was unspoken between us, but I knew that he was doing so to show a presence. He greeted all of the teachers, and to each he gave a small gift of money. Before leaving he went to see the dreaded headmistress and gave a donation towards school funds. Grandma was a great believer in showing off your wealth, for it could convince even your worst enemy to treat you more respectfully. My father also knew this to be true, for money equated to power in Sudan.

I noticed an immediate change among the teachers, but it had little effect on my fellow pupils. Sairah would be sat in her place next to Mona, and once again she would sigh and stick out her elbows and knees as I tried to squeeze past. She was gunning for trouble, and I knew that sooner or later I would have to make a stand.

Hashma was principally a Zaghawa town, so the Arabs were in a minority. But at school they were in the majority, both pupils and teachers. The Arab families came to Hashma from all over Sudan. There were traders from the north; there were the families of military officers posted to the area; and there were government employees from Khartoum.

Sairah's father was a government official, and they lived in the exclusive part of town. I had walked past it with Mona. The houses were all grand multi-storey things, built in the English style with real glass in the windows. But wherever Sairah might live and whoever her parents might be, I kept telling myself that it didn't matter. It didn't mean that she was any better than me.

It was a week into my second term when things came to a head. During eleven o'clock break Mona and I had been playing sock-ball with Najat, Samirah and Makboulah, our Zaghawa and Fur friends. I returned to class to find Sairah already at her place, and I had a suspicion she was deliberately getting there early. I asked politely if she might let me pass to my place by the wall. As she got up to let me by, there was the usual sighing and flouncing.

But as I squeezed past she forced her knees into the back of my legs. For a second I almost lost my balance, but then I caught myself on the desk and pushed back with all my might. Sairah got the shock of her life. She had no idea that a girl from the bush would stand up to her, let alone how strong we were compared to these soft city girls. I hadn't spent my childhood carrying water, gathering firewood and play-fighting only to be pushed around by a spindly, spiteful Arab city girl.

'Hey! What're you doing?' she cried. 'Idiot! Clumsy village girl. Be careful with your stupid big . . .'

I turned on her, the very look on my face shutting her up.

'Don't shout,' I told her, coldly. 'And don't try to cause trouble in front of the others. If you want to make something of it, I'll meet you after school on Thursday, under the big tree. Thursday afternoon – I'll be waiting. Be there. Otherwise, keep quiet.'

I didn't want to make any trouble. I just wanted to be free to study, and to be treated the same as the others. But if it came to fighting, then Thursday was the best day. It was a half-day, so all afternoon the school would be deserted. I only had a day to wait until our fight, but I wondered if Sairah would actually show up. She probably didn't believe that a little black girl from the bush would really stand up to her. It was time to show her otherwise.

After school Mona, Najat, Samirah and Makboulah gathered around me. They were all of the same mind: I had to deal with Sairah, or she would never let up on me. They pointed out that this was bigger than just a clash of personalities between her and me. She was an Arab daughter of an Arab teacher married to an Arab government official, yet I was coming top of the class. In that sense it was my friends' fight, as much as it was mine.

'We'll be there for you,' said Mona. 'So don't worry.'

'We'll stand by the gates where we can see what's happening,' Makboulah said.

'And if she comes with her Arab friends, then we'll fight them,' said Najat.

'But she probably won't even come,' Mona said. 'Or if she does, she'll bring her teacher mother to hold her hand . . .'

We laughed. It was typical of Mona to crack a joke to ease the tension. Knowing that I had my friends behind me stiffened my resolve. I couldn't imagine what sort of trouble I'd be in if I beat a fellow pupil, and the daughter of a teacher and a government worker. But just as with Miss Ursah, I knew that I had no choice: I had to make a stand.

The following afternoon pupils streamed out of the school gates, while I went and stood under the big tree. I had my head buried in a book, as if I was waiting for one of my friends. Out of the corner of my eye I could see Mona and the others standing in a group by the gate. None of the teachers would realise what we were up to, I told myself. I waited and waited until the school seemed to be deserted. Perhaps Sairah had chickened out.

I was just about to give up when I spotted a figure coming across the playground. It was Sairah, and she was alone. She had neither her friends nor her teacher mother with her. She marched up to where I was standing. For a second we stood facing each other, as she tried to stare me down. She was a good half-head taller than me, but I wasn't for one instant afraid of her. Finally, she glanced around at the tree and the earth and then back at me.

'What exactly did you want with me *here*?' she sneered. 'Oh, I suppose you village girls are happier meeting under *a tree*, aren't you? Feels so much more like home . . .'

It was all I could do to prevent myself from lunging at her and hurling her to the ground. I was dying to beat that arrogant sneer off her face. But I didn't want to be the one to start the fight. I wanted her to make the first move, for at least then I would have some form of defence with the teachers. When I was marched before the headmistress, as I felt certain I would be, I wanted to truthfully say that it was Sairah who had first laid a hand on me.

'Why do you treat this as if it's *your* school?' I countered. 'It isn't yours, any more than it's mine or any of the other girls'.'

'No idea what you're on about,' she replied. 'You're just trying to cause trouble – like when you pushed past so rudely yesterday . . .'

'That's a lie, and you know it! You treat that desk as if it's yours, just like you do the whole school.'

Sairah placed her hands on her hips. 'You trying to start a fight, is that it?'

'Look, it's about time you learned to share this school . . .'

'Oh, is it – and who's going to teach me? *You?* Ha ha! Good one!' She leaned forward. 'You're after getting a good beating!'

'You know what I think?' I said. 'I think you act as if you own this place for one reason only: because your mum's a teacher here.'

'Listen, I know all about you and your problems with the teachers. Refused to clean the classroom, didn't you? Job too lowly for a Zaghawa bush girl, isn't it? Well, it's news to me if it is.'

'They told you everything?' I gasped. 'Your mother and Miss Ursah . . .'

Sairah reached out and started prodding me in the chest. 'I know what a troublemaker you are. And don't you think Miss Ursah's forgotten. Or the headmistress. They're going to get you. They're going to get you . . .'

As she went to poke me again I grabbed her hands and forced them down to her sides.

'Just stand there properly and talk to me respectfully,' I told her. 'Think you can manage that?'

'Let me go!' Sairah cried. 'How dare you! You let me go!'

I did as she asked and stood back. 'That's it! You asked for it!' Sairah cried.

She lunged for me, grabbing my shirt by the neck. I heard a sharp ripping sound as she tore at the cloth. I brought my arms up under hers, knocked them aside, and grabbed her shirt. She had made the first move, so now the fight was on. I shoved her backwards hard against the tree. I could see the look of shock in her eyes as I rammed her into the trunk, trying to rip her clothes apart. But her shirt was of a far better cotton than mine, and it wouldn't tear.

Sairah grabbed my hair and started tearing it out by the roots. A surge of anger rose up inside me, as all the frustration of my school days boiled over. I was blind to the pain. I brought my right arm back and punched Sairah hard in the face. The force of it shocked her, and I seized the advantage. I tripped her, and as she fell to the ground I was on top of her, grabbing the scarf around her neck and twisting it. I was in a blind fury now. I heard a voice screaming over and over again, though I couldn't quite believe it was me.

'I'm going to kill you! I'm going to kill you! I'm going to kill you!'

My hands twisted tighter. Sairah's eyes were bulging and her face was growing ever more red. Suddenly, I glanced up and saw my friends all around me, cheering and cheering me on. Somehow it brought me to my senses a little. Sairah was from an Arab tribe and she believed she was better than us. The teachers had treated her with huge favouritism, and abused me in the process. But perhaps she didn't deserve to die. Finally, I released my grip.

I got up and stood over her as she grasped at her throat, gasping for air. I could see a look of absolute shock and terror in her eyes. Whatever else might happen to me now, I had taught her a lesson she would never forget. And it felt good to have done so. I reached out and pulled her to her feet. She glanced at me for a fearful moment, and at my girlfriends, and then she stumbled off in the direction of the main school building.

I knew that this was the calm before the storm. I braced myself for whatever was coming next. Moments later Sairah emerged with her schoolteacher mother in tow.

'Girl! You there! Girl!' Sairah's mother cried out, her face a mask of rage. 'Look what you've done! How dare you! *How dare you!*'

I felt my friends move closer, as they formed a protective group.

Sairah's mother arrived in front of us, her daughter peering out from behind her shoulder. Sairah had a mass of leaves and mud stuck in her hair, from where I had forced her into the ground. The very sight of it cheered me and strengthened my resolve.

'Ripped her shirt . . . Half-strangled her . . .' her mother gasped. 'You're like an animal! *An animal!* You get back inside that school, right now!'

'Miss, your daughter started the fight,' I told her. 'She ripped my shirt. That's how she started it. So she only has herself to blame.'

'Get back inside the school!' she screamed. 'I'm not discussing it here! Get back inside!'

I stood my ground. 'No. It's the end of school and I'm going home. Your daughter started the fight. It's her fault, not mine. If you don't believe me, ask them.' I gestured to my friends. 'They saw it all.'

Sairah's mother glanced around the faces of the other girls. Mona, Najat, Samirah and Makboulah nodded.

'Halima's right, Miss,' Mona said. 'Sairah started it.'

'You can't blame Halima, Miss,' said Makboulah.

'Look at the state of Halima's shirt,' Samirah said. 'All ripped up . . .'

'She was only trying to defend herself,' said Najat.

Sairah's mother glared at us. She was silent for a moment, her mouth tight and angry. Her mind was working overtime, trying to decide what to do next.

'Well, we'll just see, won't we?' she declared. She stared at me with ice-cold rage. 'You're in trouble, girl. *Big trouble.* Beating a teacher's daughter . . . This is something for the *headmistress.* I'll be giving her a full report. *A full report.* Come Saturday, we'll see what happens. See if your friends can help you then!'

With that, she turned on her heel and she and Sairah were gone. As for me, I had a sense that my troubles were only just beginning.

8

Resistance for Grandma

I sat in class on Saturday morning with a fearful heart. My bravery and defiance beneath the big tree had all but evaporated. Sairah was nowhere to be seen, so I knew that, one way or another, trouble was brewing. My tutor, Miss Shadhia, arrived, and the first thing she did was take me aside for a quiet word. I was wanted in the headmistress's office, she told me. I liked my tutor, and I knew in my heart that she felt the same about me.

'Will you come with me?' I asked. 'I don't want to go on my own.'

'I'll come,' Miss Shadhia said. 'But first, tell me what happened. The truth. Why did you start this fight?'

I explained that I hadn't started the fight, Sairah had. And she'd been provoking me for weeks and weeks on end. I had beaten her, that was true. But what else was I supposed to do? It was self-defence. Miss Shadhia told me that if that was the truth, then she would stick by me. As she led me across to the staff office, I felt my resolve stiffen and defiance growing in my heart. If Miss Shadhia would stick by me, it would be all right.

She took me into the headmistress's office, and there ahead of us were Sairah and her mother. As soon as Sairah saw me she burst into tears.

'There she is,' she wailed. 'That's the one who beat me . . .'

'You know, she hasn't slept for two nights,' Sairah's mother added, throwing dark looks in my direction. 'She's traumatised, and she can't stop crying. Is that any way for one pupil to behave to another, to beat her so savagely?'

The headmistress glared at me, her face like a death mask. 'Do you have *anything* to say for yourself? You can start by saying sorry to this poor child. Your behaviour is horrific, and quite shameful. You must apologise and tell her you will never do such things again.'

'I'm not saying sorry, Miss,' I replied. 'Sairah started the fight. I didn't. I was only trying to defend myself . . .'

'You will say sorry when I tell you to!' the headmistress thundered. 'That's an order. *Say sorry*. Now! Or d'you want to make things even worse for yourself?'

I shook my head. 'No. I'm not apologising. I didn't start it. She did. If you don't believe me, ask the other girls . . .'

'Look! Look! Can you see now how rude and arrogant she is?' Sairah's mother cried. 'Can you understand how she set upon and savagely beat my daughter?'

The headmistress stared at me. 'Everyone is to leave,' she announced, in a low, icy tone. 'But not you, Halima. *You* will stay here. I've never known such barefaced defiance . . .'

I felt Miss Shadhia stir beside me. 'Headmistress, I'm afraid I must object,' she announced quietly. 'You have to listen to Halima's side. I'm her tutor, and I have never known her to cause even the slightest trouble. In fact, quite the reverse is true. There were witnesses to the fight. If anyone's to be punished, surely you must hear their side?'

'Whatever the truth might be, she's a rude, impudent girl!' the headmistress snapped. 'She's shown that by defying my authority!'

'But she's a gifted pupil,' Miss Shadhia objected. 'She regularly comes top of my class. She is an example to others and a pleasure to teach. Surely it isn't fair to let an incident like this blight her academic career, especially when you haven't heard her side?'

The headmistress held up a hand for silence. 'Enough! I've made up my mind. Whatever your academic gifts, you, Halima, are clearly an impolite and rebellious girl. You are expelled from this school until further notice, or until your parents can explain your behaviour to me.'

As I stepped out of the headmistress's office, I caught sight of Sairah smirking at me. I made my way back to the classroom, knowing that I had only escaped a beating because of Miss Shadhia's defence of me. But being expelled from school was even worse. It was as if the dream that my father and I cherished was being ripped away from us.

Back in class my friends gathered around. 'What happened?' Mona asked. 'Did she beat you?'

I tried a brave smile. 'No, they didn't even touch me. I don't know how I escaped, but I did . . .'

'Wow! You weren't punished at all?'

I glanced at the floor. 'Well, I *have* been thrown out of the school . . .'

'What? They can't do that!' Mona cried. 'You weren't the one who started . . .'

Just at that moment Miss Shadhia returned, with Sairah in tow. As Sairah made her way to her seat, I heard the other girls hissing under their breaths. She plonked herself down on the end of the row, and as she did so Mona jabbed her in the ribs.

'Snitch!' Mona hissed.

'Teacher's pet!' another said.

'Snitch, snitch, snitch . . .'

'Quieten down, everyone!' Miss Shadhia ordered. 'Open your exercise books. Eyes on the blackboard . . .'

That evening I confessed to my uncle all that had happened. He is my father's youngest brother, and he is a tough, proud Zaghawa man. Even so, I didn't know how he was going to react. He listened quietly to all I had to say, and then he told me how angry he was that I had been treated so badly. It would take days to get a message to my father, and for him to come. If I was happy for him to do it, my uncle would have words with the school. He was looking forward to showing them what we Zaghawa are made of.

The following morning I found myself back at school. Sairah and her mother were inside the headmistress's room. They had come to witness my humiliation, or so they thought. Uncle Ahmed was invited in. I listened outside the door as he explained that my father lived in the village and that he was my guardian. The headmistress told him that I had misbehaved, and that he would have to punish me. She wanted to know the details of how he would punish me, in order to assess whether she could allow me back into the school.

'There will be no punishment,' my uncle announced quietly. 'There will be no punishment because none is called for. Halima has done nothing wrong. As you know, I am not her father. But she lives with my family as if she is our daughter, and we know her to be a good girl, from an excellent family. She has told me what happened. She has told me what this other girl did – first provoking and then attacking her. I think perhaps you need me to repeat it all, for everyone's benefit.'

'How can she say such things?' Sairah's mother blurted out. 'Such lies! Was she the one who was half-strangled?'

'You should keep your girls under better control,' my uncle continued, ignoring Sairah's mother. 'And part of doing so should be to treat them *all* fairly, and with an honest hand. It seems to me that you call me in here to deal with your own problems – with children fighting. Children will fight. They do so. Why make it such an issue? Is it because you can't do your job properly? I don't want you calling me in here again.'

I could hear the headmistress spluttering as she tried to find the words to respond. 'There is no discipline problem in *my* school, let me tell you. And if you're trying to imply . . .'

'Fine, then,' my uncle cut her off. 'Fine. Then punish the girl who is the cause of the wrong. If you won't do so, my niece has a right to defend herself. This girl was bad to Halima, so she defended herself. That is not wrong. Punish the girl who started the trouble. That is the end of the matter. I do not expect you to call me in here again. For what do we pay the school fees, if you cannot keep fair and good discipline?'

'Rest assured, your fees are fair for the service provided,' the headmistress snapped.

'Indeed, so I hope,' my uncle replied. I heard a chair scraping on floorboards as he got to his feet. 'Now, we've all wasted enough of our time on this issue. I am not going to demand to know the punishment for this one, this one who started the fight. I am going to leave that in your capable hands. Likewise, I will leave it in your hands to treat my niece fairly. I hope very much that I shall not be needed again. Now, good day to you all.'

I stepped back from the door. I couldn't believe how well my uncle had defended me in there. The headmistress had been rendered speechless. Uncle Ahmed was my hero. He came out of the room, gave me a cheeky grin, and wandered off to find the loo.

'This family! These people!' I heard the headmistress declare. '*Look* at how they behave! These Zaghawa! *Who do they think they are?* Do they think that no one can punish them?'

'You know, you handled that very badly,' Sairah's mother remarked. 'Very badly! We should have beaten her while we had the chance. Now you have called the family, and there's nothing we can do!'

'You're blaming *me*?' the headmistress retorted. '*Me*? It's your daughter who started this trouble in the first place . . .'

With Sairah's mother and the headmistress having a heated argument, I stole away from the door. I laughed to myself, thinking how my uncle had turned the tables on them. In him I truly had a champion.

The other children in the class were amazed at how I had

turned on Sairah. I'd been as quiet as a mouse until then, and I was seen as being something of a class swot. However well I did in my exams, I knew that each of them would think twice before crossing me in the future. I had shown that, deep inside, I was a Zaghawa warrior. In their different ways Grandma Sumah and my father would have been proud of me.

From this moment on, the other black girls and I decided we would take no more abuse. '*Arab hagareen* – the Arabs treat us like animals,' we told each other. From now on, if anyone tried to abuse us we would band together and act as one. No matter whether they were pupils or teachers, we would stand together against them.

The first test of our new resolve wasn't long in coming. There was an Arab girl in secondary school who we'd meet each afternoon on the path. She must have been thirteen or fourteen years old, and she just marched ahead as she saw us approaching and shoved us aside. Several times we'd tried saying 'hello' to her, but she'd simply scowl at us.

'Hey, you – hold up a minute!' Mona announced, the next time we saw her. 'Have you ever looked in the mirror? You have a donkey's face!'

That stopped the girl in her tracks. '*What* did you say? I hope I didn't hear you properly!'

'Why don't you ever bother to return our greetings?' I countered. 'Don't you know how rude that is? You see us on the path but we don't exist, is that it?'

'You bad, impolite girls!' she exclaimed. 'What rubbish d'you think you're saying?'

She reached out to grab Mona, but before she could do so we picked up sticks and clods of earth and started to pelt her. She cried out, more in shock than pain, and started to run. We chased after her, cheering, until she had disappeared around the corner. That was our second victory, but our triumph was to be short-lived.

Unfortunately, the Arab girl lived next door to one of our teachers. Once she had described her attackers, the teacher knew exactly who we were.

The following morning at assembly the headmistress announced that six girls had beaten a girl from the secondary school. We each had to step forward, as she gave us six cracks on the back with a stout stick. It really hurt, but none of us so much as let out a cry or a yelp. We knew if we did, the others would hear it and laugh. I stood up straight as I walked back into line. I noticed that some of the Arab girls were sniggering. I looked them right in the eye – letting them know that I'd seen them and wouldn't forget it.

After my tutor, my favourite teacher was a young Arab lady called Aisha. She taught English to the older girls, and I was really looking forward to starting her lessons. Often, Mona and I would walk part of the way home with her, and she was always chatty and kind towards us. One day Miss Aisha had a big pile of exercise books and we offered to help her carry them. This time we went all the way to her house, and it turned out to be one of the posh, English-style homes in the exclusive quarter.

She invited us in. She flicked a switch on the wall, and as if by magic lights in the ceiling lit up. We washed our hands with running water before being treated to a slice of cake and some pop. As we ate, I looked around at the smooth walls and the smart, glossy furniture. The walls of my uncle's house were of rough, home-made mud blocks, whereas here they were of bright red bricks. In the rainy season we would add a fresh layer of mud to the outside, in the hope that it would prevent the walls being washed away. But there was no danger of such a thing happening to this building.

As I looked around at Aisha's beautiful house, I realised that we inhabited separate worlds and lives, ones that only ever collided at the school. Each of these houses had electricity and water, things that the rest of the town's inhabitants could barely dream of. I wondered why these houses seemed reserved for Arab families. They were a minority in Sudan, so how was it that the best homes and the best jobs were reserved for them? I remembered what my father had told me – that the British colonists had given all the power to the Arabs. Well, from what I could see little had changed since then.

Each of these 'Arab houses' had a team of servants cooking and cleaning. Invariably, those servants were black Africans. The Arabs did little work themselves. Often the women wouldn't even go to the market: they each had a driver, and they would send him with a shopping list. They had a life of indolent luxury, and that was the life that Sairah's family led. So when I had turned on her at school, it must have been almost as if one of their servants had done so. That is what had made it so unbearable for them.

The next time Mona and I walked past the exclusive district, I picked up a stone and hurled it over one of the fences. As Mona and I made a run for it, there was the sound of glass shattering behind us. I wondered why I had done that. It was because I resented those Arabs their luxuries. I wanted to break their windows and break into their cosy lives. I wanted them to know the harsher side of life that we lived on a daily basis.

Reports of my rebellious activities started filtering back to my uncle. He told me that it was right to stand up for myself, but that I didn't want to get a reputation for being a troublemaker. At the end of my second term my father came to collect me, and when my uncle told him the story of my fight with Sairah and the Arab teachers, he laughed fit to burst. My uncle asked him how it was that he had such a tough daughter. Any girl who had grown up around Grandma Sumah was bound to turn out like this, my father explained.

On the drive home we passed by the local school, and I caught sight of the barefoot children sitting under a tree. Before I could stop myself, I found myself thinking that I was better than them. If there was a storm their lessons would have to be cancelled, but at my school lessons continued regardless. And while they had only the one teacher, we had the lovely Miss Shadhia for maths, Miss Aisha for English . . . I realised that I felt different now. I felt worldly wise and superior, as if I had lost much of my village innocence.

When I got down from my father's Land Rover, I was acutely aware of how smart my school uniform must seem. I felt oddly dislocated – as if I didn't fit in any more. Yet at the same time I knew that I wasn't part of the town. Over the next few days I tried to cover up my insecurity by boasting to the other kids. My school had a roof, proper buildings, everyone wore smart uniforms and we had lots of clever teachers. It was miles better than theirs.

Eventually, the neighbours' children started badgering their parents to be sent to the big school. As soon as my father heard about this he sat me down and gave me a stern talking to. I was not to tease the others, he warned. Not all families were as fortunate as us, and most didn't have the money that we did. I shouldn't be so arrogant and so conceited, he told me. I apologised. I felt ashamed. But I still didn't feel as if I fitted in.

I tried to rekindle my friendship with Kadiga, but things were different now. She would be getting married in three years' time, whereupon she would go to live in her husband's village and motherhood would quickly follow. Our lives were going in opposite directions. It was the same with the other children. They treated me as if I had abandoned the village and rejected their ways. Perhaps this was their way of getting back at me.

I had always felt so at home in the village, with my people all around me. I had always felt as if I was safe, and that no one could look down on me. At school I was always so eager to return to the simplicity of the village. But now I was here, I almost felt as if I wanted to return to the big town. I felt as if I was living in two worlds, as if I was split between two people – the simple village girl and my big-school, city-girl persona.

I think my father must have picked up on some of my disquiet. One day he returned home with a black box beside him in the Land Rover. As soon as I saw it my heart leapt for joy. I knew exactly what it was: it was a TV. I used to love watching TV at Mona's place. The first time I saw these tiny people moving around in a black box I thought it was magic, especially when I realised that I could actually hear them talking.

At Mona's house we'd lie on the floor, and the adults would lounge on the beds, and often we'd fall asleep in front of the TV. We'd watch anything – children's programmes, cooking, even football – until the screen went blank. We felt that if we missed anything we'd never get to experience it again. Since returning home I'd found myself getting bored with the long evenings spent by the fireside with nothing to do but talk.

Our TV set was given pride of place in the centre of our living area. My father wired it up to a car battery, and as it flickered into life it was as if he had brought a little bit of the town into the village. A music show was on, with drummers playing and women dancing. Mo, Omer, my mother and I settled down to watch. We had stopped eating and drinking and chatting, and we stared at the flickering blue-grey light, the noise of it filling our ears.

For the first half hour or so Grandma was with us. She tried to chat away and poke fun at what was happening on the TV, but all she got in reply was a series of grunts. We remained glued to the screen. Eventually she lost patience, jumping to her feet and declaring in an angry, bitter voice that the TV was an evil abomination. Still no one responded, and so Grandma went and stood right in front of the screen. Now she had our attention.

'This cursed thing!' she declared. 'Look at you – like ghosts, or zombies!' She turned on my father. 'And you – you spend your money on a curse! *On a curse!* This is *haram* – this dancing and people with skimpy clothing. We should spend our time as a family, talking and eating and telling stories. Not watching this rubbish!'

No one said very much. We were used to Grandma's tantrums. All we hoped was that she would go away and leave us to watch in peace. But Grandma was having none of it.

'You!' she declared, pointing at me. 'Go and fetch some wood. The fire's almost finished. And you, Mohammed, go and fetch some fresh water.'

'But we've only just started watching,' I complained. I reached over and grabbed the last of the wood and threw it onto the fire. 'There! Now can I see?'

'What rubbish is this?' Grandma cried. 'This *haram* TV! Children lying around and refusing to obey their elders! It teaches them nothing but the very worst!'

My father could stand it no longer, and he cracked up laughing. 'It's just a television . . . Everyone has one in the big towns.'

'It's just *nothing!*' Grandma retorted. 'You carry on like this and you'll damage your mind, and you'll damage your children! Look at you all.'

'Well, I just hope one day I catch you watching it!' my father retorted. 'It'll be just like the radio. At first you never like anything I bring. Then you decide it's the best thing ever, and that it was all your idea in the first place . . .'

At that, Grandma stomped off angrily to her hut. As she did so we fell about laughing. My father was being naughty, but what he said about the radio was quite true, of course.

Word about the TV spread around the village like wildfire. As evening approached on the second day, children started arriving in droves. When there was no room left for anyone to sit, adults began taking the standing room. My father connected the battery and turned on the TV, and a deep hush settled over the crowd. Fuzzy voices echoed out of the black box, as row upon row of little faces stared into the eerie, flickering light.

Some of the children screamed in surprise when music blared out or the tiny people spoke in loud voices. At the fence a row of old people were peering over, gazing in disbelief at the scene before them. Like Grandma, I guess they were trying to work out what witchcraft my father might be up to now. It was made all the more mysterious in that the crowd of children half-obscured the TV's screen from view.

My mother went around giving the children biscuits and cups of milk. Some families had brought their evening meal with them, and they proceeded to have a makeshift TV dinner in our yard.

A week after the arrival of the TV something like a hundred people tried to crowd their way in. They were mainly children, and some had travelled from many miles away.

As more and more arrived, I heard a distinctive cry of rage. Grandma had finally lost her patience with all this TV madness. She came charging out of her hut with a big stick, driving the nearest before her. She beat a path to our gate, where she stood barring the way and resolutely rejecting all who came before her.

'No! No! Go away!' she cried. 'There's no more space! No space! Go home! Go home!'

All that night Grandma remained on guard. And in a strange way she seemed to have found a role for herself in our post-TV world: she had become the keeper of the gate. Yet the children were not to be put off so easily. Their first response was simply to come earlier the following evening. But Grandma changed her tactics to deal with this new threat. Those who had been one night would be turned away the next.

Grandma would peer into a new arrival's face, before declaring: 'You came yesterday! Why are you coming again today? You go home!'

But while one group of children was being refused entry at the front, others would be shinning up a tree at the back and leaping into our yard. Inch by inch, the ground would be taken up – some sitting, some standing, and some lying on rugs that they had brought with them. The tide of watchers just seemed unstoppable.

No one ever argued over which channel to watch, as there was only ever the one. Finally, so many kids crowded onto my bed that it collapsed with a loud crack. Of course, once we realised that no one was hurt we fell about laughing.

Grandma came storming over. 'I told you! I told you! This evil thing! I told you – it will damage your home, your mind, your beds – *everything!*'

Our house had become like the village cinema. Sometimes I'd joke with the others to bring some money next time or Grandma wouldn't let them in. But there was no way that my father would ever have dreamt of charging anyone. It just wasn't in his nature to do so. Week after week it went on like this, until a man on the far side of the village purchased a much bigger TV set and started to charge people for watching it.

When she heard about this, Grandma declared what a clever man he was. Our TV remained free, though, and lots of the village kids still came to watch. It was only a black-and-white thing, but to them it was like magic. Most of the children couldn't understand a word, for there was no Zaghawa language programming. So I'd translate for them what was being said, and they soon got to know most of the shows off by heart.

My favourite was an English children's programme badly dubbed into Arabic. There were two sisters who were trying to find their long-lost parents. Officers from Scotland Yard came to help, riding on horseback and wearing smart black uniforms. The most amazing thing was that each of the sisters had her own handsome boyfriend. No wonder Grandma thought that the TV was teaching us the wrong, *haram* things.

If a cartoon came on we'd shout to each other: 'Come! Come! Film Cartoon has started!' Even the adults loved the cartoons. Our family favourite was *Tom and Jerry* – though we nicknamed it 'Mo and Jerry', with Omer being Jerry the mouse. Whenever we watched we'd each choose to be one of the characters. Sometimes we'd argue about who was going to be whom.

Strangely enough, Grandma's hatred of the TV barely seemed to diminish with time. She loved her radio set, but she treated the TV with real loathing.

Now and again I wondered why this was so. Part of me knew that some of what Grandma had said was true. Unlike the radio, the TV killed all conversation. If Grandma had been in charge the TV would have been banned, and we would have learned far more from talking to her of an evening. She was a brilliant mathematician, adding and subtracting in her head without ever making a mistake. It was from Grandma that I had inherited my gift with maths.

Whenever my father was away Grandma would still try and put her foot down. She'd hear one of us switching on the TV and come charging over to chase us away.

'Don't sit in front of that evil thing!' she'd yell. 'Stop it! Stop it!'

If my father was away in the Land Rover we'd have no car battery to power up the TV, and then Grandma would come to find us and prod us with her stick.

'Ha! Ha!' she'd declare gleefully. 'So what're you going to watch today, a blank screen? Time to sleep early! Or maybe this family can actually learn to *talk* to each other again!'

One evening I was watching a music show with my father, when suddenly he jumped to his feet.

'Look, look!' he exclaimed, jabbing a finger at the screen. 'Rathebe! It's Rathebe – your namesake!'

Sure enough, a caption declared the performer to be Dolly Rathebe, the black South African jazz singer. Her hair was a wild afro, and her arms and legs were covered in bangles. She was singing a raunchy, funky jazz song, and strutting her stuff as she did so. Because she was singing in English, I couldn't understand a word.

'You named me after her?' I asked in amazement. 'Why? Look at her. She's wild!'

My father laughed, his eyes shining with excitement. 'You only see her *image*, but I can understand *the words*. She sings about the rights of the black man to Africa. She sings about Nelson Mandela's struggle, about the black man's fight for freedom in South Africa. And what the white man is to South Africa, the Arabs are to Sudan.'

My father was an avid watcher of anything to do with race and politics in South Africa. He reckoned that the South African resistance offered a model for how we Zaghawa, the Fur and other black African tribes should resist the Arab domination of our country. He was keen to share with me his dreams of a free and golden future for Sudan.

And in me, little Rathebe, he had found a disciple who was eager to learn.

9

The White Eyelash Attack

By the end of our first year at school Mona, Najat, Samirah, Makboulah and I had got the measure of the Arab girls. There were still arguments, of course, but we had learned to stand our ground. They tried telling us that all things from the village were bad – that it meant poverty, sickness and ignorance. We countered that the city was empty and unfriendly, a place where no one cared for their neighbours. The city was dangerous, like a wild animal. But in the village you could relax among family and friends. At the end of such discussions we'd conclude that we lived in a parallel universe to them.

The Arab girls still tried to scold us if we spoke in our tribal language. They tried telling us that our Arabic was polluted by our native tongue, and poked fun at our pronunciation. But all we had to do to retaliate was to start abusing the Arab girls in our tribal language. We'd tell each other that one had a face like a horse, or another had a nose like a crooked bird's beak. In no time at all we'd be killing ourselves laughing. While they didn't understand the words, the Arab girls got the gist of what we were saying, and it drove them wild.

The Arab girls teased us that we had no freedom to fall in love – we just had to obey our parents and marry whomever they chose. They said that we village girls had to break free and live. We accused them of being loose and immoral, of going out with boys before they were married. We even hinted that we knew that they might do things with men prior to marriage. Certainly, the teachers allowed us to have no contact of any kind with boys. Making friends with boys was strictly *haram* – forbidden – as school was simply for study.

The boys' school was just nearby. Whenever we went out to buy our lunch the boys might be there, getting their food from the stalls. When they caught sight of us they would whistle or catcall. We'd pretend to be angry, but deep inside it was thrilling to get such attention from handsome boys in their smart uniforms. Our teachers would get angry, but what could we do about it? Boys would be boys, and we weren't exactly provoking them.

— ~ —

With the completion of year one our lessons became more varied. From Miss Aisha, the English teacher, we learned about weddings where the bride would be dressed all in white. I found it odd that she would wear such a dull colour: red was dramatic and drew attention. Perhaps because English girls had white skin the men believed white was the most beautiful colour. I asked Miss Aisha if this was so, but she explained that white was believed to be the colour of purity, and that was why they were married in white.

We learned about Big Ben and the Houses of Parliament, and that England was the birthplace of democracy. We saw pictures of London with huge tower blocks going high into the sky. We read about the great works of English literature. But at the same time our history teacher taught us how the British colonised Africa. They came to Sudan bringing education and hospitals, but they took our gold, our oil and our agricultural exports in return. If we understood the British then we would know how to fight them, our teacher explained, just in case they ever tried to colonise Sudan again!

Our second year drew to a close with proper end-of-year exams.

I had been coming top of the class in most subjects, but there were three classes in our year, and I wondered how I had done overall. The day of the exam results each class went to sit outside. My heart thumped fiercely when the headmistress read out the names of the top ten pupils in our year. I heard my name – *Halima Bashir*. The other girls jumped to their feet. But was the dreaded headmistress really going to congratulate me, her least favourite pupil?

I felt someone at my side. 'Go on, Halima,' my tutor, Miss Shadhia, urged me. 'Go on. You're top of the year.'

I walked forward, the other girls making way for me. I saw the headmistress force a smile as she bent to shake my hand. She passed me my certificate and hung a golden medal around my neck. Then she turned me around to face the crowd. As she did so, the girls broke into a deafening round of applause. I felt as if I was in a dream.

'Well done, Halima,' I heard her murmur, as she rested her hands on my shoulders. 'Well done. Top of the year. I'm so glad our little . . . problems are all behind us now.'

When my father arrived to take me back to the village he couldn't believe the news. I saw how happy I had made him, and I knew it was as much a victory for our tribe as it was a personal triumph for our family. I felt tears of joy at his happiness. I couldn't believe that I, his little daughter, could have made him so fulfilled.

My father declared that he was going to buy me a special treat. Within reason, I could have anything I wanted. I chose a fine gold chain, and I wore it with joy in my heart as we drove back home to the village.

As soon as we arrived my father announced the news – that I had beaten all the Arab city girls to come top of the year. My mother was amazed, and even Grandma seemed suitably impressed. But as for Mo and Omer, they reacted badly, especially when they caught sight of my shiny new gold chain. Why did I get all the attention, they demanded. Why did I get all our father's gifts? Why couldn't they go to the big school?

Mo had just started at the village school. My father had promised to send him to the big school if he did well, but his early results were hardly impressive. He had been coming tenth or lower in his class.

'You should learn a lesson from Halima,' my father declared. 'You came tenth because all you wanted was for me to buy you some toys. You have to *want* to learn, to burn for it. You have to hunger for it, like Halima. She studies because she loves to . . .'

Mo and Omer stomped off, ignoring the last of my father's words. Later, I found out that they had scribbled in my exercise books and drawn rude pictures. My mum called Mo and Omer and asked who was responsible. They both denied it, each blaming the other. Eventually my mum lost her temper and started to beat them both – but that just meant that my brothers resented me all the more for it.

Unbeknown to me, Omer had decided that I had an unfair advantage at school: my white eyelash. It was this that gave me my brains. And so he hatched a plan to get rid of it. He told Mo that he, Omer, would hold me down while Mo had to cut it off. But Mo asked why he had to be the one to cut it. Omer told him that it was because he was older, but Mo refused. Omer scoffed at him, and declared that he would do it, then.

The day after my return from school they came for me. I was carrying a basket of washing out to the back of the house when Omer called me over. 'Come, Rathebe, come! I've got something to show you!' As I went to look he stuck out his foot and tripped me over. The instant I hit the ground he was on my chest, while Mo pinned my arms and legs down. As Omer bounced on my stomach and tried to squeeze the breath out of me, I screamed, presuming that this was just a particularly nasty episode of play-fighting.

But then my cries froze in my throat as I spotted a big, sharp carving knife glinting in the sunlight. I stared up at Omer as he forced the knife closer and closer, a fierce madness burning in his eyes. Omer was barely five years old, but he was fearless and strong. I tried to push his knife hand back, but Mo kept dragging at my arms. As I weakened, Omer's free hand shot forward and grabbed my eyelid, and he thrust the knife downwards.

'Help!' I screamed. '*Help!* He's going to kill me!'

'I'm going to cut it!' Omer yelled. 'Then we'll all be the *same*! We'll all be *equal*!'

He slashed with the knife, the blade flashing past with a horrible tug at my eye socket. I felt a bolt of pain as Omer let out a yell of triumph and thrust something aloft.

'The white eyelash!' he cried. 'I've cut it! I've cut it!'

He threw the tiny piece of white aside, and turned back to me. 'Now to finish it!' he yelled. 'Dig it out! Slice it! Finish it!'

He reached forward with the knife again, and I felt a wave of fear wash over me. But all of a sudden I caught a blur of grey to one side of him, followed by a deafening crack as Grandma's big stick made contact with the side of his head. An instant later Omer was lying in a dazed heap on the ground. Grandma whipped her hand down and scooped up the fallen knife. As Mo tried to make a run for it she grabbed him by the hair and hauled him backwards.

'What in Allah's name is going on?' she cried. She brandished the big carving knife. 'You think this is a toy? Do you? You want to play the knife game with Grandma!'

Mo burst into a flood of tears. Seconds later my mother and father arrived on the scene. At the sight of the carving knife they were horrified. Each of them started to quiz a blubbering Mohammed on why his younger brother was trying to kill me. As for Omer, he was sitting where he had fallen, dazed and confused. Grandma had hit him a fierce whack, and he was too far gone to answer anyone's questions.

Omer had managed to slice off a good length of my white eyelash, but other than that it appeared to be intact. My father let out a deep sigh of relief, but the fallout from the attack was only just beginning. My mother had words with my father, telling him that in future he had to bring a present for each of the children, not just for me. Otherwise, Omer was mad enough and jealous enough to really hurt me.

And my father had to stop making such a fuss about my white eyelash. It was true that he was forever going on about it – how it brought us such good fortune and me such knowledge. Then my mother turned to me. I had to stop bragging about my presents and teasing my brothers. It was true that I did taunt them. I'd dance in front of Mo and Omer, holding up a present and singing: 'Look what I've got! Look what I've got!'

Well, it was all very well my mother playing the peacemaker, but what about the villain of the piece – Omer? Why wasn't he getting a lecture? He was the one who had taken a knife, set a trap for me and stabbed me in the eye. Yet, so far, not a word had been said. I pointed this out to my mother. Grandma's blow with the stick was enough punishment for now, she declared. As for how my parents would deal with his hot temper, they didn't know. Omer was like a wild animal, and it wasn't the first time that they had despaired of him.

My mother and father were seriously worried. At times, their youngest child seemed overtaken by bouts of enraged madness, during which he seemed capable of almost anything. The only thing they could think of doing was to consult the village Fakir for help. Without breathing a word to Omer, that is exactly what they did.

The Fakir fetched an egg, rolled it all over my mother's body and broke it into a glass. He studied the egg to discover whether someone had put the Evil Eye on Omer. If the egg looked up at him with the appearance of an Evil Eye, then he would know that

131

they had. He would break another egg and try to discern the person's name. Often, it would take three eggs to get it all sorted. Sure enough, the eggs revealed that Omer was under the influence of an Evil Eye.

The Fakir prepared a special *hijab* for Omer to drink, called a *mehia*. He wrote some verses from the Koran on a blackboard, and washed them off into a glass. The water he decanted into a small bottle, to which he added some extra potions. My parents thanked the Fakir and returned home. But as soon as Omer spotted the *mehia* he knew what they'd been up to, and he refused to drink. No matter how they pleaded and threatened, he wouldn't drink. Finally, Grandma lost patience and went to fetch her big stick.

'Drink it! It's good for you! *Drink*!' she ordered. 'What is it with you refusing to drink? You like being crazy, is that it? You think the rest of us like living with a mad boy?'

'Look at all these,' Omer countered, lifting up his robe to reveal several *hijabs* strung around his waist. 'Have they done any good? No! So why will this drinking one be any different?'

'Ungrateful boy!' Grandma scolded. 'Imagine how wild you'd be without wearing those! You'd be totally insane. Now drink, or do I have to . . .?'

Suddenly Omer grabbed the bottle and flung the contents down his throat. 'There!' he declared. 'Not that it will make any difference . . .'

Shortly after the eyelash attack I started experiencing intense pains in my stomach. I was vomiting up my food and nothing would stay down. Grandma took me to see Halima, the traditional village medicine woman I had been named after. Halima was as kindly and gentle as ever. She massaged my stomach while mumbling some spells, and then she started to spit little puffs of air over me. With each puff she murmured, 'Evil Eye – out! Evil Eye – out! Evil Eye – out!'

She took a china teacup and heated it over the fire. She placed the hot cup on my bare tummy, inverted, so that it formed a seal, and started to suck the badness out of me. As she did so, I felt a warm glow rippling through me. After that the vomiting eased, and I was soon better. To this day I still believe in the Evil Eye, and the power of *hijabs*, medicine women and the Fakirs.

The Fakirs in our village were carefully chosen by the community as men of good character and truly wise. They were blessed with the ability to wield the power of God. It was dangerous to do so, unless you understood how to use the Holy Koran in conjunction with ancient spells and other traditional law. But for every good Fakir there was invariably a self-proclaimed bad one. These men used dangerous and dark powers – black magic and devilish arts – to achieve people's worst desires.

I'd been home from school for a month or so when I witnessed the terrible harm such bad Fakirs caused. I had a cousin called Mousa, who was in his early twenties, and like most young men he was impetuous. One day he went to consult a bad Fakir concerning a quarrel in the village. The Fakir prepared a spell to use against his adversary, but at the very moment of casting it the spell fell upon Mousa instead. For weeks on end Mousa locked himself away in his hut, and the only person he was able to speak to was his elder brother.

His parents took him to see a good Fakir, but he could do nothing. He needed to know the name of the bad Fakir who had cast the original curse, and the name of the intended victim, before he could undo the spell. Unfortunately, my cousin was too crazed to be able to tell him. Eventually, they flew Mousa all the way to Nigeria, where the Fakirs are renowned for their power in lifting curses. But even they were unable to do anything for him.

Whenever we visited their house, Mousa would be all hunched up in his dark hut, his face twisted into a grimace of pain. He looked so unhappy and I felt so sorry for him. I even tried asking him who it was who had cast the bad spell, and who was the intended target, but Mousa just mumbled confusedly. Finally his family took him to the hospital. The doctors tried giving him all sorts of medication, but nothing worked – proof in itself that Mousa's madness was caused by an evil Fakir's spells.

Time passed quickly, both in the village and at school. I reached my eleventh birthday, and I felt more than ready to move on to the secondary school. But first I had to pass my exams, without which I couldn't graduate to high school. Every pupil in the country had to sit them, and the results would be compared across the country. I studied harder than ever, and once the exams were completed I waited with my friends to hear the results. If any one of us had failed it would break apart a fellowship that had seen us triumph over such adversity.

The first I heard of the results was a pounding on the door of my uncle's house, early one morning. It was Mona, and she had raced over to be the first to tell me. She had been watching TV with her parents, and my name had been announced as being one of the top five students for the whole of Darfur. She hugged me tight and we danced for joy. I couldn't believe it. It was inconceivable. *One of the top five.* There were hundreds and hundreds of schools across the region.

We hurried into school. I asked Mona if she knew how she had done. She shook her head and grinned. It didn't matter – she was sure to have passed. What mattered was that I, a black Zaghawa girl from the bush, had beaten every single Arab girl in our school.

Upon arrival at the school gates I was mobbed by teachers and pupils alike. Everyone had heard the news – all except me, as my uncle couldn't afford a TV.

We gathered for one of our last ever assemblies. The headmistress stood at the front as I took the place of honour in the roll call of results. I was given a gold-embossed Koran, and a prize of some money. But what mattered most to me was that I had beaten the system. I had proved to them all that race was no arbiter of talent or intelligence. I left that school, which had caused me so much heartache, being rewarded by the headmistress for being her star pupil.

That evening there was a party at my uncle's house. Mona, Najat, Samirah and Makboulah were there, as were many of my other friends. Some of the Arab girls even deigned to visit, although Sairah had left the year before to go to another school. But best of all was when my father turned up. He'd heard the news on his radio, jumped into the Land Rover and driven all day to be with me. He was overjoyed that his name, his family name, had been on the news. And he was so very, very proud of me.

The party went on long into the night. When the last people had said their goodbyes, my father took me out onto the veranda. I was proud that I had come number five in the province, I told him, but if the truth be told I regretted that I wasn't number one. Still, I had shown that a black African girl could beat those from rich, privileged families. My father took my hand in his and we sat there in silence, both of us filled with a blissful happiness.

It was then that my father told me about his dream for me – how he wanted me to go to university to train to be a medical doctor. I had proven that I had the flair to make it, and if he worked hard then he could afford to fund my studies. I was the only one of his children with the talent to do so, he confided in me. Mo and Omer were a great help on the farm, but in truth neither cared much for school or studying.

A medical doctor. Could I really be a medical doctor, I wondered. Sometimes Mo, Omer and I used to play a game where we'd act out what we wanted to be when we grew up. Omer would be a tough soldier, yelling and making fierce thrusts with a sword. Mo would act as if he were a driver, holding an imaginary steering wheel and changing gear. As for me, I'd ask my brothers what was wrong with them, so I could make them better.

Then we'd have to argue who had the best job. 'I'm the best because I'm going to kill people,' Omer would say. 'Me – I'm driving people,' Mo would declare. 'Without me no one can go anywhere.' 'But the doctor is the best,' I'd argue. 'When you get ill, I will help you get well again.' We'd make whoever was declared the loser the donkey, and they'd have to carry the winner around on their back.

My father went on to confess that he was disappointed in Mo and Omer, for neither had any interest in the wider world, the politics of our country, or even the struggle of the Zaghawa people. Outside his family, these were my father's consuming passions. Our present rulers had stolen power, my father told me, his voice laced with a quiet anger. The people should choose who was to govern them, not a bunch of military men in plastic uniforms. Our military rulers were overshadowing the country's bright future.

By the time we got back to the village a second party had been organised. Half of the village seemed to have watched the announcement of the exam results on my father's TV set, and everyone was invited. By now, Mo and Omer seemed to have reconciled themselves to the fact that academia was not for them, and they seemed happy for me. It was a wonderful party, and I felt so proud to have achieved even this much for my village.

During my final term at junior school my mother had given birth to my baby sister, Asia. Baby Asia was quiet and gentle, just like Mohammed had been. She was still very much a bundle of rags, but it was clear that she was going to take after my mother.

She had big eyes, just like her, and her hair was going to be long and lustrous. Of course, I felt a touch of jealousy, as I was no longer the only daughter. When I saw my father cooing to her, I felt a stab of envy. But the age difference was such that it soon passed: I was approaching my twelfth birthday, whereas Asia was just a little baby.

＊＊＊

During the long summer holiday the rains were especially good, and the trees became heavy with fruit. In the farms around the village there were mango, guava, orange and lemon groves. There was such an abundance that we reckoned the farmers could spare a little. The trouble was that each farmer was jealously guarding his trees, just in case any pesky children came looking to steal his fruit.

One morning Grandma told us to go and fetch her some lemons and mangos from a nearby farm. She didn't openly instruct us to steal them, but we got her meaning. We knew that farm well. There was an old man looking after it, so we weren't especially worried. We sneaked down there, and the old man was nowhere to be seen. We started hurling sticks and stones into the branches, knocking down the ripest fruit.

As we gathered the fallen lemons and mangos, we heard a roar of anger from behind us. We tried to make a run for it, but powerful hands grabbed Omer and me from behind and knocked poor Mo to the ground. Suddenly, we were staring into the face of a young and very tough-looking Zaghawa man.

'Throwing stones and damaging my fruit trees!' he thundered. 'You bad children! Stand in line, while I decide what to do with you.'

He took a couple of steps backwards and glared at us. 'I know you, don't I? You're that Grandma Sumah's lot. No wonder! I bet she sent you. Well, speak up!'

'No one sent us,' Mohammed wailed. 'No one sent us to do anything.'

'He's right,' I added. 'We came of our own accord.'

As for Omer, he just glared at the man in a stubborn silence.

'Well, you can stand there until someone comes for you,' he announced. 'I'll bet that Grandma sent you – and I'm not letting you go until she comes to explain herself.'

All morning we were made to stand beneath the fruit tree, under the watchful gaze of the angry man. But there was no way Grandma would come for us, of that I was certain. She was far too smart for that. If she did, it would be akin to admitting that she'd sent us to steal some fruit. The angry man could then demand payment, and he might even try to claim compensation for his damaged trees.

Eventually, the angry man lost patience. He gave us each a sound beating and sent us on our way. When we got home Grandma showed us no sympathy whatsoever. Instead, she scolded us for failing in our mission.

'Go and try another farm,' she ordered. 'And this time, try not to get caught!'

We went to Kadiga's house and recruited her and her brothers to help. Then we headed for another farm. We split up into two teams. Kadiga's gang went ahead, deliberately revealing themselves to the old man guarding the farm. We watched from our hiding place as he raced after them, yelling for the thieves to get off his land. As soon as he was out of sight we rushed in and grabbed as much fruit as we could. It was lying on the ground in neat heaps.

We made our getaway and headed straight for the prearranged meeting place. Kadiga and her gang had managed to outrun the old man, and we divided the spoils between us. We took the plundered fruit to the market-place, where we sold half to one of the traders.

The rest we took home for our crime boss – Grandma Sumah.

10

Cousins in Love

Towards the end of my summer holiday there was a big wedding in a neighbouring village. The groom was a close cousin, and we all had to go to support his side of the family. My father was away in his fields, so we would have to travel there in a big truck that doubled as the village bus. Twice weekly the truck would do a circuit of all the neighbouring villages, including ours. Most passengers would crouch on the open truck bed or stand gripping the sides. But the best was if you could get a seat inside the cab.

I didn't want to travel to the wedding on the truck's rear, as it would ruin our nice clothes. Passengers would carry a wild assortment of luggage with them: cages of chickens, goats on a string, sacks of maize, old bicycles, even the odd cow. Whenever the truck hit a bump everything would fly into the air. More often than not you'd end up on your back with a goat on top of you and a cage of chickens on your head. It was impossible to arrive at your destination looking even remotely neat and respectable.

Luckily, Grandma had spoken with the truck driver and booked three seats in the cab. As a result, we arrived at the neighbouring village in fine fettle. That evening the groom had his head ritually shaved. There was singing and dancing and drumming, as we celebrated the groom being cleansed of his body hair in preparation for the wedding.

Of course, the bride price had been set many months before. The groom had already paid the bride's family a quantity of gold and a number of animals. He had also bought a new set of clothes for the bride's family members, so that they could look their best on the wedding day. For their part, the bride-to-be's family had built a house for the newly-weds and furnished it completely, even down to the kitchen things.

The day after the head-shaving ritual we headed over to the bride's family home. We took our places on rugs on the floor as we waited for the bride to appear. Everyone kept asking when we would get to see her, but it turned out that there was a problem. The bride's family said that, somehow, the bride had been spirited away in the night.

'Perhaps there will be no wedding at all,' the bride's grandmother announced dramatically.

We all knew what was going on, as this was a regular charade. The bride's family had hidden her in order to extort some last-minute money out of the groom. The bride's mother tried to maintain a dignified silence, as the grandmother did the talking.

'Perhaps we could find her and talk her round,' she declared. 'But you will have to pay something, to help us persuade her.'

The grandmother named an extortionate price as the fee to deliver the bride. But on our side we knew that the bride price had already been paid in full. The bride's family were dressed in their fine clothes, all of which had been bought by our side. We refused to pay up, and so the arguing and the bargaining began.

Grandma Sumah loved these fights and she quickly rose to the challenge. She marched out in front of the bride's family.

'Shame on you!' she declared theatrically. 'This is shameful! How can you behave like this? Soon we will be one family. Let us pay this money, but proceed with the wedding first. This delay is a deep shame . . .'

The bride's family knew what Grandma was up to: as soon as the bride was delivered, all thoughts of paying would be forgotten.

'No! No way!' the bride's grandmother countered. 'The shame

is on you, for refusing to help us. Family or no family – you have to pay now.'

The argument went backwards and forwards, our grandma facing off against their grandma. So far there had been no food or drink served. The bride's family were holding back the wedding feast in an effort to force us to pay up. But all that seemed to matter to the adults was the fight over the money. Finally, I could bear it no longer.

'Eya, I'm hungry,' I complained. 'When can I get something to eat?'

My mother told me to keep quiet. She was known as a great negotiator in these situations – a peacemaker and a go-between. But as for Grandma Sumah, the bigger the fight the better as far as she was concerned. Eventually the bride's family agreed to accept all of the money that our family had with us. But the grown ups on our side hid some of their money in their clothes, so that they wouldn't have to hand over everything.

In our culture, if a wedding goes ahead without any fighting people don't really enjoy it. We always remember the weddings with the biggest fights and the most heartfelt making-ups.

Once money was handed over the wedding feast was served, but it was well after midnight by the time we were finished. In spite of the hour my cousin refused to eat. He couldn't relax until he had seen his bride. She was an only daughter and very beautiful, and he knew that her family would try to extract every last advantage from the situation that they possibly could.

He asked his friends to go and search for the bride. At first, no one would show them where she was hidden. But then they paid off the bride's best friend, and she took them to the house. Still the bride refused to come, unless her family said that it was all right for her to do so. Eventually, the groom lost his patience and he and his friends carried off the bride, taking her across the village to the wedding house. The groom knew that once he had her in that house, it was all over: no more money could be demanded of him.

At the last moment the bride's family realised what was happening. They placed their biggest, fattest women in the doorway of the wedding house, to prevent the bride and groom from entering. Both sides faced off against each other, chanting as if they were about to go to war. But the groom's party played a trick. As the groom pretended to try for the front entrance, his friends smashed down the fence at the rear. They hoisted the bride on their shoulders and carried her inside, crying out their victory as they did so.

The bride's family knew when they'd been beaten, and they welcomed the newly-weds into their home. The drummer – the *mayee* – picked up his drum, made from cow skin stretched over a hollowed-out tree trunk. The wood was decorated with carvings of beasts, birds and mythical spirits. A strap on the drum went around his neck, and he stood as he drummed. As each new person entered the wedding house, he beat out a deep, pounding rhythm, calling out their name and their lineage, and their family's most famous exploits.

Every few seconds the new arrivals threw some money at the drummer. It would fall at his feet, or even stick to his brow with the sweat that was pouring off him. The drummer had a boy with him, whose job it was to scuttle about and collect up all the money. The drumming went on for an age – until those being welcomed ran out of money to throw at the drummer, or until the drummer ran out of grand things to say about them.

When all the guests were present, the drummer stood in the middle of the dance floor. The women formed one line, the men facing them. As the drummer took up the dance rhythm, each man would step forward to choose a dance partner. The chosen woman would come dancing out of line, holding up her scarf to half-cover her face, as she peered at the man and decided whether she wanted to dance with him or not. If the woman refused, the man would be left isolated on the dance floor, and everyone would laugh at him.

Mostly, she would accept, and then the couple would start to dance around and around the drummer, faster and faster as the rhythm grew in power, pirouetting like a pair of birds, whirling about each other but never quite touching. As more and more dancers joined them, they started to sing a song that came from deep within their hearts.

> *All we are here,*
> *All we are here,*
> *We are Zaghawa,*
> *We are Zaghawa.*
>
> *From the Coube clan,*
> *From the Towhir clan,*
> *From the Bidayat clan,*
> *We are Zaghawa.*
>
> *We are the warriors,*
> *We are the people,*
> *Nobody can overreach us,*
> *No one can beat us,*
> *We have our tribe around us,*
> *Our family around us,*
> *Our children around us,*
> *Our lands around us,*
> *Our camels around us,*
> *Our cattle around us,*
> *We are Zaghawa.*
> *We are Zaghawa.*

The party lasted all night, until it was time for the bridegroom's breakfast. A sheep was slaughtered, and the bride's mother prepared the first meal for her new son-in-law. Using a fine white flour she made a special *acidah* mash. She part-filled a coffee cup with distilled butter oil and heated it over the fire. The more of the hot oil that the *acidah* soaked up, the more successful the marriage would be. The newly-weds had to feast on the butter oil mash, together with a spicy stew made out of the sheep's intestines.

Once the breakfast was over, the wedding was declared complete. It was then time for us to return to our village, but the truck that was supposed to take us home had broken down. My mother took us to a relative's house, to see if there was any other transport available. After two late nights I was exhausted, and I fell asleep on their rugs. I awoke in the early afternoon to discover that one of my cousins, thirteen-year-old Sharif, was offering to take us home in his donkey cart. It was a long way but he reckoned we could make it by nightfall.

'Don't worry,' he declared, brightly. 'I'll get you home.'

'What happens if the cart breaks down?' I objected sleepily. 'It'll be dark, and we don't know the way.'

'You're a typical city girl, aren't you?' Sharif teased. 'That's what comes of going to the big school. It's made you weak and soft . . .'

'You've been spoilt by that father of yours!' Sharif's mother added. 'He drives you around in that nice car and you've forgotten how to walk!'

I tried to object. 'No I haven't, and no I'm not . . .'

'Look, I know you're used to travelling by car,' Sharif interrupted. 'It might not be as fast or as comfortable, but my cart is just as reliable. I'll get you there all right.'

Before I could say another word it was agreed that Sharif should drive us home. But I didn't really like this cousin of mine very much, especially after he'd teased me about being a soft city girl. I didn't like his looks very much, either. He was dressed in a boring old robe, just like all the other simple village boys. I had decided that I wanted to marry a cultured, educated man from the city, a modern man who wore a smart suit and a tie.

The journey in Sharif's donkey cart was uneventful, if uncomfortable. By the time we reached home my father was already there. He thanked Sharif for bringing us and insisted that he should stay the night, for he wouldn't have him returning in the dark.

After we'd eaten my father announced that he had some surprise news for me. One of my cousins had asked if he might marry me. He was a teacher working in a local school, and because he was an educated man his family believed that it would be a fine match.

'What do you think, Rathebe?' my father asked, with a twinkle in his eye.

'I hope you said no! How can I go to university and everything if I'm married?'

My father laughed. 'Quite – and that's exactly what I said. I said you had to get a proper education, and maybe we'd think about marriage later.'

'How did this cousin react?' I asked.

I couldn't help but be curious. And in any case, I reckoned that Sharif was paying a little too much attention, as if he had an interest somehow. I wanted to show him that I was a long way from ever getting married, and that any hopes that a village boy might have were unlikely to be fulfilled.

My father shrugged. 'He was very angry. The family were very angry. They took it as an insult. They told me that daughters weren't for educating. They said you should get married and have kids and take on some responsibilities.'

'Well then, I'm doubly glad you said no. My life would be at an end. I'd be stuck at home, with no study and no life . . .'

My father went on to tell me a story about one of his nieces. Her father had refused an offer of marriage, but the would-be groom had kidnapped her. They searched for her far and wide, but her 'husband' had taken her to a distant village. For years the family had no contact with her, and then one day she returned to the village with her 'husband' and son. Her father was extremely angry, but her 'husband' proposed a settlement: he handed over some money and animals, and eventually they put their differences behind them.

'I'm telling you this story for a reason,' said my father. 'The man we rejected will be angry. We should keep our eyes and ears open and be on our guard. Anything is possible. The way they see it, we have slighted them. So the sooner we get you off to that new school, the better. Once you're away, I'm sure it will all be forgotten.'

I needed no further urging – I was more than ready for my new school. My girlfriends from junior school had all passed their exams, so at secondary school Mona, Najat, Samirah, Makboulah and I were able to re-form our gang. We had made it quite clear by now that we weren't to be pushed around, and we faced few of the problems that we had before. In any case, my own personal success had set a black girl from the village at the pinnacle of academic achievement – so who could possibly try to claim that we were somehow inferior?

My father was becoming increasingly active in politics now. He had volunteered as a local organiser, raising support for his democratic party to win at the forthcoming elections. When his party leader, Sadiq al-Mahdi, was elected President of Sudan, my father was overjoyed. But his happiness was to be short-lived. One morning there was a shock announcement on the radio: soldiers had seized power in the country. Sudan's short democratic spring had been cut short, and it was as if my father's dream had died.

My father became angry and despairing. The President, Sadiq

al-Mahdi, was a fair man who had felt keenly the neglect of the black African tribes in Sudan. Yet he had been thrown into gaol. Those who had seized power were calling themselves the National Islamic Front. They declared that they were 'a government of Islam', their mission being to purge Sudan of all un-Islamic thoughts, actions and peoples. They would turn Sudan into a pure Islamic state ruled by Islamic *shariah* law.

They promised to quadruple their efforts to defeat the black African 'unbelievers' in the south of the country. They called on all young men to join this 'jihad'. Anyone who refused to volunteer would be rounded up for military service. My father knew what a government of soldiers and Islamic extremists would mean. He knew that this was truly going to be a government of the Arabs for the Arabs. His instinct told him that this was the beginning of a terrible time in Sudan, one in which the whole country would be plunged into war. And the people of Darfur would not escape unscathed.

So worried was he that he decided we should leave the country. We should go to live across the border, in Tchad. But my mum and Grandma refused. He was overreacting, they said. In any case, what would happen to the children's studies? In the coming months we heard of several families that had fled to Tchad. They were getting out while they still could, my father argued, and we should follow their example. But my mother and Grandma refused to leave our people and our village, and so we stayed.

My father's worries threw a dark shadow over my school days. Much as I might try to concentrate purely on my studies, I saw things differently now. Whenever I passed by the exclusive district of town, I looked at those grand people in their grand houses and I was torn. On the one hand I wanted what they had. On the other, I knew that among their number were the men who had stolen power and shattered my father's dreams.

Early one morning I found myself in the market-place buying

some food. I wanted a little salad and some bread for my lunch. Suddenly, a quarrel erupted out of nowhere. The market traders had been listening to a radio news bulletin about the war in south Sudan. The rebels had scored a minor victory. A muscular black man was in a heated exchange with an Arab, as they argued about who was fighting on the side of right.

'Idiot! What do you think?' the Arab yelled. 'You think we will allow you black dogs to beat us, to rule over us? Is that what you believe?'

The black man just stared at the Arab, his eyes flaming anger. For several seconds neither spoke, and then the Arab man exploded.

'*Abeed! Abeed!* – Slave! Slave!' he yelled. 'Take your eyes off me! *Abeed!* You're nothing but a black slave. Get yourself away from me before there's trouble!'

The black man sprang at him, and with one blow he knocked the Arab to the ground. The other market traders tried to hold him back, but he was wild with fury. He smashed his fist into the Arab's face, and I was both elated and fearful. Part of me wanted the black man to pound the Arab's head into the dust so that he never got up again. But part of me feared what the consequences would be if he did.

I turned to leave, but as I did so there was a screeching of tyres and a police Land Rover ground to a halt. Six Arab policemen rushed over, their batons drawn. With barely a moment's hesitation they started to give the black man a savage beating. He went down under a hail of blows. I watched in horror as they pounded those heavy batons into his back and head, hearing the hollow thwack of wood on bone. They dragged the bloodied black man into the rear of the Land Rover, and roared away from the scene.

I felt rage boiling up inside me. Not for one instant had they tried to find out who was at fault in the argument. All they had done was beat the black man, while allowing the Arab to go free. I heard murmurings of anger all around me as market traders and customers commented on how unjust it all was. A ruthless Arab elite was ruling the country, and they didn't even try to disguise their racist policies. It was the law of the jungle now. The strong would beat the weak, and the country would end up in flames.

I walked away from the market-place, my mind in turmoil. The Arab man had openly called the African man a 'black dog' and a 'black slave'. That meant that he had also called *me* a black dog and a slave – for the African man and I were the same colour, with similar facial features. What was it about the difference in the shade of the colour of one's skin that made the Arab believe he was superior to me? What was there in a sharper, more pointed set of facial features that made him believe he was my master?

I was confused and enraged and hurt and scared. I was born this way. It was who I was. I wasn't about to change.

It wasn't long before my father's fears took concrete form in our own home. A new TV programme had started up, called *Fisah hart el fidah* – Voice of the Martyrs' Battlefield. This was a daily bulletin showing graphic and bloody images of fighting in the south of Sudan. The first time I saw it I was horrified. I asked Grandma what it was all about. Grandma simply adored the clash of warfare and the noise of battle being portrayed: she explained that Muslims were fighting the unbelievers, which was the right thing to do.

But whenever I saw it I had terrible nightmares. One day I was watching in horrified fascination, together with my brothers and some of my friends in the village. Grandma was there, her eyes glued to the screen as she soaked up the violence and the bloodshed. But when my father realised what we were watching he strode over and angrily snapped off the TV.

For the first time ever I saw him turn on Grandma. 'Why do you let the children watch such things? Such evil and violence? You are an elder! You are wise with the years. You of all people should know better!'

For once Grandma was lost for words. She had never known my father speak to her like this.

'How can you be *proud* of that war?' he demanded. 'You know nothing about it! *Nothing!* It is a wrong war, a bad war, and an *unholy* struggle.'

'But the TV says it's a jihad,' Grandma tried to object. 'Holy warriors fighting against infidels, people who have no faith . . .'

'A jihad? *A jihad?* What lies!' my dad cut in. 'I'll tell you what it is: it is propaganda made by those who stole power in this country – that's what it is. It is a pack of lies made by a bunch of criminals, murderers and thieves.'

There was an uncomfortable, embarrassed silence.

'I'll tell you about your so-called "infidels", shall I?' my father added. 'There's four million of them have fled to refugee camps, just to escape those brave "holy warriors". Mostly they're women and children. A great many of them are Muslims. You go to kill your fellow Muslims, you slaughter women and children, and you call that *a jihad?*'

My father pinched the skin of his arm. 'And all of those "infidels" are black African people, just like us. So think before you fill the children's heads full of propaganda, rubbish and lies.'

My father stalked off into the shadows. Grandma hadn't really considered what was right or wrong in this war: she just enjoyed the images of fighting. I watched as a shadow passed across her face, and then she hitched her shawl over her head and turned towards her hut. She walked away in silence, and I thought for the first time in my life that Grandma looked old. I knew how much she loved and respected my father, and I knew how much his words must have stung her.

But my father was right, of course. And this was a far bigger issue than simply what was shown on TV. Recently, government agents had been going around Zaghawa villages recruiting young men to go and fight in this so-called jihad. They picked easy victims: the orphans, the young men with no education and no work. And it was in this TV show, *Fisah hart el fidah*, that Zaghawa families were learning that their loved ones had been killed – as the bodies of the 'martyrs' were paraded in front of the cameras.

Whenever my father heard of any men tempted to join up, he tried to persuade them not to. Most of those recruited were simple village boys, and they were brainwashed in special training camps. It was a bad, *unholy* war, from which few would return alive, my father explained. There would be no holy martyrs, no honour in such death. It was hardly a befitting end for a Zaghawa warrior. And, worst of all, we black African Zaghawa were being made to fight our black African brothers. It was all so wrong.

My father hated the idea of brave Zaghawa warriors wasting their lives in this way. We needed them for the next battle – a battle that he knew in his heart was coming.

11

Dream to Be

In order to get a place at university to study to be a doctor I would have to achieve the highest possible marks at secondary school. All my previous achievements would be as nothing if I failed. So I forced my father's worries to the back of my mind, and concentrated hard on my studies. While I couldn't yet help with my father's political dreams, at least I might achieve his academic ones.

My years at secondary school flew past. Seemingly in no time at all I was eighteen, and facing my high school leaving certificate exams – a nationwide test across all subjects studied. If I failed to achieve over 70 per cent, my chances of securing a place at university would be zero. And in order to make it to medical school I would need an exceptional mark. With the exams fast approaching I studied as I had never done before.

The exam results were announced first by the Minister for Education, on national television. He named the top thirty students in the country, but I was not among them. Every one of those top achievers was from a school in Khartoum. I headed to school and joined my friends waiting at the gates for the headmaster. As soon as we saw him we rushed over, begging to be told how we had done. But he shrugged us off angrily.

'All of you – all of you have failed!' he cried. 'Failures! Failures! Only two did well. Only two! The rest of you – failed!'

I couldn't believe it. It was a disaster! I hoped and prayed that I was one of the two lucky ones. The headmaster made us wait the whole morning for details of the results. We knew why he was so angry. The more pupils who got a university place first time round, the higher the points the school would score, and the bigger the headmaster's pay bonus would be. This year had not been a good earner as far as he was concerned.

Just prior to lunchtime the grim-faced headmaster had us form up in stiff ranks on the playing field. The name of the girl who had achieved the top mark was announced first: it was Rehab, one of the cleverest of the Arab students. She had achieved 89 per cent, a good pass by anyone's standards. I was truly worried now. My heart pounded as I waited to hear the second name, hoping beyond hope that it would be my own.

'Second, with 88 per cent – Halima Bashir!' the headmaster called out, his brows scanning the faces in front of him.

I felt a wild mixture of emotions surge through me as I stepped forward to receive my pass certificate. On the one hand I was overjoyed to have passed and to have the chance of going to university. On the other, I berated myself for letting Rehab beat me by one percentage point. And I knew that for me the struggle was far from over. Medicine was the hardest of all subjects for which to gain a university place, and my results still had to stand up nationwide. Eighty-eight per cent just might not be good enough.

Where had I gone wrong, I wondered. My subjects had been geared towards the sciences, as that was what was required to study medicine. Just as soon as the results were pinned on the notice board I went to check. I ran an anxious eye down the list: I'd got top marks in chemistry, biology, English, Arabic, maths and Islamic studies. It was physics that had let me down, the one subject that always did seem to confuse and confound me.

As Mona, Najat, Samirah and Makboulah gathered around to congratulate me, I could see just a hint of envy in their eyes. This was the beginning of the end of our fellowship, as none of my friends would be going through to university this year. That afternoon, Mona and I shared one of our last walks home from school. She confessed to me her big secret: her exam results didn't matter much any more. Her parents had told her that there had been an offer of marriage from a cousin. They had accepted. Mona's education was over.

All through her schooling they had encouraged Mona to do well and to take a place at university. But her husband-to-be was an uneducated trader, and he had refused to countenance her continuing her education. I felt so sorry for Mona. She hadn't done that well in her exams, but the very knowledge that she was being married off would hardly have encouraged her. I was so glad that my life hadn't followed the same pattern as hers – that my father had had the courage to refuse my cousin's offer of marriage.

Thursday marked the end of the week and the end of my days at secondary school. My father arrived in the Land Rover and we set off for the village. On the long drive home I confessed how disappointed I was with my results. But my father urged me to be happy. Eighty-eight per cent was easily good enough to get me to university. If I couldn't get a place in medicine, then we would try for something else. He was so proud of me, and I should be proud of myself too.

Back in the village everyone was so happy that I had passed. The sense of joy was infectious, and I started to feel as if maybe I had done all right. No one from the village had ever been to university, so simply getting a place would be a great honour. Normally, village girls would be married off long before they could ever think about university, and the village boys would be hard at work earning money to support their families.

My best friend, Kadiga, was married with a little boy now. She had moved away to her husband's village and I hadn't seen her in five years. I decided to visit her, to tell her my news. But it was a bittersweet reunion. Kadiga tried to make light of things, yet we both knew that there was a huge gulf opening up between us. She had been married at the age of fourteen, and she was proud of her first-born, a little boy called Mo. Laughingly, she told me that we would have to remain best of friends, so I could become the family doctor.

'Our lives went in very different directions, didn't they?' Kadiga remarked, quietly. 'I got married, you went on to study. I have a good husband, but he told me that wives weren't meant to study. I should be looking after children. So I stopped. But I'll make sure my boy goes to school, and maybe even university, just like you.'

More than ever before, now I felt as if I was no longer of the village. My education had alienated me, setting me apart from those who had been my childhood friends. Somewhere deep in my heart I regretted it, but this was the path that I had chosen.

Back at home I filled in the forms to apply for my university place. I opted first for medicine, and failing that, law. My third choice was to study economics. My father took the forms with him to Hashma town, and he fed them into the applications system. It would take many, many weeks for us to hear, and so the long wait began.

It was during this time that we received some terrible news. Grandma's estranged husband had gone off to fight in the civil war in Tchad, taking Grandma's two sons with him. Grandpa had a second wife in Tchad, of course, so he was fighting alongside his family. But there had been a massive battle in the Tchadian deserts and all three of them had been killed. In one blow, she had lost her husband and her sons.

Upon hearing the news Grandma's strong face just seemed to

collapse in on itself. She broke down in tears, and nothing we could do seemed able to comfort her.

'My man! My man! My children's father!' she wailed. 'My sons! My sons! I've lost the only men in the world. All men are dead now. All men are perished . . .'

This was the first time that I had ever seen Grandma cry. To see her openly reveal her heart like this was a real shock for me. Grandma had treated her estranged husband so harshly, yet here she was mourning his death as if he had been her one true love. She had never stopped loving him – that much was clear from her grief. It had been her pride and her hot temper that had prevented her from being reconciled with him. Now he was dead and they would forever be apart, and her two sons had perished alongside him.

We dressed ourselves in the traditional white robes of mourning. Visitors started arriving to pay their respects. The women removed their shoes at our gate, in deference to the dead, before joining us in our lamentations.

'They were such good men,' they comforted Grandma. 'We'll miss them. We'll miss them.'

Normally, the bodies of the dead would be wrapped in white perfumed robes and placed on a funeral bed – an *angrheb*. The bed is covered in a white burial shroud – a *bhirish* – and left in a hut so that people can pay their last respects. Before sunset the body is taken to the graveyard, as a Muslim has to be buried upon his or her day of death. The men carry the *angrheb* out of the village, the women running after and trying to touch the body one last time. Upon arrival at the freshly dug grave, the body is lowered into the ground using the *bhirish* – the white robe, which wraps the body like a funeral shroud.

But in this case Grandpa and his two sons had been buried where they had fallen, so the funeral in our village was largely symbolic. For three days the visitors remained at our house, forming a party of mourning. Grandma, my parents, my siblings and I had to remain in mourning for a full forty days and nights. Forty is a sacred figure for Muslims. This is because the Prophet Mohammed went out into the desert wilderness for forty days, and that's when he heard the word of God and received his holy teachings.

During those forty days of mourning I witnessed Grandma start to wither away. It was almost as if she had nothing left to live for. She kept going on and on about how her men were dead and there was nothing left in her life. All was empty. All was bereft of hope. Grandma stopped eating properly, and she stopped being angry. She even stopped beating the children. Instead, she became quiet and gentle, as if she was scared of losing what family she had left.

At times I felt so sorry for Grandma. She had had such a hard life, and now this. She started spending time at the mosque, praying for the souls of the dead. But the most worrying thing was when she started to give her possessions away. Her precious possessions – things that she had hoarded for years and years – were handed out to family and friends as if she didn't need them any more. It was as if her very spirit had died, as if Grandma had given up the will to live.

Towards the end of those forty days we were all in need of some good news. It came in the form of an early morning visit from an excited neighbour, one of Kadiga's uncles.

'I heard your name!' he cried out. 'On the radio! Halima Bashir! In a list of students accepted into university in Khartoum!'

'Oh my God! Oh my God! But which degree course? Which one?'

'The medicine one,' Kadiga's uncle announced. 'The medicine! You're going to train to be a doctor!'

I couldn't believe it. I thought perhaps that Kadiga's uncle had misheard it. My dad cursed the fact that he had missed the radio announcement himself. He decided to drive to Hashma, to check directly with the Ministry of Education, and set off immediately. I wanted to go with him, but he told me I had to stay behind. I was still in mourning and it would be unseemly for me to go.

Two days later my father returned. He got down from the Land Rover with the biggest smile I had ever seen. He held out his arms to me. Kadiga's uncle was right, he announced. I had secured a place to study to be a medical doctor.

Mo and Omer did their best to be pleased, and little Asia seemed content to soak up the general happiness. Even Grandma seemed lifted out of her gloom a little. I heard her and my mother boasting to the other women about the ills that I could cure, as if I was already a medical doctor. I hoped I would be up to the seven years of intensive study that now lay ahead of me. I hoped that I would prove myself, that I would live up to my father's dream. And I hoped that I would make friends and be happy far away in the big city.

I was halfway through my holidays by now, and my first term at university wouldn't start until the following May. I had eight months to kill. I spent the time at home helping to cook, wash and do the other chores. My mother and father chose a whole new wardrobe for me, and we went on several trips to Hashma to buy books for my studies. But most of the time there wasn't much to do, and I grew overweight and unfit. I felt my brain cloying with all the inactivity. It was time that I left to commence my studies.

It was time that I moved on to pastures new.

PART THREE

Desert of Fire

12

Medical School

The evening prior to setting out for university my mother made me remove my gold jewellery, to leave with her for safekeeping. In the boarding house there might be thieves, she said, so it was best to be careful. Early the following morning my father and I said our goodbyes. We drove to Hashma, and made our way to the train station. My father had travelled to Khartoum before, as that's where he'd purchased the Land Rover. He knew it would take us a good few days to get there.

I had with me a green metal trunk, which was in reality an old ammunition case that we'd bought at the village market. Inside I had packed all the food that my mother and Grandma had prepared for me. There was dried *kissra* – the flat sorghum pancakes; there were roasted groundnuts and sweet cakes; there was dried, spiced lamb meat; and even a few dried locusts that Grandma had saved from the last big swarm time.

All of this was crammed in among my university clothes, and a pretty *muslaiyah* – a Muslim prayer rug – that my father had bought for me. The *muslaiyah* had a picture of a mosque woven into it, finished in a rainbow of bright colours. On top of everything I'd packed a beautiful new *bataniyah* – a thick bed cover. My mother had woven it from sheep's wool, and it was to keep me warm during the months of the cold season.

The train puffed out of Hashma station shortly after midnight. My father had booked a first-class cabin for the ride to Khartoum. There were four bunk beds, and we were sharing it with a married couple. They were friendly and the beds were comfortable, and we had my mother's food to sustain us on the journey. But in spite of the fact that everyone else was soon snoring away, I was too excited to think about sleep.

At some stage I must have drifted off, for I awoke to sunlight streaming in through the cabin window. Each time the train came to a station people rushed along beside it, holding up trays of food at the window. There was fresh fruit, dried fish, juicy dates and chunks of barbecued chicken. Others were selling live goats with their feet bound together, or cages of live chickens. Arms reached out from the train, money changed hands, and the animals were passed through windows and into the carriage.

The train pushed onwards towards Khartoum, the landscape becoming a flat, dry-brown wilderness with a few scraggy trees. Here and there a faint pathway snaked through the scrub towards a distant village. But there was little other sign of life here. It was very different from the green, leafy place that was home. We passed through a series of towns, each of which seemed bigger than the last, and in places there were grey factories by the side of the tracks.

As the train rattled along my father talked to me quietly about how I should try to live my life at university. It would be the first time that I had stayed in a place so far from home, a place where we had no close relatives. I should keep myself to myself, and I should be careful. I should study hard and be wary of others – at least until I had got a measure of what they were like. I should make friends only with those that I could trust.

On the evening of the third day a blanket of velvety darkness descended over the flat, featureless landscape. Up ahead I caught sight of an orange-pink glow, the horizon lit up within the darkened bowl of the desert. The very sky seemed as if it was on fire. Those were the lights of Khartoum, my father explained. As the train was sucked into the big city I felt myself engulfed in its blocky, concrete darkness. The windows of the many-storeyed houses stared out at me like a thousand empty eyes. How would I ever survive here, I wondered. How would I make this my home?

The train clanged to a halt at the dimly lit station. For a second or so I sat there, glued to my seat, and then my father grabbed my green metal trunk and called for a taxi. We drove in silence across the dark city to the house of a Zaghawa friend of my father. After a sleepy welcome I was shown to a room where I could rest. I lay awake for what seemed like an age, staring out at the weird, pulsating glow of the city, my ears full of the roar-hum of the traffic. The city seemed to eat and to breathe and to move, almost like an animal – an animal that seemed never to need to sleep.

The next morning my father's friend drove us across to the university. It was the induction day, and each of us first-year students was to be interviewed by our head of faculty. Mine was a friendly looking man called Dr Omer, of mixed Arab–African appearance. He greeted me and asked where I was from. What did my father do for a living? Why had I chosen to study in his faculty? I told him that my dream was to become the first ever medical doctor of the Coube clan of the Zaghawa tribe. There was no doctor in our village, and I hoped one day to return there to practise medicine.

Dr Omer seemed to enjoy my answers. He told me that it was a worthwhile dream for a young woman to cherish. If I studied well, there was no reason why I shouldn't achieve it. With an encouraging smile and a few scribbles of his pen, Dr Omer confirmed that I was registered to study for a degree as a medical doctor. I breathed a sigh of relief. If all the university staff were as gentle and supportive as Dr Omer, my time here would be an enjoyable one.

I went with my father to find the university boarding house. All being well, this would be my home for the next six years. It turned out to be a fine building. Like others we had passed on campus it was of recent construction, with strong brick walls, wooden shutters on the windows and a polished concrete floor. It had a shiny, galvanised iron roof, insulated on the underside with thick wooden boards. But I was surprised to find it almost completely deserted. Where were the other students, I wondered.

The lady who ran the boarding house showed me around. I chose the top bunk in a row of beds in one corner of the dormitory. I placed the contents of my metal trunk in the wooden cupboard beside it, or at least those things that would fit. I had to share the cupboard with whoever might take the bunk next to me. So all my mum's gifts of food had to stay in the metal trunk, which was pushed underneath the lower bunk bed.

There was only one other person present in the dorm, and like me she was in the company of her father. I asked her why it was so empty. Had we got the wrong day? Perhaps we were too early. She gave me a smile. She'd been worried about the same thing herself, she said. But it was the right day for induction. Perhaps the other students would turn up the following day, when our lectures were scheduled to start.

The girl's name was Rania. She came from the Mahass tribe, a mixed Arab–African people who are related to the Nubians of north Sudan. Like me, she was a very long way from home. I warmed to her immediately, and even more so when I discovered that she was studying medicine.

My father did his best to settle me in for the night. Before leaving, he asked Rania to look out for me. He was going to spend the night at his friend's house, then take the train back to Hashma the following morning. He gave me some money for my keep, urging me to look after myself, to study hard and be happy. As he did so I could see the tears welling up in his eyes. Whether they were tears of pride or of sadness at our parting, I didn't know. I hugged him tightly, as the tears streamed down my own face.

'Don't cry, Rathebe,' he told me. 'Everything will be okay. You'll like it here. And you've got Rania. You've made your first friend already.'

'I know, Abba, I know,' I sniffed. 'It's just . . . It's just I've never been so far from home. I'll miss you all so much . . .'

'I'll come to visit whenever I can. Whenever I can get up to Khartoum, Rathebe, I'll come.'

I held onto my father, hugging him as tightly as I could. I was reluctant to let go. I knew he meant what he said about visiting, but I also knew how difficult it would be for him to do so. Finally he prised my hands away and with a kiss to the top of my head he was gone, striding off into the shadows and waving his good-byes. That night Rania and I slept huddled together in the deserted dorm, sharing one mattress for comfort.

The dormitory proved to be stuffy and hot, even though we were the only students present. What would it be like at the height of the dry season, and when the beds were full? I was glad that I'd got a top bunk. I couldn't bear the thought of sleeping in the claustrophobia down below. That first night a heavy shower of rain drummed on the tin roof, beating out a deafening rhythm. But at least it took the worst of the heat out of the air.

In the morning Rania's father returned, and he invited me to join them for breakfast. He was a teacher back in their home village. As with my father, it was his life-long dream that his daughter would study medicine. Rania's father was a kind-hearted man. His daughter and I were already the best of friends, he told me, so I was like a second daughter to him now. It was easier for him to travel to Khartoum than it was for my father. So when-ever he came to see Rania, he would also be coming to visit me.

Barely had we finished eating when a stream of new arrivals began filling up the dorm. Rania had bagged the bunk opposite mine, and the other beds were quickly taken. Rania's father took us on a stroll around the campus to escape the crush. He pointed out how new and smart the buildings were. Apparently the entire university was barely six years old. A tree-lined avenue led into the campus from the main road. It ended at a large dining hall, with lecture halls branching off to either side.

I marvelled at the wonders of the university – this vast house of intellect and learning. There was a giant, ultra-modern lecture hall, which could easily house our entire year. It had microphones for the students, and rows of desks facing a raised lecture platform. All 700 first-year students would have their lectures here. Our first year would be spent doing a foundation course, which covered just about every subject one could imagine. Those who passed the foundation year would move on to study their specialised degree subject.

I quickly settled into a routine. Each morning I'd breakfast with Rania, and then we'd rush over to the vast lecture hall to secure the best seats. We dormitory students had an advantage over those who lived off campus, as we had less distance to walk. In those first few weeks I fell in love with the university. I adored its studious air, coupled with the atmosphere of freedom and respect for all that emanated from the academic staff. No one looked down on anyone because of their skin colour, their tribe or their status in society.

Of course, it wasn't perfect. There were regular power cuts, which meant that the loudspeakers and the microphones in the vast lecture hall stopped working. At times like those it was vital to be as near to the front as possible, so as to be able to hear the lecturer. The city power stations were old and crumbling, hence the shortages in supply. And, of course, I missed my family. But the excitement of being at a place where Arab–African rivalry seemed a thing of the past almost made up for being so isolated from them.

There were still clear differences between village girls, like Rania and me, and the Arab city girls. For example, I didn't have a single photograph of my family, for there were no cameras in our village. But most of the girls were able to tape up glossy pictures of their parents next to their beds. At night they would stare at the photos, and sigh, and lament being separated from their families and sleeping in such a bare, uncomfortable place.

One night I awoke to one of the girls having a terrible fit of hysterics. I rushed to her bedside, together with Rania and some of the others. Why was she so upset, we asked. Was there some terrible news? She turned her distraught, tear-stained face towards us. She had received a letter from her parents, she said. Upon reading it she had realised just how much she missed them. I asked her where her family lived and when she might see them again. It turned out that her home was just across the city, and she was planning to visit at the weekend.

I had little sympathy. I couldn't for the life of me grasp what she was moaning about. She would be seeing her family in a few days, whereas I didn't know when I would next be seeing mine. At the end of the term I would return to my village for the long summer holiday, but between now and then there wouldn't be enough time, or money, for me to do so. The spoilt city girls outnumbered us some ten to one, but we seemed far more self-contained and robust and able to cope with the rigours of dormitory life.

There was no running water in the dorms. For Rania and me it was no great effort to lift a bucket of water from the well and carry it balanced on our heads to the wash tank. But the city girls complained bitterly. They were incapable of lifting such heavy loads, they said. They begged us to do it for them. We laughed. Why on earth should we? They may have had black servants at home, but we weren't about to be their campus slaves. Some took to flirting with the male students, in an effort to persuade them to fetch and carry their water.

———— ————

May, our first month at university, rapidly rolled into June. The heat intensified, the iron-roofed dorm becoming like a baking oven. Eventually, Rania and I decided to drag our mattresses outside onto the grass. It was far, far cooler out there – and it was what we would have done in the village. Gradually, the other girls followed suit. Eventually, even the precious Arab city girls were sleeping outside. The boys had their own dorm, and they had taken to sleeping outside theirs just as we girls bedded down outside our own.

One night I awoke to the terrifying sensation of a big hairy hand resting on my face. For a horrible instant I thought it must be one of the male students. But then I realised what it was, and if anything it was even more terrifying. It was a *karaba* – a giant flesh-pink spider with long hairy legs. It is called a camel spider in English, and it secretes an acid that burns the skin. Normally I wasn't afraid of insects. At home we'd even catch scorpions, remove their sting and play with them. But we didn't have any *karaba* in our village.

They were the most revolting creatures that I'd ever seen. They had an unearthly, alien look about them. They were the size of a person's hand, with a horrible flesh-pink abdomen full of an ink-black liquid. From the head end projected two long claw-like pincers that I imagined they used to hold their victims while squirting acid onto them. But most frightening of all was the fact that these spiders could run and jump at lightning speed. We'd all seen them chasing after students as if to pounce and attack them.

And now I had one on my face. If it squirted out its fluid, the acid would be in my eyes. In an instant my hand shot up and I smashed it away. But a moment later I heard a terrified cry. The *karaba* had landed on one of the girls, and she had started screaming hysterically. Luckily, it didn't have the chance to squirt its poison onto her before it was bashed aside once more. But no matter how hot the weather became, that poor girl refused ever to sleep outside again.

We also had chameleons on campus – large, tree-dwelling lizards that catch insects with their sticky tongues. Chameleons can change their colour to blend in with their background. I used to delight in picking one up from a tree and placing it on the ground, and watching it change from a green leafy colour to the sandy-red of the soil. I especially liked doing this whenever the Arab city girls were around. They'd be making yucky faces at the chameleons and crying for their mothers – as if they were dangerous dinosaurs or something. They couldn't believe that I could pick one up and handle it so easily.

In fact, the city girls were even terrified of frogs. This was a problem, as we had to dissect frogs in our biology classes. As we had to provide our own frogs for dissection, Rania and I would go out and catch them in the nearby streams and rivers. We'd grab them with our hands and pop them into a plastic bag. But the city girls refused to do so. Instead, they used to pay street boys to go and capture the frogs on their behalf.

Even then the frogs had to be readied for the dissecting table. The city girls used to beg us to do this for them. We'd laugh and tease them mercilessly, but usually we would help. First, you had to give the frog some chewing tobacco to eat, which would render it unconscious. Then you'd slice it open and pin it out flat on the dissecting board. The male students were forever stealing the chewing tobacco, and it reached the stage where the professor refused to provide us with any more until they stopped.

The Arab city girls couldn't believe what our lives had been like prior to university. They couldn't accept that we'd played in the mud, made toys from soil and caught and eaten insects – for if so, how had we possibly ended up studying medicine at university? It was quite impossible. In comparison to Rania and me, they had led privileged childhoods – with electric lighting, running water, food to buy in the shops, and servants to tend to their every need. Plus they'd had many more years of education than we had: from the age of two onwards they had been to nursery, followed by junior school.

I guessed that there had to be things that the city girls knew which we didn't, but I couldn't for the life of me see what they were. The only department in which they seemed to be more knowledgeable was boys. Prior to going to university I had never had a boyfriend. We village girls believed that your husband should be your one and only partner. From the very earliest years this was what Rania and I had had drummed into us.

But the city girls found this very old-fashioned. They would lounge around on the grass with the male students, chatting and laughing. Sometimes they'd try to get Rania and me to join them, but I was always very shy. Occasionally, late in the evening, one of the Arab girls would quietly slip away with one of the male students. Rania and I would exchange glances. Their families had sent them here to study, but look what they were doing!

There was a funny, crazy Arab girl called Dahlia who was forever teasing me. She accused me of having no heart because I didn't seem interested in boys. Whenever a boy tried to make advances I would tell him to go away. But with her, a few nice words and she'd fall head over heels in love. It wasn't fair, Dahlia declared. While she had to go and hunt for a man, my family would do it for me. Her parents were useless. And with an ugly face like hers, what chance did she ever stand of getting her man?

For those parents who really did worry about their daughters, there were always the Islamic universities. They offered the same courses, but the lectures were segregated by sex. Our university wasn't at all like that – only the boarding houses were segregated. My father could have sent me to an Islamic university, but his priority was to find a good place of study. People in the village used to say that 'you can't put the firewood next to the fire' – meaning that boys and girls were best kept apart. But my father trusted me, and he had his own progressive ideas.

Back in the village, people were convinced that I'd been left behind by the marriage train. Who would want to marry me now, they argued, when I was so over-educated? I didn't need all this learning to have children and look after the home. But my father disagreed. He argued that a woman should be able to depend on herself in life, not solely on a man. People wondered where he had got such radical ideas. But I was happy with his views, of course, and I felt that I was different from the other Zaghawa girls.

There was one big advantage that the city girls had over us country girls – and it came as a complete shock to me. One night in the dorm Rania and I were telling the others about our circumcision time. They were both horrified and fascinated. They told us that this had never happened to them. At first I didn't believe it: I had just presumed that all girls went through their cutting time. So Dahlia offered to show me. Sure enough, her womanhood was intact.

I was amazed. Hadn't the other girls at school laughed at her, I asked. Wasn't it unclean to be left like that? And how would she ever find a husband? Dahlia laughed. Many of the girls at her school were like her, she said. It was how God had made us, so what could possibly be so wrong with it? And which of the boys at the university would turn her down, just because she had her full womanhood?

In fact, it was a great advantage, she said. We girls who had been circumcised – we didn't know what we were missing. What we had been born with was a gift from God. How could it possibly be right to go through all the pain and bloodshed of circumcision, risking infection or death, and knowing that childbirth might present us with a real problem in the future?

The more I thought about what Dahlia had said, the more I suspected that she was right. It was inexcusable. My circumcision was inexcusable. To put a small child through the hell of that life-threatening pain and injury was simply inexcusable.

The more I studied human anatomy at university, the more I realised the horrible long-term effects of what had been done to me as a child. All parts of the body are designed with a specific function in mind. To replace soft, pliable flesh with a tight ring of scar tissue could only cause problems in adult life, in particular with childbirth. I may have been different from most Zaghawa women, in my education and my independence, but I certainly wanted to have a family. Yet the chance of my child – or even me – dying during childbirth was massively increased because of my circumcision.

And then there was the pleasure issue. Dahlia hadn't been totally explicit about it, but she had said enough to make me understand. Rania and I had lost more than just a physical attribute – we had lost a sensual one also. And our lives would be forever the poorer for it.

The more I thought about this, the more I felt angry and cheated somehow. My family and my tribe had taken advantage of my girlhood innocence and stolen something precious from me. I had been an unsuspecting child, and they had convinced me that what they were doing was right, that it was a wonderful part of my growing into womanhood. In fact, they had been stealing my very womanhood from me.

But there was no way back now. What had been done could not be undone. The one thing I vowed to myself was that if I ever had a daughter, I would never let anyone steal her womanhood.

She would go through her life blessed by what God had given her, and as nature certainly intended her to.

Dahlia was quite open about what she wanted from a future husband. She wanted to marry for love, and to share the responsibilities with her husband on an equal basis. She wouldn't start a family until her career was properly established. She would have her law degree, and so she would be quite capable of earning half the family income. The more I listened to her, the more a lot of what she said made sense. I was no longer a blinkered village girl, and at least some of the city-girl ways were rubbing off on me.

Dahlia loved trying to shock me with stories of her teenage years. I was scandalised – yet also secretly thrilled – to hear how she had chased after the boys and kissed them. How she had tried drinking alcohol, and several times had ended up quite drunk. How she'd lied to her parents so she could go out to discos and nightclubs, dancing wildly and partying long into the night. But the worst was when she tried to tell me about some of her adventures with the city bad boys.

'No, no, no – don't tell me any more,' I said, pretending to block my ears. 'I don't want to hear!'

'You see what a different life we live!' she exclaimed. 'Come and stay in the city with us. Your father could pay your living expenses, at least until you're earning enough as a doctor. Do it – and then you'll truly be free.'

I shook my head. 'My family would never accept being so separated from me. And I could never force them to live in the city. Just three or four days and they'd be more than ready to leave. They say it's overcrowded, with unfriendly people and bad air.'

'You don't need your family,' Dahlia countered. 'You can live here on your own.'

'Let me tell you a story,' I replied. 'One time my whole family had been staying in Hashma, with my Uncle Ahmed. A thief came in the night. We woke up and ran after him, but none of the neighbours did anything to help. In the village, if you heard someone chasing a thief you'd rush to their aid, no matter which house he had tried to rob . . .'

Dahlia shrugged. 'So?'

'The story's not finished yet. The next day the neighbours came and asked why we had been screaming in the night. My mum got really upset with them. "We had a thief in the house, and you didn't help! Shame on you," she told them. "Why didn't you come to our aid, like you would have done in the village?" They didn't know what to say.'

'So? So it's a nice, quaint story. What's it got to do with you coming to live in the city?'

'If I came to live in the city, I'd not be with the people – the village, the community – that I grew up in. And I can't move the village to the city in one lump, can I?'

Dahlia laughed and shook her head. 'Sounds like you'll always be a country girl!'

My first three months at university were a challenge, a revelation and a joy to me. I was among my academic peers, and I was tested and stimulated by being so. I had made good friends, and I even found myself enjoying the company of the male students. I was looking forward to the years of study that lay ahead, eager to learn and to advance myself. There was little sign here of the dark powers that had seized control of our country, little sense that my father's fears might come to pass.

It couldn't last.

One morning towards the end of our first term, I awoke to sense a strange electric tension in the air. A buzz of whispered conversation was going round the dorm. It turned out that the dreaded secret police had arrived on campus. There were scores of them in plain clothes, plus their regular colleagues in khaki-green uniforms. As yet none of us had any idea why they were here – but we all felt in our hearts that it couldn't be for any positive reasons. We dreaded whatever was coming.

We headed down to the lecture hall under the dark gaze of these men. The Dean of the university was there to address us, which in itself was highly unusual. He was looking drawn and haggard. He gave a short address in which he explained that a *nephirh* – a state of national emergency – had been declared across the country. He was sorry to tell us that the university was to be closed immediately, and until further notice.

The Dean left the podium and one of the plain-clothes officers took his place. In a strident, badgering tone he proceeded to inform us that the country was in crisis. The National Islamic Front needed volunteers to join the jihad in the south, otherwise the infidels would overrun the country. All people of the right age must volunteer to fight. Women were not allowed to take up arms, but they could join the jihad in an auxiliary role. As for the young men, jihad was no longer voluntary. It was their obligation to fight.

Those who agreed to fight for a year would be treated well. Their studies would be fast-tracked, and they would graduate early with good results. Jihad was superior to academic study, and so it was only right that the jihadists should be rewarded. All universities were being closed until further notice, so there was no possibility to continue studying. The only option was to join the jihad on behalf of the country and for Islam. Any who refused would lose their place at university, the security officer declared in a menacing tone.

As he finished speaking a video started playing. It showed bloodthirsty scenes from the *Fisah hart el fidah* TV programme, accompanied by patriotic and religious music. The faces of the martyrs were paraded on the screen, as the music swelled to a heroic intensity. Mothers spoke of how proud they were that their sons had been martyred for the cause. The final minutes of the video urged all men to join the jihad and all women to support them.

As I watched, I felt sick in my heart. I knew from my father what a pack of lies this all was. I knew what the people of the south were fighting for. Many were Muslims, just like us, and I knew that they were fighting for the return of democracy. Few of the students supported the National Islamic Front. All we wanted was to continue our studies in peace. Yet here we were, being bribed and threatened into fighting an unjust and unholy war.

The video ended with scenes of officials handing out money and gifts to the mothers of the so-called martyrs. The security officer informed us that he and his colleagues were ready to sign up 'volunteers'. In the deathly silence that followed there was practically a stampede for the door. We herded out of the lecture hall with downcast eyes. As we hurried away, we could feel the hostile stares of the security men boring into our backs. The very sense of it sent shivers up my spine.

There was only one thing to do now, and that was to get away as fast as possible. Back in the dorm many of the students seemed frozen with shock. What were we to do, they cried. Should we try to leave? Would they try to stop us? I told them to pull themselves together. We should all of us go, and as quickly as we could. The longer we stayed, the more risk that one or more of us would be forcibly taken to join this 'plastic jihad'.

As quickly as I could I threw some essential items into a travel bag. Rania and I decided to travel to the station together, whereupon she would take a train north to her village and I would head west towards my own. If anything happened on the way, perhaps one of us might be able to raise the alarm. As we hurried across campus, we could see uniformed men locking shut the lecture halls with massive padlocks and chains. It was such a depressing sight. My heart sank.

All my dreams of learning had been so suddenly shattered.

13

University of Jihad

Four days later I reached home. I had taken the train to Hashma, and the truck back to the village. Of course, my parents weren't expecting to see me, and they were surprised and more than a little worried. I explained some of what had happened, trying to gloss over exactly why the university had been shut down. My mother had anxiety in her eyes, and I didn't want to make matters any worse. As I finished speaking she burst into tears.

'Look at you! Look at you!' she sobbed. 'So thin, like a skeleton. Bad food and studying all the time – just look what it's done to you.'

'I'm fine, Eya,' I replied, giving my mum a hug. 'I've just slimmed down a bit, that's all. I was fat when I left the village.'

'Nonsense, Rathebe, nonsense,' Grandma cut in. 'You think we want you wasting away to nothing? We need you to be healthy and strong and to do well at your studies – our doctor daughter! All that time away – what you need is some good home cooking!'

I was glad that Grandma seemed to have recovered her good spirits. But why were they all so keen to stuff me full of food? I didn't even feel hungry.

'Look, I ate some bread and fruit on the truck . . .'

'You think you can survive on *that*!' my mother exclaimed. 'So thin, so thin-looking . . .'

I shrugged and gave a little laugh. It wasn't food that I was lacking – it was my studies, my wonderful university studies that had been so unexpectedly cut short. If anything had made me thin and pinched-looking it was that. Still, my mother and Grandma wanted to do something for me, and feeding me up was the best they could think of. I would speak to my father later, and have a proper talk. He, I knew, would understand.

'Get your money and take her to the market,' my mother announced to my father. 'Get her a plate of meat. She has to eat meat, so she can regain her strength.'

My father rolled his eyes at me and hurried off to fetch his money from the hut. He went to start his Land Rover but I told him that I'd prefer to walk. As we strolled through the village I started telling him exactly what had happened. I saw a shadow pass across his face. All of the universities were facing problems, he told me, and in some cases it was even worse.

We headed for the restaurant in the village market-place. It was a simple, basic place of wooden uprights topped off by a grass thatch roof. The meat was prepared out at the front on a huge wooden block which was buzzing with flies. I chose to have a plate of flash-fried camel liver, which was my favourite dish. If you tried cooking it properly it would go hard as a stone, so it had to be eaten practically raw. We took a table and tucked into our plates of spicy meat, together with a fresh onion and chilli salad.

My father lowered his voice and leant across the table to me. My cousin Sharif – the young man who had many years ago driven me home from the wedding in his donkey cart – was at another university in Khartoum. That one had also been shut down, but the students had gone onto the streets to protest. The police had broken up the demonstrations, beating the students and driving many into the river. Scores had drowned.

Sharif was all right, my father assured me, but he'd been arrested and questioned, which meant that he was now a marked man. The secret police would have a file on him, which was a big worry. Several times now Sharif had travelled to the south of the country, my father explained. He'd gone there to see for himself the reality of the war. He had even met the rebel leader, Dr John Garang.

Sharif wanted to ascertain whether the students might take up the fight in Khartoum. And if so, what help might Dr John be able to provide? I was amazed. Dr John was the legendary black African leader of the southern peoples. How was it that Sharif, the village boy with the donkey cart, could be moving in such circles? He was older than me and he had been at university longer, but even so it was quite a turnaround for the boy from the bush.

My father's worry now – and that of all Sharif's family – was that his arrest might prompt the secret police to probe him more deeply. If they did, they might discover his contacts with the rebel leader and his visits to Dr John's camps. And if that happened, Sharif was as good as dead.

My father finished his food and left me in the café to enjoy some sweet mint tea, while he went to find a couple of choice goats for Grandma. Grandma's constitution wasn't what it used to be, and my father reckoned a couple of nice animals might bolster her spirits. The mint tea arrived in a little glass, together with a box of sugar cubes. I took three and dropped them in. They lay on top of the mint leaves, dissolving slowly. As I watched them disappear, I wondered what on earth was happening to our country.

On my way through Hashma town I'd been forced to wait for the truck for several hours, so I had gone to see my old school friend, Mona. She had a little baby daughter now, which had made her very happy. But in a frightened voice she had explained to me how the soldiers had been around her part of town, trying to force the men to go and fight in the jihad. Her husband had gone to hide in his village, leaving poor Mona with the baby.

And then there was Sharif. My country cousin had grown into a young man with dreams to lead a rebellion. How had that transformation taken place? And what sort of country was it where universities – places of learning – became the breeding grounds for armed revolt? Part of me felt proud of Sharif, and I was more than a little intrigued as to what he might be like now. Surely he must be so different from the boy in the white robes who had eagerly offered us a ride home in his donkey cart. Perhaps one day I might find out.

As I considered the risks that Sharif had taken, part of me felt guilty – guilty that I was doing nothing to stand up to those who were destroying our country. When they had closed our university I had fled home to my village. Had some of the other students tried to make a stand? Had I deserted them? I kept telling myself that this wasn't my struggle. I was a woman, and all this politics and war was for men. More importantly, my priority was to study. I wasn't about to give up on that just because we had a bunch of madmen running the country.

My father returned, and he showed off the two strong goats that he had with him. I finished my tea and we set off on the walk home. But the larger of the goats didn't appear to be very happy. It was digging its hooves in and shaking its head from side to side as my father pulled the string. A tug-of-war ensued, which neither side won. Finally, my father grabbed the stubborn goat by its horn and handed me the string of the more co-operative one.

'Rathebe, you still remember how to hold a goat?' he asked, his eyes twinkling.

'What's that supposed to mean?' I retorted, in mock anger. 'Why on earth wouldn't I?'

My father shrugged. 'Well, big city girl soon to be a doctor and all that . . . I was just checking.'

We laughed. My father wrestled the troublesome goat into a submissive stance and started dragging it along by its horn. For a few minutes it tried to struggle, before realising that resistance was hopeless. As we wandered along I started to feel sombre again: my father's joking had raised a laugh, but it had also hit on a sore point.

'Abba, d'you really think I will be?' I asked, quietly. 'D'you really think I will be a doctor?'

He stopped, and gazed at me with his gentle eyes. 'What d'you mean, Rathebe? Of course you will.'

'But they've shut the university. It's closed until further notice . . .'

My father reached out and took my hand. 'Don't worry, Rathebe, they can't keep it closed forever. They need doctors and lawyers and engineers in this country and they know it. So don't worry. By the end of the summer they'll be forced to reopen, you'll see.'

I nodded. My father's words had cheered me up a little.

'Now look what you've done,' my father declared. 'You've dropped your string and the goat's wandered off . . . Lucky it's the well-behaved one. Think you can manage this devil-goat, while I go to fetch it?'

When we reached home Grandma was overjoyed to be presented with the two strong goats. She immediately declared that we should slaughter one of them, and prepare a feast to welcome home our 'doctor daughter'. I tried to object that I was a long way from being a doctor, but Grandma was having none of it. Mo and Omer were called, and Grandma passed them the devil-goat to be taken away for slaughter. Mo would hold the goat down while Omer administered the cut to the throat with his sharp dagger.

As they led the goat away, I reflected on the way Grandma had changed since Grandpa's death. For most of her life the very idea of slaughtering one of her precious goats for a spontaneous feast would have been unthinkable. She would have seen such behaviour as unforgivably profligate and wasteful. Now all that had changed. I remembered when she had made us eat the goats that had died from an unknown disease. That was about the height of generosity with the old Grandma. It would take me a while to get used to this softer, kinder version.

Grandma, my mother and I jointed up the meat with a big machete and a couple of sharp daggers. There was never much blood, as the goat had been bled to death after having its throat slit. This was the way that an animal had to be killed to be *halal* – acceptable – for a Muslim. It may sound horribly cruel, but I knew that Omer would have talked to the goat and said prayers over it, calming it down before he dispatched it to the afterlife. He had a gentle, natural way with animals that belied his warlike nature.

'You never used to slaughter your goats like this,' I ventured, taking a peek at Grandma. 'What's got into you?'

Grandma shrugged. 'This life doesn't last forever.' She was slicing up the goat's liver into dice-sized pieces. 'I know when I was your age I thought it did, but it doesn't. So, best make the most of it while we're here, for you're a long time dead afterwards. Now, take this goat's liver, fry it in some spices and go and serve it to your father . . .'

With the summer holiday drawing to a close my father's predictions came to pass. The national emergency was declared over and the universities reopened. I said my goodbyes to my family and travelled back to Khartoum, my hopes riding high that all would be as it was before. Upon arrival, I was overjoyed to see Rania, Dahlia and my other friends. We had an excited, gossipy reunion. But there were a handful of bunks that remained empty. We soon learned that these were the girls who had gone to join the jihad. In the boys' dorm there were yet more bunks that were empty.

Much as we tried, it was hard to recapture the joy and the spirit that had possessed us during our first term. There was a shadow hanging over us. In part it was the memory of the forced shut-down of the university; in part it was the ongoing absence of those students who had gone to fight the 'plastic jihad'. We knew that there was nothing to stop the authorities from doing the same again, and next time the methods used to 'recruit' for this war of deception and lies might be far more forceful.

The campus had become a heated rumour mill, and every week there were reports that yet another student had died fighting. Some of the Arab students became angry at the blacks and the southerners for bringing death into their lives. I tried to keep out of it, to keep my head down and to study.

After the baking summer came the rainy season, and the cool downpours were very welcome. They took the heat out of the campus, both physically and in terms of our anger and confusion over the 'plastic jihad'. Gradually, we tried to forget all that had happened. But the rains brought other, unexpected problems. One afternoon in October a huge swarm of insects blocked out the sun. Within minutes a thick carpet of giant locusts had settled upon every inch of the ground. This was a plague of biblical proportions.

Dahlia and the other Arab city girls were totally horrified. As for Rania and me, we had to resist the temptation to collect up handfuls of the insects and fry them for dinner. We could just imagine how the other girls would react if we did. The swarm stripped the leaves from the trees and the grass from the ground, and when all the green matter was gone they turned their attention on the university buildings themselves.

In no time at all they were munching away at curtains, seating and even our bedding. It was impossible to sleep without a mosquito net, and it was impossible to wash without first clearing dead and dying locusts out of the water tank. Finally, the city girls decided they could take no more. The locusts were making them ill, they complained. Scores of them went home. In no time Rania and I were pretty much alone in our dorm.

We had a *khawaja* from Germany teaching us chemistry, and he became obsessed by the swarm. On the one hand he hated walking among the clouds of insects that rose at every footfall; on the other, he was fixated by the locusts' ability to chomp their way through the entire campus, stripping it bare. Ten days after the arrival of the swarm an aircraft flew over, dropping a fine mist of chemical spray. We stayed inside the dorm to avoid the nasty, choking ammonia smell. The German professor was equally amazed at the piles of dead locusts that now littered the ground, and he started to photograph them.

At the end of our first year we had to sit our foundation exams. Those who passed would go on to study their chosen degree subject. Those who failed would either have to resit the year or leave. I was nervous as to how I would fare. Before now, I had always been up against girls from the provinces, but here I was being tested against students from Khartoum and some of the other major cities.

The morning that the exam results were posted Rania and I rushed down to discover how we had done. I elbowed my way through the crowd of students and nervously ran my eye down the list of names. I found my own, only to discover that I had come somewhere in the middle of the year. It was a pass, but hardly a good one. I was relieved to have got through, but disappointed. Rania's mark was a little lower than mine, but still a pass.

As we studied the results I suddenly realised that the names of those who were away fighting the 'plastic jihad' had been included on the board. I simply couldn't believe it, especially when I realised that they had each been given a mark far higher than my own. I stared at the board with mounting anger. Ringing in my head were the words of the security officer who had addressed us on the day of the university shut down: 'Jihad is considered as superior to academic study,' he'd said, 'and so it is only right that those who fight should be rewarded.'

So this was their reward! Without being present for most of the year, and without even turning up to sit the exams, they had been given top marks. I was furious. I felt as if the university had betrayed me. I felt as if the grand ideals that it supposedly stood for were all just a pack of lies. What was the point of studying, if this was to be the reward for honest endeavour? I turned to Rania, jabbing my finger down the list of names.

'High pass marks,' I snorted. '*For them.* For the plastic jihadists! I can't believe it. I just can't believe it!'

Before Rania could respond, a male voice cut in. 'Why can't you believe it? If you spend all your time buried in your books, it's no wonder you don't know what's going on!'

I turned to find Ahmed, one of my fellow Zaghawa students, standing behind me. He was in his third year, and his family were traders in Khartoum. I didn't know him that well, but I was aware that he was involved in political activities at the university. A few times he'd tried to engage me in political discussions, but I'd always shrugged him off, telling him that I was here to study. Rania and I wandered away disconsolately. Ahmed fell into step alongside us.

'Well done on passing,' he remarked. 'But it's time you opened your eyes, don't you think? There's no point in trying to pretend this is simply a place for academic study. It isn't. It is a recruiting ground – both for those dumb idiots who support this regime, and for those of us who oppose it.'

'And what about those of us who don't want to get involved?' I countered.

Ahmed shrugged. 'Then don't get involved. Bury your head in the sand. But you'd better prepare yourself for more favours for the jihadists, like those fraudulent exam results, and more trouble for those of us who refuse to join their jihad. Better get used to it.'

'D'you think they'll be back again?' I asked. 'Those men who closed the campus . . .'

Ahmed snorted. 'You really think they ever left? Look around you. *Open your eyes.* They're here. They have their people every-where, talking to the gullible, showing their videos, recruiting, recruiting, urging students to go to war and be "martyrs". No need to sit any exams, they say – *come and fight.* No need to read any books, they say – *learn to shoot a gun. Write your name on the exam papers and leave the rest to us.'*

In Ahmed's smouldering anger I reckoned I could see some of my cousin Sharif's reasons for becoming the rebel spirit that he had. But still I refused to get involved. Instead, I returned to the village for the end-of-term break and tried my best to put such troubles to the back of my mind. I was about to start my studies in medicine proper. The dream was that close to being realised. I didn't want anything to jeopardise it.

The medical degree breaks down into four subjects: general medicine; surgery; paediatrics (the care of children); and obstet-rics and gynaecology. I had already decided that I wanted to specialise in the last one – the care of women during pregnancy and childbirth. This was where the need was greatest in our village: I had seen so many cases where babies had died during childbirth and mothers had become terribly ill.

During my second year I had to study all four subjects, and I knew I would face exams at the year's end. In each subject I would be awarded either an excellent, a pass or a fail. I would need to pass all four subjects, achieving excellence in obstetrics and gynaecology, to be able to specialise in that area of medicine. I spent large amounts of time secreted in the library, poring over medical books and cramming. I did my best to avoid Ahmed and others involved in the political struggle, keeping my head firmly on my studies.

I acquired the reputation of being a boring swot. Most students believed that I had not the faintest interest in politics, or even the vaguest sense of the trouble that was brewing across the country. The only context in which I showed a spark of dissention was human dissection. As part of our studies in surgery we each had to complete a course in the cutting and identification of the parts of the human body. We broke down into teams of four, the university providing each team with a human corpse on which to work.

Each cadaver was kept on a rack in a giant freezer. It was immediately plain for all to see that the corpses were exclusively black Africans. Our corpse had the most amazing face, with a mass of dot-scarring in a swirling pattern over cheeks, nose and forehead. Rania remarked that this was the scarring of the Nuer tribe, one of the main rebel groups fighting in the south. With black, gallows humour we named our corpse James, as we reckoned that would be a suitable name for a man from the Nuer tribe.

I asked the laboratory technicians where James had come from. All the corpses came from the Capital Cadaver Collect, but how exactly did a corpse end up there? Various explanations were offered. Some were houseboys to Arab families; they had died, and upon their death no relatives could be traced, so they were donated for dissection. Some were refugees who had fled the fighting in the south. Others had died in road traffic accidents, and as no family came forward they were sent for dissection.

Finally, I asked the question that was foremost in my mind: why were there only ever black Africans? The lab technicians confessed that they didn't know why, and this troubled them. On one occasion some Nuer people had turned up, demanding to know why their son had been sold for dissection without their knowledge. The lab technicians felt terrible about this, but what could they do? Their job was simply to fetch corpses for dissection from the Collect, not to check on the provenance of the bodies.

The more I dwelt upon this the angrier I became. If some were victims of road traffic accidents then surely Arabs also died in such accidents – so why didn't we get their bodies? Why only ever black Africans? I discussed this with Rania, Dahlia and the others, and it built into a big issue among the students. At one point we were even considering boycotting the dissection course, but we realised this might jeopardise our studies.

'If it wasn't for us black Africans the Arabs couldn't feel so superior,' I fumed. 'They need us – they need someone to keep down, to keep under them.'

Rania agreed. 'They're just playing games with the blacks in this country. They don't give a damn about us when we're alive, and even less when we're dead!'

How horribly full of foresight those words were to prove.

14

Rumours of War

I knew how valuable my qualifying as a doctor would be for the people of our village. That gave me the strength and fortitude to persevere with my studies, and I did well. There were several further shutdowns of the university, but luckily the Medical Faculty was largely left alone. Perhaps someone realised that doctors were needed in the country, and that to send medical students to fight in this futile, murderous war wasn't very wise.

I became increasingly fascinated by the traditional medicines used by Halima the Fakir and by Grandma. I had good laboratory facilities at my disposal, and I decided to determine what medicinal value such cures might have. I was particularly interested in the ointment made out of burned pigeon faeces, which was used to treat cuts and burns. Then there were the scores of plants, shrubs, bark and roots that Halima and Grandma took from the forest. Each time I went home I gathered a few more samples.

Some of these village cures had no medicinal value whatsoever. When someone had jaundice the medicine woman would burn their skin with a knife heated over the fire. Six or seven times she would apply the red-hot knife, the smoke and steam sizzling up from the skin. If you had a bad migraine, the medicine woman would use the hot knife on the side of your head, or on your neck if that's where the pain was. There was every chance that this would make things worse, especially as the burns so often become infected.

There were other ailments that were treated by traditional 'cutting' – but invariably the so-called treatment proved more dangerous than the illness itself. If a child had whooping cough their throat would swell into a big goitre. The medicine woman might decide to cut it in an effort to try to 'drain' the goitre. But the goitre was in reality a swollen gland, and as often as not the child would die from the bleeding, infections and trauma.

One lady in our village had given birth to seven daughters in a row. Her husband had decided to take a second wife, as he desperately wanted a son. Then, to the joy of both parents, their eighth child was a boy. But he soon developed whooping cough, and so the medicine woman had cut the goitre. The bleeding refused to stop and eventually the boy had died. The distraught father had accused the medicine woman of murdering his son, and the mother had never really recovered her peace of mind.

But several of the herbal cures did seem to have merit. Grandma would make a paste out of the *birgi* shrub, to heal wounds. When I tested the *birgi* plant I found it to contain cutins – natural chemicals that promote healing. The drying and burning of the plant simply rendered it into a fine powder, so that it could be more easily applied and absorbed into the wound.

I reached my final year at university proud that I had come so close to achieving my father's dream. But early one morning I awoke to the tramping of heavy boots just outside the dormitory window. Word rapidly spread that the security men had locked the boarding house. No one was being allowed to leave. For several minutes I crouched in the darkness, worried sick that this was it – that they were going to forcibly carry us off to the jihad. I vowed to myself that I would resist.

One or two of the city girls had mobile telephones, and they managed to contact their parents. They found out the gist of what was going on. Word was passed round the darkened dorm, whispered from student to student. Fighting had broken out in my area, Darfur. A group of rebels had attacked the airport at El Fasher town. Dozens of soldiers had been killed and several aircraft destroyed. After the attack, the rebels had melted into the desert. It was seen as being a major victory for the Darfuri rebels, whoever they might be.

Soldiers had been ordered onto the streets of Khartoum and all the major cities, as the National Islamic Front feared a nationwide uprising. Security men were posted at every university, to ensure that the trouble didn't spread. The parents of the city girls were urging them to return home as soon as they could. But with all students locked in their dorms, there was clearly no way that any of us were going anywhere just yet.

'The Africans, the Darfuris – they're trying to crush the Arabs!' Dahlia whispered. 'They killed lots of soldiers. They're saying it's a big defeat for the government . . . Can you believe it? This isn't the south. *It's Darfur*. It's *that* close to Khartoum!'

'You know something – I *can* believe it,' I replied. 'And *I* am a Darfuri, or had you forgotten? I'm also a black African.'

'But this isn't people *like you*,' Dahlia hissed. 'I mean, you're a model student. You don't *support* what they're doing.'

'Listen, if you keep the black people down under your boot for so long, what d'you expect? In their own country! D'you expect them to be happy? D'you expect them to do nothing?'

Dahlia was gazing at me in amazement. Some of the other Arab city girls had gathered around. They were equally astonished. I was the goody-goody swot from the library. I was the perfect student. How could I be saying such things? I suppose I was emboldened by the news that my people were fighting back, and maybe that was why.

'Look, this is war,' I told them. 'And it's a war that may come right to Khartoum. *To Khartoum*. And if it does, d'you think I won't be supporting my tribe, my people, my fellow black Africans?'

'But we're all friends,' Dahlia objected. 'There's no trouble between us. There never has been. Doesn't that count for anything?'

'There's one thing you have to understand,' I replied. 'You have trodden us down for too long. You can try to ignore it, but it's true. You treat people worse than animals, and eventually they will turn and bite you.'

Dahlia and the others stared at me. Their astonishment had turned to apprehension. Perhaps they had never heard such fighting talk. Perhaps in their privileged lives, in their plush houses with their black servants, they really did have no idea what was going on. But that was no excuse. Did they never talk to those servants? Ask them why they were so hopelessly poor? Ask them what had destroyed their happy lives and forced them to flee as refugees to Khartoum? Ask them how they had ended up as fourth-class citizens, barely any better than animals?

By mid-afternoon the security men had relented. Students were being allowed out to get food and to wash. Many took the opportunity to return home. In no time, the campus was empty. All that remained were the village girls like Rania and myself. The people of Darfur had finally shown their hand, and proven how strong they could be. How far would this go, I wondered. Would they fight their way to Khartoum, and topple those who had stolen power? Would they return this suffering nation to an open, civilised and democratic one?

<hr>

Two weeks after the attack on El Fasher airport, life at the university had returned pretty much to normal. The Arab students trickled back and we resumed our studies. There were barely four months to go until our final exams, so there was little time to dwell on what had happened. But the attitude of Dahlia and the other Arab girls had changed. They were distant towards me now, and in a way I wasn't surprised. I had shown my teeth, revealed my claws. I was no longer the quiet little swot in the library. I was the enemy within.

Further reports of fighting filtered in from Darfur, but the news was worrying. The army was counter-attacking, burning and destroying whole villages. The fear of an imminent takeover of the country was receding. There was little being reported in the media, but rumours came via word of mouth and there were scores of horror stories. We heard of whole villages being massacred. Innocent men, women and children were being gunned down. Increasingly, I was worried for the fate of my own village, and my own family.

There was a great deal of tension between the black African and Arab students now. The trust and friendship that had once existed had almost completely broken down. Occasionally, Dahlia would ask me if I had news of my family, or if everything was all right in my village. But there were others who breathed not a word of concern.

Just prior to our final examinations I managed to get a call through, using a public phone box, to Uncle Ahmed in Hashma. The fighting was far away from our area, he reassured me, and my family weren't in any immediate danger. I tried to put my worries to the back of my mind as I readied myself for my exams. But even as I did so, I knew that my dream of becoming a doctor had somehow turned sour. At a stroke, war seemed to have over-ridden everything, making the years of study seem somehow so irrelevant.

My final-year tutor, an Arab academic, tried to encourage me. He told me that I was on course for a top degree mark. I had attended each and every one of my lectures, and he knew that I stood to do well. Those students who skipped lectures used to rely on copying their lecture notes from me.

The three weeks of back-to-back final examinations were hell. At the end I was completely exhausted, but I felt confident that I had done well. All that now remained was for me to pass my oral exam – my viva.

The viva is like a one-to-one interview, and I knew it could make all the difference in getting a top mark. As I stood before my tutor and the external examiner, I felt confident that they would back me with a strong recommendation. The external examiner asked me a few questions, all of which I answered easily. Then he turned to my tutor and asked how my attendance had been at lectures. Just for an instant I saw my tutor hesitate, his eyes flickering in my direction, and then he gave his answer.

'I'm afraid that's the one area where this pupil has failed to excel,' he remarked. 'If the truth be told, there were many times when she failed to attend. As her tutor I have looked into this, and I understand that she had a similarly poor record with all lectures.'

I stood there in shock, refusing to believe what I had just heard. Barely a month ago my tutor had been congratulating me on my attendance record, and urging me to do my very best. Yet here he was telling the external examiner a pack of lies. The external examiner fixed me with a severe eye, but I figured I could detect just the hint of an amused sneer.

'Being a medical doctor is a huge responsibility,' he remarked. 'In fact, I cannot think of another degree qualification that carries such onerous responsibility. Your studies are about saving human life. You must ensure you know your subject inside out. Failure to attend lectures is a serious matter.'

'But I . . . I did attend,' I replied. I glanced at my tutor in confusion. 'I did attend. I attended everything . . . All of my studies. In fact, I can't think of a single lecture that I missed . . .'

I saw the examiner bend to his desk and scribble a note onto my viva. 'Your duty as a doctor is not only to uphold life,' he remarked, without glancing up at me. 'It is also to be truthful . . . Thank you, Miss Bashir, your viva is over. You may go now.'

I turned to leave the room. As I reached for the door handle I felt hot tears of rage pricking my eyes. Just as soon as I stepped out of the room my friends were around me, asking me what had happened. Rania wiped the tears away from my face as she tried to comfort me. Her viva was coming next. At least now she knew what to expect.

'The tutor's a coward,' Rania told me, as she gave me a reassuring hug. 'A coward and a liar. No one has a better attendance rate than you. Everyone knows that. You know what this is all about? It's their way to make sure you don't get a top mark. That examiner's been put there by the government, and your tutor's scared of him, that's all.'

Several of the other students agreed. With Darfuris rebelling across the country, how could they let me, a Darfuri, come at or near the top of my year? I had been marked down as a shirker and a liar in my viva – that's how they had got me. In due course I did graduate, but it was with a middling mark. I wasn't surprised: it was what I had expected. Yet I still felt cheated and betrayed, as if the system and the country were against me.

In contrast to the way I had so often dreamed of receiving my medical degree – in a blaze of happy glory – it was a sad, empty affair. My parents didn't even attend my graduation, and neither did I. The very day that I heard my result I set off for home. There were few goodbyes that I felt like saying. I had an emotional parting with Rania, and I said as warm a farewell as I could to Dahlia. But all I really wanted to do was to reach home and see that everything was all right. That was what was foremost in my mind.

Together with a dozen other students from Darfur – Zaghawa, Fur and others – I set off on the train journey back to Hashma.

Ahmed, the Darfuri student and political activist, came with me. Our conversation was forever about our fears for our village and our families. Fear was like a corrosive acid eating away at us. We talked continuously about the war and the fighting and who was going to win. Each of us prayed that our own village had remained untouched by the killing.

We all hoped for the best, while secretly fearing the very worst. I prayed to God to protect my family and to keep the war away from them. As I retraced the journey that I'd first taken with my father, some six years earlier, I reflected on how things had changed. Then my heart had been full of bright hope and dreams for the future. Now it was full of a dark apprehension and dread.

Upon arrival at Hashma I searched the crowded platform for my father. I'd phoned through to Uncle Ahmed, asking my father to meet me. Suddenly I spotted his distinctive figure easing through the crowd. I broke into a run, leaving my green metal trunk abandoned on the platform, and flung myself into his arms. Thank God! Thank God! At least my father was all right. And by the looks of him all was well in the village.

We hugged for what seemed like an age, and then my father held me at arm's length, gazing into my face. I had worked so hard to achieve the dream that he had shared with me when I was a little girl. And now, sixteen years later, I had done it – I had achieved the impossible. I had returned to him as Halima Bashir, MD. But did it mean anything any more? Did it matter? Was it even worthwhile?

I searched my father's face for something – for a sign, perhaps, that it was all still valid, still worth something in this crazed country that was tearing itself apart. And what I saw there made me blush, as a warm rush of happiness surged through me. My father had tears in his eyes. Tears of happiness and pride. He seemed completely lost for words. But it didn't matter. Words weren't needed any more. His look had said it all.

My father slung my trunk over his shoulder and beckoned for me to follow him to the car. We stepped out of the station and I glanced around me. The town seemed different somehow. What was it? There were no obvious signs of the war – no soldiers on the street, no tanks rumbling past, no aircraft overhead. Then I realised what it was: it was so quiet, and so tense. People hurried past, their heads bent and eyes furtive and distrustful.

As soon as we were in the privacy of the Land Rover, I asked my father if everyone was all right.

He smiled briefly, keeping his eyes on the busy road. 'Don't worry, Rathebe, everyone's fine. Mo and crazy Omer are helping me with the livestock. Your mum's looking after the house. Grandma's been ill, but she's recovering. And little Asia's at secondary school now, but she's nowhere near as gifted as you.'

'So there's been no trouble?'

'No. None. None whatsoever in our area.'

'But we heard all these terrible things – villages being bombed, houses burned, people killed.'

'Not in our area. In fact, you'd hardly know there was a war on . . .'

I felt overwhelmed with relief. The dreaded war hadn't so much as touched our village. I was returning home a proper medical doctor, and perhaps it was going to be a happy home-coming. I glanced out of the window as we rattled though the bush, and there were no signs of the horrors that we had heard of. There were no plumes of smoke in the distance, no burning villages, no long lines of fleeing refugees, no bodies rotting in the sun.

I told myself to relax, to put my fears behind me. For a while my father and I talked about my degree. I told him about my cowardly tutor and how I had been cheated in the viva. A pass was still a pass, he smiled. But the conversation kept getting dragged back to the war. It overshadowed everything. At present the fighting was concentrated around Al Fasher and West Darfur, my father said. It had yet to touch our part of the province.

'When our people attacked the Arab forces they did very well,' my father said. 'But the tables have been turned. Our people are being hit hard now.'

For a moment I was shocked to hear my father refer to the Darfuri rebels as 'our people'. This was more than I had ever said at university. But these were the people who had taken up arms to fight for our rights, so why shouldn't we refer to them as 'our people'? I listened hard as my father continued talking.

'At first we outsmarted them. The rebels came out of the mountains, attacked, and melted away again. They stuck to the hills and valleys where the soldiers couldn't use their tanks and helicopters. So you know how they responded? They attacked the villages instead.'

'We heard rumours,' I said. 'It sounds so horrible. *So horrible.* That's why I was so worried . . .'

'It is a living nightmare, Rathebe.' My father turned to me, his face dark with anger. 'Imagine – they refuse to fight us fairly, face to face as men. Instead they attack the innocent women and children. The murderous cowards. People run and try to escape, for if you stay they just kill you. Villages are burned and looted, even the livestock stolen.'

'But what can we do to stop them?'

'How can you stop them? It's only now that people are waking up to the danger. People are trying to band together, to find weapons, to join the rebels. But of course you need money, especially for weapons. And it takes time . . . So far the fighting has been in the west, but we fear it will spread to our area. We fear that it is coming.'

My father paused, leant forward and tapped the fuel gauge. The needle wobbled, then dropped to indicate the tank was a quarter full. It was forever getting stuck, and if you forgot it was easy to run out of petrol.

He glanced at me, pain etched in his eyes. 'You know how bad it's got, Rathebe? In some places whole villages have gone to live in the hills. They're living in the mountains to try to avoid the killers . . . A few weeks ago we talked about whether we should do the same. But the old people, your grandma included, refused to abandon the village. They opted to stay and fight. Better to be brave than to run, they said. So we're staying – at least for now we are.'

'What did you want to do? What did you say?'

'I said it was fine to talk of bravery, but it was guns that we needed. I said that if we waited for the fighting to reach us it would be too late. But I understand why people want to stay. It's our land, our houses, our farms. It's our community. I don't blame them.'

'So what now? What do we do next? It's all so horrible . . .'

'Don't get me wrong, Rathebe,' my father cut in. 'We need to shake off the past. For too long the Arabs have abused us and this is the start of the fight for our rights. I'm happy it's started – this is a good thing. I just hope and pray that we succeed. We'll know we have won when we take our rights, when we have true equality.'

The men of the village had started a watch duty, my father explained. Day and night someone was on guard to warn of an attack. They had marked out the best escape routes, in case the women and children had to flee to the forest. People kept talking about trying to get some guns, but how did simple farmers become gun dealers overnight? In any case, where was the money to come from? My father was the richest man in the village, and he could hardly afford to arm everyone, even if the weapons could be found.

Everyone was hoping and praying that the soldiers wouldn't come, while at the same time trying to ready themselves for an attack. Fear was stalking our village – fear and horror and evil. A darkness had descended upon my home.

It was terrifying, and totally chilling.

15

Medicine Woman

The morning after my return I awoke late to a hubbub of voices outside. I emerged from Grandma's hut with a sleepy yawn. A line of people snaked away from the gate and down the street. I wondered what was going on. My father was organising a welcome home party, but it wasn't supposed to start until the following evening.

'What's this?' I asked Grandma, trying to stifle another yawn.

'What time d'you call this?' she countered, with a smile in her eyes. 'You've kept your patients waiting long enough. I'll prepare some breakfast, while you do your rounds.'

For a moment I stared at Grandma in confusion. What was she going on about? What patients? And then I realised that the woman at the front of the queue was pointing at me. She lifted up her *tope* to reveal a swollen abdomen, and motioned for me to go and take a look. Oh no . . . I glanced at Grandma, half in amusement and half in horror.

'Go on,' she urged. 'What're you waiting for? Six years studying and now's your chance to get your hands on some real patients. Go on – *Doctor* Halima Bashir.'

As I made my way across to the group of waiting women I felt myself cringing with embarrassment. How was I going to explain that in spite of being a doctor, I couldn't cure most of their ills? I felt hopelessly inadequate. My father had set up a little table by the gate. On it was a stethoscope and a blood pressure monitor that he'd purchased in Hashma town. As I sat down behind the desk I was painfully aware that my family were watching, their pride like a fire burning all around me.

The first woman stepped up, her stomach thrust forward. She pointed at the black rubber coil of the stethoscope. 'Put that one on me and tell me what's wrong.'

I tried a smile. 'Well, first I need you to tell me what you think the trouble is.'

She snorted. 'Anyone can see that. My tummy is far too big. Just put that one on me and tell me what's wrong.'

'Look, it doesn't work like that. It doesn't talk to me. It can't tell me what's wrong.'

'Huh! Calls herself a doctor . . .' she remarked, to the woman behind her. 'Look, I've been pregnant before and it was never like this. Look at the size of me! I mean, is there a monster in there or something?'

She was speaking at the top of her voice, and the rest of the women cracked up laughing. 'Like I said, put that one on me and tell me what's wrong.'

'All right, I'll try. But I can't do everything. You may still need to go to hospital . . .'

I placed the earpieces in my ears, and the cold metal of the stethoscope against the soft skin of the woman's stomach. As I did so she flinched.

'Watch out! It's freezing! Are you going to freeze my monster baby, is that it?'

There was more laughter from the ladies. I soon discovered what the woman's 'problem' was. She was carrying twins. I could hear each of their wonderful little hearts hammering away. As far as I could tell they both sounded perfectly healthy. I felt a warm glow of happiness coursing through me, as I listened in on their world. This is what I had trained for.

I sat back and smiled. 'There's nothing wrong, and there's no monster in there. You're carrying two babies, that's all. You're going to have twins.'

The woman threw up her hands in amazement. 'What rubbish! Two babies! It's my stomach and I can tell you there's only the one in there.' She turned to the woman behind her. 'I told you she was too young to be a real doctor, didn't I?'

The other woman peered at me for a second. 'She does look very young . . .'

'Let me show you,' I suggested. 'Here, give me your hand. Now, there's the first head. Can you feel it? And now, here – here's the second. That's two heads. Two babies. Like I said, you're going to give birth to twins.'

'Well, I don't know . . . The second "head" felt just as much like an arse to me . . .'

The pregnant woman wandered off, the rest of the ladies dissolving into fits of giggles. 'Did you hear what she said . . . Felt like an arse . . . She's a one . . .'

And so my first genuine patient had been dealt with. As more of the women presented themselves, I realised that with many there was nothing the matter. Most complained of 'blood pressure', as they wanted me to use the blood pressure monitor on them. With each I did so. Few if any had the slightest idea what their blood pressure should be, but in any case they went away happy. They had seen the doctor, she had used the new-fangled gadget on them, and they'd been told they were okay. That was good enough for them.

One old lady demanded to have both the blood pressure monitor and the stethoscope 'treatment'. I tried explaining that neither machine actually did anything, they were just tools to better arrive at a medical diagnosis. But the old lady was having none of it. Why shouldn't she have both, she demanded. She was feeling ill enough to warrant it. I tried getting her to explain to me exactly what was wrong, but she just told me that whatever the machines could cure, that was good enough for her. It was what she'd come for.

'Just touch me here with that machine,' she said, indicating her stomach for the stethoscope. 'And here with that one,' she added, indicating her arm for the blood pressure monitor. 'Once you've done that I just know I'll feel better.'

I did as the old woman instructed, and she went away as happy as could be. The line dwindled to just a few remaining patients. I glanced up to catch my mother and Grandma watching me, as proud as proud could be. I asked Grandma if she might make a cup of mint tea, as I was parched. I excused myself from the last of my patients and went to take a break. My father, Mo and Omer came and joined us.

'There's nothing wrong with half of them,' I muttered. 'So don't look so impressed. Anyone could do it.'

'It doesn't matter,' my mother said. 'Look how happy you're making them.'

'But it isn't a game,' I objected. 'It's medicine. It's serious. I can't just pretend to treat people.'

'You're doing a fine job,' Grandma remarked, happily. 'I don't know what you're worried about. Maybe you got it wrong with the twins, but with the rest of them . . .'

'It was twins!' I snapped. 'That's the best diagnosis I've done all morning! It's the rest that worry me. Even if I do find high blood pressure or something, I can't treat it. They'll still have to go to hospital . . .'

'Well, you're making people happy, and that's never a bad thing,' my father said. 'If you can make an occasional diagnosis at the same time, so much the better. The lady with the twins will go away and think about what you said, and she'll see sense. Don't worry.'

As we were talking, Omer wandered over to the table and picked up the stethoscope. He popped the earpieces into his ears, and brought the listening device to his mouth. Then he placed his one free hand on his pelvis, his thumb tucked into his belt, and started to gyrate his hips in a provocative manner. He was eighteen years old, and he was a fine-looking young man. As the remaining patients gazed at him in bewilderment, he opened his mouth and started to sing – doing his very best Elvis Presley impression (although the lyrics weren't quite right).

> *Uhuhu! Uhuhu!*
> *I'm all shook out. I'm all shook out.*
> *Uhuhu! Uhuhu!*
> *I'm all shook out. I'm all shook out.*

With each successive 'uhuhu', Omer flicked his pelvis around in a wild gyration. For a second or so I was beside myself with anger. How dare he turn my surgery into a stage to perform his crap pop songs? I glanced at the line of waiting women. There was consternation written all over their faces. And then I caught Omer winking at me as he did another pelvic thrust, and I cracked up laughing. I just couldn't help myself.

'Look, I'm a famous singer and this is my microphone,' he announced to the waiting women. 'It's transmitting my song all over the world. You have to guess who I am.'

'My brother's not right in the head,' I remarked, as I went to reclaim my table. 'He thinks he's Elvis, the famous American pop star who died many years ago.'

By the time I had finished with my patients I was exhausted. I had charged nothing for my services, of course. I would never have dreamed of taking money from anyone in the village.

The day after my village surgery I went to visit the family of Halima the medicine woman. Sadly, Halima had died during my final year at university. We mourned Halima's passing, and shed a few tears as they told me the story of how she had died. Halima had become very ill – so sick, in fact, that she could no longer treat herself. This was the time we call *sinya nee* – when someone knows they are about to die. Within two days of her *sinya nee* time coming, Halima had peacefully passed away. Hers had been a gentle dying.

I said my farewells to her family and made my way back to our house. As I wandered through the village it felt different somehow. It was quieter, and it felt tense and fearful – almost as if it was waiting. Every day the elders were meeting, trying to work out how to better organise the defence of the village. They kept debating whether it was better to run and hide or to stand and fight.

I reached a group of old women chatting by the roadside. I paused to listen to their conversation. They were talking about when the Zaghawa had fought the Arab tribes in ancient times. Always we had won, one old woman pointed out, so why would it be any different this time? It was different now because the Arab tribes had powerful people behind them, another answered, giving them guns and machines to fight. Without that they would never have the bravery, or the foolishness, to attack us.

Even the little children seemed to be preparing themselves for war. I spotted one group hiding by the roadside. Suddenly, they jumped out and pounced on their friends, crying: 'The Arabs are coming! The Arabs are coming!' Children screamed and scattered in all directions. I just hoped to God that scenes like these might never become a reality in our village.

A few days later a neighbour came to our house. She was totally distraught. She had been to visit her village, which was situated on the far side of the Jebel Marra, in a green and fertile region. But when she arrived all she found was a deserted, burned-out ruin. She had discovered some of the village children, plus a handful of adult survivors, hiding in the hills. But as for her family, no one knew where they were or what had happened to them. The survivors had told her the story of the attack on the village.

The Arabs had come at dawn, riding on horses and firing machine-guns. Many villagers had escaped and fled into the hills, but many more were caught and killed. The Arabs brought their families with them and settled in the village, eating all the food and slaughtering the livestock. If any villagers tried to return to their homes, they were gunned down. No one could understand where the Arabs had got such powerful weapons. When they had eaten their fill, the Arabs had set fire to the village and left.

My father reacted to our neighbour's story with a burning anger. It was clear now that we would have to defend ourselves, he declared. If we died trying, so be it. We would be doing so for the coming generation – that one day they might be free. In spite of his fighting talk, I detected an enormous sadness within him. His politics, his belief in democracy, his hopes for the future of the country – all of it had failed, for now it was war.

As for the rest of my family, they reacted in different ways.

Predictably, Omer was all fire and bravado. 'You just watch – when they come I'll kill them all!'

Mohammed snorted in derision. 'When they come you won't kill anyone. You'll run and hide.'

Omer brandished his dagger at Mohammed. 'You'll see – I'm not scared. I'll fight and save the village.'

Mo turned to me. 'Why did they start this fight? It's as if they want to destroy us. We were living in peace. What did we do to them?'

'Its simple, Mo. They want to take the land for themselves. They always have done. So you'd better get ready. But if the Arabs come, I bet you'll be the first to run.'

Mo shrugged. 'Well, what are you going to do? Whatever you do, so will I.'

'I'm going to fight,' I told him. 'We all are. Me, you, Abba, Grandma – we all are. We don't have much choice.'

'Okay, I'll stay and fight if you will.'

'If you don't the Arabs will come and steal your new bicycle!' I teased. 'How would you like that?'

Mo and Omer both had new bikes that my father had bought them. They used them to cycle out to the farms to check on the livestock. Few people in the village had a bicycle, and they were a real status symbol. If there was one thing that might persuade gentle Mo to fight, it was the thought of the Arabs nicking his bike. But really I was teasing Mo and trying to cheer him up, for he did look very confused and fearful.

Word about the raid went around the village like wildfire. The attacks were still far distant from our area, but even so it all felt horribly real. The men broke out the few weapons that we did have – a handful of hunting rifles inherited from their grandfathers. Some of the ancient guns didn't even work, but their owners still stalked around the village looking fierce. Zaghawa knives and swords were sharpened, and the Fakirs made up special *hijabs* with the power to render their wearer bullet-proof.

In spite of the atmosphere of imminent war, life had to go on. For me that meant waiting to be allocated a place where I would work my year as a trainee doctor. The Ministry of Health would be writing to me, posting me to one of the teaching hospitals. I waited for three months for my instructions, but none came. At first I passed my time running my makeshift surgery, but eventually my stream of patients dwindled to a trickle. Either I had treated all the ailments that I could, or they had lost faith in me.

I knew that life couldn't go on like this forever. I shared my disquiet with my father. Why didn't I volunteer to work in the hospital in Hashma, he suggested. If I did, perhaps the whole family could move to town, which would get us away from the dangers now facing us.

My father was torn between his loyalty to the village and his fear for his family. He said that I'd have to persuade my mother and Grandma, if we were to move to Hashma town. We still had a house there, so the move would be easy enough to make. But they would have to be talked round. Choosing my moment carefully I broached the subject with my mother. My suggestion of moving to town didn't go down very well.

'Oh, so you want to change your skin, do you?' she demanded. 'You want to forget your roots, to turn your back on who you are?'

'What's that supposed to mean?' I countered.

'You want us to go and live in the Arab town among the Arabs? The very people who are trying to kill us?'

'It's not like that. There's lots of tribes living in town. Anyway, it's only temporary . . .'

'Go and speak with your grandma about it. Go and tell *her* you want to abandon the village – just when everyone needs us. And you a trained doctor, and so able to help your people!'

'Look, you've only ever lived here, in this remote place. A change, something different – it's not so bad. Why won't you even try? You don't know how people live there . . .'

My mother's eyes flashed anger. 'I told you, go and speak with your grandma! Or didn't you hear me? You think I'm the soft touch – well, go and try your arguments on her.'

Without my mother's backing I knew there was no way that I would ever persuade Grandma to leave the village. I abandoned the idea. But a few days later I overheard my mother talking about it with Asha, one of her best friends. I didn't like Asha one bit. She was horribly small-minded and old-fashioned. They were chatting across the fence. My mother was expressing doubts as to whether she was right to refuse to move to town.

'You know, she thinks we'll be safer there,' my mother ventured. 'And she can work in the hospital as a doctor.'

'Ah, this is a big mistake,' Asha said. 'Your daughter wants you to follow her everywhere! It isn't right.'

'You think so?'

'Look, your daughter went off to the big city and she spent too long there. Too much city life. Too many books. She got a bit unbalanced in the head.'

'But why d'you say that?'

'You know what the city's like. You don't know your neighbours; you eat alone; someone dies and no one goes to the funeral. You can't live like that. It'll destroy you. But your daughter thinks it's okay? Come on . . .'

'Perhaps you're right.'

'Remember that funeral in Hashma? Remember? None of the neighbours bothered to turn up. Not one. Without the people from the village there would have been no funeral. You want to make the same mistake as them, and all because of your daughter's crazy ideas?'

'But my husband's all for it. He says the main thing is the family's safety. He's got a point, hasn't he? Plus in town she can get a good job in the hospital . . .'

'Look, just find her a man – that'll sort her out. I mean, how old is she? And still not married? All of her friends have three or four children by now. She'll soon be too old for anyone to want her. That's no life for a woman. Even if she reaches the sky with all her studying, she'll still come back to the village in the end. And for that she needs a man.'

Asha's views were typical of many in the village. I heard her telling my mum that I needed a man to tame me. Then she offered to go and have words with my father, but my mother said that he nearly always took my side. Asha said that that was the problem then – how could they hope to 'tame' me if I always had the backing of my father?

I'd heard enough of this rubbish. As noisily as I could I showed myself and stomped across the yard. As I did so, Asha quickly changed the topic of conversation to the state of her maize crop. I stormed out of the gate, giving her one of my hardest stares. If looks could have killed she would have died on the spot. I was especially angry because barely a week ago I had treated Asha in my surgery for a lesion on her foot.

Eventually I decided to try for a voluntary placement at the hospital in Hashma. I would move to the town on my own if I had to. My father drove me in his Land Rover and we went to speak with Dr Salih, one of his Zaghawa doctor friends. Dr Salih was a specialist in obstetrics and gynaecology – my chosen field – and he agreed at once to have me as his ward assistant. He was short of staff, and my help would be invaluable.

At first I wanted to live in the junior doctors' quarters, but Uncle Ahmed insisted that I stay with them. My father agreed that it might be better, at least for the first few months. I got to work immediately, helping Dr Salih deliver babies and looking after the mothers and newborns. Dr Salih was very distinguished-looking, and slim as a rake. The other junior doctors and I used to joke that one puff of wind might blow him away.

I loved dealing with the young mums and bringing their babies into the world. And I was fortunate in that Dr Salih was a gentle man and an inspiring teacher. I was now doing exactly what I had dreamed of during all my years of study, and I was so happy. I almost forgot about the troubles menacing the village. But they never quite went away. The worry was always there, a dull aching pain that was forever eating away at me.

A month after I started work a letter finally arrived from the Ministry. It stated that there were staffing deficits in the accident

and emergency ward, and I was being allocated a training placement there. The man in charge was Dr Rashid, an Arab from the
Berti tribe. It was his job to teach me the ins and outs of the new
ward. He was a true professional and I quickly warmed to him.
He often gave me the chance to work by myself, leaning over my
shoulder and gently guiding my hands.

Dr Rashid dealt with his patients regardless of their race, colour
or creed. But the new ward was full of tension and trauma. There
was an endless stream of blood and guts and horror, and the work
was tough and exhausting. Yet I knew that I could cope. Fairly
quickly I realised that we were treating the victims of the conflict
that was spreading across Darfur. As soon as I understood this,
my worries for my family returned with a vengeance.

Of course, no one declared openly that they had been injured
in the fighting. There was a police unit stationed inside the hospital
itself, and every patient had to submit a form to them before they
could be treated. The form had to be signed off by the doctor,
and it recorded the patient's injuries and how they had been
sustained. The system was designed to identify any Darfuri rebels,
so they could be seized from the hospital and arrested.

But there were exceptions to these rules. Some of the wounded
would come in with a police escort. In these cases we were told
that we were permitted to treat them without any forms. These
injured men were the Janjaweed – a name that means 'the devil
horsemen'. They were the Arab tribesmen who were being armed
by the government to attack our villages. But it would take me
several weeks to work out that this was so.

And by then I was already deep in trouble.

16

Accident and Emergency

I spent my time swabbing bloody wounds, cleaning wounds, suturing wounds and plastering broken limbs. With each patient I learnt more about the war and the fighting. Some of the injured were black Africans, while some were from the Arab tribes. I was treating people from both sides of the war.

There were few black African doctors at the hospital, and I realised that I could help my people by ensuring that they were treated properly. This gave an added sense of urgency to what I was doing. I began working longer and longer hours. I started coming to the ward in the evenings, so I could listen to 'my' patients' stories, and comfort them. I moved out of my uncle's place into the hospital dormitory, so I could be near them.

Gradually word spread that there was a young black African doctor at the hospital from whom injured Darfuri villagers could seek help. I learned of the full horror of the war. With the Zaghawa patients in particular I could talk freely, as none of the other medical staff could understand our language. Most were simple villagers – men, women and children caught in the crossfire. They told me how the war was spreading fast. The dreaded Janjaweed were on the march, with the full backing of the military and the government.

One terrible day a distraught mother arrived with her two small boys. One was nine years old and one was just six, and their little bodies were horribly burned. I asked her what had happened. The Janjaweed had attacked her village. The boy's father had been gunned down in front of them, his sons being thrown into the burning hut alive. As I cleaned and dressed their burns, they were screaming for their mother and begging me to stop. I felt hot tears of pain and rage welling up in my eyes. My heart died inside.

Their mother had gone to wait outside. But even from there she could still hear their screams. Eventually she could bear it no longer. She came back in, and without a word she sat down at their bedside and grasped each by the hand. Every morning and every evening I cleaned and dressed their burns. But I had no anaesthetic with which to kill the pain, as it was in preciously short supply. Each time the boys cried and cried, and their mother was torn apart by it. But there was nothing more that I could do to help.

The trickle of war-wounded quickly became a flood. One horror story merged into the next. A small Zaghawa boy had had the whole of the side of his face torn off by gunfire. Where his eye once was there was now an empty, gaping hole. There were horribly burned and disfigured faces, and children with legs that had been roasted raw in the fiery huts. And there were scores and scores of ragged, bloody gunshot wounds. I'd had no idea what a bullet could do to the human body: it was sickening.

A father from the Fur tribe brought in his young son, still dressed in his school uniform. He was paralysed, and he kept falling in and out of consciousness. His father just sat there, weeping, as he told me his story. The boy had been walking to school when the Janjaweed had attacked. His school friends had been gunned down, and the little boy had tried to run. But a bullet had hit him in the back, knocking him to the ground. A gunman had ridden up to him and fired into his body, the bullet smashing through his side. The little boy had been left for dead.

But somehow, he'd clung onto life and his father had found him. Incredibly, he had survived the long journey to the hospital. When I examined him, I realised that the second bullet had severed his urethra. We couldn't treat him properly in our provincial hospital. The last I saw was the two of them being prepared for transfer to a hospital in Khartoum. I had no idea if the little boy would even survive the journey, let alone what the future might hold for him if he did.

I befriended a kindly old man who had worked at the hospital for many years. His name was Kayan, and he was the head nurse. He was from the Massalit tribe, a black African people from the north of Darfur. This was the area bearing the brunt of the fighting. Daily he saw his people arriving with terrible wounds. He told me that he wanted to go and fight, but he knew he could do more good staying here and helping the victims. He taught me all the ins and outs of the hospital system, and together we worked to help those patients most in need.

Kayan taught me the true meaning of compassion. He was willing to help anyone, no matter whose side they were on. If an Arab had been injured while attacking a village he would treat them regardless, for they too were in need. They had become victims. Kayan pointed out that the Arab tribes were being armed and driven by the government, which meant that they were not the real enemy. The real enemy was the government, and those murderous madmen who had set the Janjaweed loose in the first place.

━━ ⚊ ⚊ ━━

I was working so hard now that I only had time to eat, sleep and work. That was all my life consisted of. I'd take a few hours off on a Friday and try to catch the TV news, in the doctors' quarters. Or I'd seek out Uncle Ahmed for news of home. But all other topics of conversation were gone: all we could talk about was the war. All people could think about was how to safeguard their families and their homes. Life itself had been put on hold: no one was going away to study, or getting married, or even trying to have children.

This went on for three exhausting months, each day bringing more shattered bodies and broken lives. Then one day a young newspaper reporter arrived at the hospital. It was lunchtime, and he hung around the hospital canteen asking questions of the medical staff. He was trying to get the doctors to give him their impressions of the war, from everything they had seen in the hospital. At first I did my best to avoid him. It was impossible to know who to trust. Anyone could report you to the security services, at any time.

I watched the young reporter work his way around the canteen. The other doctors seemed to be speaking with him quite openly. He was taking their names and scribbling quotes into his notebook. So when finally he reached my table I agreed to hear him out. He asked me my name and on which ward I worked. He told me that I must have seen a lot of war-wounded, as I worked on accident and emergency. Surely it had given me an insight into the nature of the conflict. I agreed that it might have.

'Everyone is saying that the black Africans attacked the government,' he said. 'D'you agree with this? D'you agree that this is the basis of the conflict?'

I considered his question for a second. I knew that I couldn't say what I really wanted to, for to do so would be suicide. But perhaps I could give him a series of half-answers that would point towards the truth, without actually incriminating myself too much.

'Well, yes and no,' I said. 'It's more complicated than that. Historically the Arab tribes were nomadic, with no land and no livestock. Now they want to take land and livestock for themselves.'

'So it's fighting for control of animals and water and land – those are the reasons?'

'In a way, yes. But like I said, it's complicated. In our area, the Zaghawa, there is a lack of good water and little health provision. And the government does little to help.'

'So, you're Zaghawa? The Zaghawa are a famous warrior tribe. Are you fighting for your rights, is that it?'

'Well, if you are attacked you have to resist. If you don't resist you'll be crushed. It's that simple.'

'So, you're in favour of the fighting?'

'As I said, you have to resist or you'll be crushed.'

'In that case, do you want the fighting to continue?'

'No. I want there to be peace. I want the fighting to stop. It is causing terrible, terrible suffering.'

'And once there is peace, what then?'

'Well, then the government should provide the right kind of support and development for the Darfuri people.'

He glanced up from his notes. 'Regardless of which tribe they are?'

I nodded. 'Yes. Regardless of which tribe they are.'

He smiled briefly, and checked his notes. 'It's Dr Halima Bashir, right? Thanks. Something may appear in the paper, I don't know. Have to get it past the editor first . . .'

The reporter moved to the next table. I finished my meal and went straight back to work. I had a long line of patients waiting for me. I didn't dwell on the interview for too long. I'd seen other doctors speaking with the reporter for far longer than I had. And I'd said little that might incriminate me. My short interview with him was quickly forgotten.

Two weeks later I saw a group of policemen making their way around the ward. I didn't think anything of it. In the late after-noon they usually did their rounds, in case of any trouble between patients. I carried on with my work, and then sensed them come to a halt behind me. I turned. There was an odd, sinister feeling in the air. I noticed there were four men in plain clothes together with the uniformed policemen. I knew immediately who they had to be.

'Dr Halima Bashir?' the senior uniformed policemen asked. 'Dr Bashir?'

I nodded. It was an odd question. He knew perfectly well who I was, as we'd spoken many times before. He was one of the policemen stationed in the hospital to deal with the forms. He half-turned to the plain-clothes officer at his shoulder. 'Like I said – it's her.'

'You are to come with us,' the plain-clothes officer announced flatly.

'Why?' I asked, trying not to let my fear show. 'What d'you want with me?'

For a long moment he just stared at me. I imagined his dark, dead eyes behind the mirror sunglasses that he was wearing. All four of them were wearing mirror shades. Sunglasses, and dark Western-style suits: it was their ultra-macho, ultra-cool uniform. It was the same look that they'd had on the university campus when they'd come to shut it down. It would have been laughable, were it not so terrifying.

'Don't ask questions,' he rasped. 'Just do as you've been ordered.'

'Can I at least change?' I was wearing my 'scrubs' – latex gloves, rubber boots, a white gown and a hair net.

'Fine. Change. But quickly.'

I made my way to the staff changing room, my heart pumping fearfully. I stripped out of my scrubs. My hands shook as I tried to peel off the bloodied gloves. My mind was racing. What had I done? What had I done to attract their attention? Wherever they were taking me, I knew in my heart that it wasn't going to be good. What on earth had I done?

I followed the four of them out to their waiting car. It was a shiny new Toyota Land Cruiser, white, with dark-tinted windows. I sat in the rear, with one of them on either side of me. Their apparent leader – the one who had done the talking – took the seat next to the driver. As we pulled away from the hospital no one spoke a word. The windows were so dark that no one could see in. Few would have witnessed my departure, and I prayed for a safe return.

The driver pushed the vehicle fast through the traffic. Each of the men stared ahead, saying not a word. Minute after minute this went on, and the effect was totally chilling. Where on earth were they taking me? And why? What had I done? What had I done to provoke them? I knew these people were capable of anything. The secret police were notoriously brutal and they were all-powerful. Were they going to hurt me? Or torture me? Or worse? During that long silent drive I tried to prepare myself for whatever was coming.

We passed by Hashma market-place and an image flashed into my mind. It was of a black man being beaten for standing up to an Arab who had openly called him a slave. The policemen had smashed him around the head and dragged him away. Perhaps they had come for me for similar reasons. Perhaps it was because I was saving the lives of black people injured in the war. Perhaps it was because I had become *known* for doing so. Perhaps I was being punished simply for helping my own people.

We left the centre and headed into the suburbs. I couldn't bear the silence any longer.

'Where are you taking me?' I asked.

No one answered. I tried asking again.

'Shut up,' one of them snapped. 'You are not allowed to ask anything.'

Even as I had asked that question I knew the answer. Deep down inside I knew what our destination would be. Everyone in my country knew where people were taken. It would be to a 'ghost house' – a place that looked just like any other residence, but was a secret detention centre. They used such places to hide and 'disappear' their victims.

The dark, silent journey lasted for forty minutes or so. The driver clearly knew where he was going, for no one gave him any instructions. Finally, we stopped outside a totally innocent-looking single-storey house. It had a painted wooden fence surrounding a large leafy garden. The vehicle crunched to a halt on the gravel driveway.

'Get out,' the man in front ordered.

I got down and glanced around me fearfully.

'Follow me,' the front man ordered. 'And quietly. Don't do anything stupid. Don't try to shout or scream. No one will hear you. And even if they do, they won't help.'

I was taken to a dark room, bare but for a single light bulb hanging from the ceiling. There was a desk and two chairs, one facing the other. Otherwise, it was empty. I was ordered to sit. The man in charge sat opposite me, while the others took up positions in the corners of the room. Silence again, as the man opposite just stared. All I could hear was the sound of their breathing; a foot crunching on the floor. A cigarette lighter flared; the room darkened again. But the noise of my pounding heart drowned out everything.

It was me who finally broke the silence. 'Why . . . Why am I here?'

Suddenly, the standing men were screaming at me.

'SHUT UP! SHUT UP!'

'SILENCE!'

'KEEP YOUR STUPID MOUTH SHUT!'

'NO QUESTIONS!'

Silence once more, dark and terrifying. My ears ringing with their screams. My heart pounding as if it was about to explode. The man across the desk staring. The dull light from the single bulb cast his eye sockets into deep shadow, like the mask of a skull. The face started speaking now, the voice quiet and drained of all spirit and emotion. His features were devoid of any expression, as lifeless as the words that came at me.

'Look at me carefully and listen to what I have to say. I don't want to have to repeat myself. I don't want to say it twice. I don't want you to miss a single word.'

I looked at him. I tried to be brave. 'Who are you to pick me up like this?'

More screams from the walls.

'SILENCE!'

'WE TOLD YOU – NO QUESTIONS!'

'SHUT UP! SHUT UP!'

'KEEP YOUR STUPID MOUTH SHUT!'

'You are the Zaghawa doctor!' the face opposite me yelled, his finger jabbing at me, his features an instant mask of rage. 'You are this Zaghawa doctor! This Zaghawa doctor woman! Don't deny anything! We know everything. *Everything*! We know it all!'

'So why are you questioning me?' I countered, trying not to let my terror show. 'Why bother? What's the point if you know everything?'

More screams came from the walls. More rage, threats and abuse. Then the sound of heavy footsteps approaching from behind. I flinched as I waited for the blow to fall. A crack on the desk in front of me, as a heavy folder was dropped in front of my eyes.

'Better learn some respect . . . Dr Halima Bashir,' the face opposite hissed. He picked up the file and read my name from the front of it. 'Dr Halima Bashir, the Zaghawa doctor. The Zaghawa doctor who spoke to the newspapers . . . Silly. Very silly, Doctor. You are a silly, silly little girl. You have a very long tongue. Very long. It has got you into trouble.'

I gripped the edge of the desk to steady myself. So that was it – the interview. Something must have appeared in the papers. But what had I said that could have caused me to end up here? I hadn't said anything. In a way I felt relieved. I knew that I had treated scores of wounded rebel fighters in the hospital – fighters who'd claimed to be injured villagers. I had been terrified that the security men had found this out, and that I was here on charges of supporting the rebels.

Still, I was petrified. I wanted to run and to hide. But I hadn't seen any knives or guns yet, or any other weapons. So perhaps they weren't about to torture or kill me. I told myself to be strong, to hide my fear. If it showed, they would feel all-powerful, and I would seem defenceless. I would be at their mercy. I had to try to resist, to put up a front.

'So, I spoke to the newspaper man. Is it forbidden to do so? Did I say anything so wrong?'

'You really don't know?' the face opposite sneered. 'You really think you are *allowed* to speak out? *Permitted to?* You really think you are allowed to make trouble? *To make trouble*. We have the power to do anything to you. *Anything*. Don't you know that?'

'But what did I say . . .?'

'What party are you a member of?' The Face cut in. 'Tell us. No one speaks out unless they are a party member. So, which party is it? Or perhaps it is a rebel group? Is that what it is? Tell us. If it isn't a political party, it must be a rebel group, isn't it?'

'I'm just a medical doctor . . .'

'Don't lie!' The Face again, snarling now. 'You think you can lie to us? We know everything! We know it all! We know you give medicines to your people. We know you help them. We know you are the black Zaghawa doctor they all come to see. So, make it easy on yourself. Tell us the truth. Tell us – who are you involved with?'

'My job as a doctor is to cure . . .'

'Idiot! Idiot girl! You think we are stupid? You think we don't know? I'll tell you what we know. We know what you told the newspapers. We know . . .'

The Face ranted on. He wasn't allowing me to say a word in my defence. I wasn't here to speak. I was here to feel their power over me, to taste their anger and their hatred, and to know the chill, cringing dread of absolute fear. Each time I tried to speak, either the Face would cut me off or the standing men would scream at me. So I gave up. I stopped speaking. I sat there in silence, as the Face ranted and raved and threatened.

Finally, the Face produced a sheet of paper from the file. 'Now, Doctor, you have to sign this. This says you will never speak to a newspaper about anyone or anything ever again. You will never speak about anything. *Anything*. And if you disobey – then we will deal with you. You understand? Tell me you understand.'

I nodded. 'Tell me!' he snarled. 'I want to hear it.'

'I understand.'

He pushed the paper across the desk at me. 'Now, sign!'

'SIGN!'

'SIGN!'

'SIGN!'

'SIGN! SIGN! SIGN! SIGN!'

The screams from the walls were deafening. I grabbed the pen and scrawled my name with a shaking hand. The instant I lifted the pen from the paper The Face snatched the document away from me.

'Now go!' he spat at me. 'Get out! I don't ever want to see your ugly black face again.'

The drive back was as silent as the drive out had been. Two of them came with me, the driver and one of the standing men. They dropped me at the market-place without a word. I stood on the pavement and watched the vehicle speeding away. As it disappeared into the traffic, I felt my knees buckling. I leant against a car. I breathed deeply, trying to steady myself. A wave of nausea swept over me, and an instant later I was vomiting into the gutter.

Eventually, I was recovered enough to move. I set off towards the hospital, passing by the ugly concrete hulk of the football stadium. I felt a surge of cold anger sweep over me. I knew now that I was a part of this war, and that it was a part of me. For the men who had seized me this was a war against my people, and anyone who helped them was their enemy. They had picked me up simply to terrify me, to force me to stop helping my people. And they had left me in no doubt of what would happen if I continued.

As I walked, I realised that this was only the beginning. I would not change. I would not stop helping my people. Anyone who came to the hospital in need of my help would get it, no matter which tribe they were from. But I would have to be more careful. There would be no more talking to newspapers. And I would have to be more secretive – for someone at the hospital had reported me for helping the black African war-wounded.

Who was it, I wondered? Which of the medical staff had they bribed, blackmailed or frightened into spying on his or her colleagues? For a moment I wondered if it was Kayan, the kindly old man who was the head nurse. It was with him that I had shared my innermost thoughts, hopes and fears, and we had both been complicit in treating the black African war-wounded. But as quickly as I considered this, I ruled it out. No way would I believe that of him. It could be anyone else at the hospital, but not Kayan.

It was late evening by the time I arrived back at the hospital. I headed straight for the dormitory, as my head was swimming and I didn't want to have to speak to any of the others. I collapsed onto my bed in the room that I shared with the half-dozen other female doctors. Thankfully, the room was deserted. I lay there alone and in silence as I contemplated what had happened to me, and what I should do next.

One of the ways in which the human body reacts to shock is with sleep, and I slept the sleep of the dead. The following morning one or two of the other doctors tried to ask me what had happened. I told them that I didn't want to talk about it. I was too worried about who I could trust. But I did ask if they had seen the report in the newspaper. They had. They told me that I had been quoted, along with a number of the other doctors, but that none of us had said anything so controversial.

In spite of what had happened to me, Kayan and I continued to treat *all* the war-wounded, just as we had done before. I warned him that we couldn't talk freely in this place, for it was impossible to know who to trust. Kayan agreed with me. You couldn't even trust your own brothers and sisters, he said, those who had come from the same mother as you.

Everyone was turning against everyone, and the country was in flames.

17

Mission to Mazkhabad

A few weeks later my father came to visit. I was overjoyed to see him. I had confided in no one about what had happened to me, and I was dying to tell my father. But instead, we sat around with Uncle Ahmed as they discussed the war. There had been several small-scale attacks in our area. These were hit-and-run raids, and the villagers had chased the raiders away. But it was still very worrying. By the time my father had finished speaking I had decided to tell him nothing of my own problems. He had more than enough to deal with.

Shortly after his visit I was called to the office of Mr Rashid, the hospital manager. He offered me a seat before reading from a letter that he had in front of him. It had come from the Health Ministry – I could see the Arabic lettering reflected in his thick, heavy glasses. The letter instructed me to take up a new post in charge of the regional clinic in Mazkhabad.

Mazkhabad is a village in the remote north of Darfur. Why was I was being transferred, I asked Mr Rashid, and why to such a remote location? He shrugged. He didn't know. But my name had come up and I had to go. In fact, I was directed to leave the following morning, so this would be my last day working at the hospital.

'I'm sorry, Dr Bashir,' he said, glancing up from the letter. 'It's as much of a surprise to me as it must be to you.'

'But surely, I'm not yet experienced enough to run my own clinic?'

He shrugged. 'I agree. No junior doctor should be sent to a remote area without first having the full range of training.' He turned the letter towards me. 'But look – the instructions come direct from the Ministry, so there's little I can do . . .'

'But I don't want a transfer. I'm happy here. I didn't ask for one. I'm not ready for it.'

He nodded, sympathetically. 'It's unprecedented. And your work here's been excellent. I'm sorry to lose you. But there's nothing that I, or you, can do about it, I'm afraid.'

I was speechless. What more was there to say? He handed me the letter. 'Here, take this. I've enjoyed working with you, Doctor, I really have.'

As I made my way back to the ward I had few doubts as to why I was being sent away. I looked around me at the injured men, women and children. So many of them were the black African victims of this war, and so many of them were relying on me. What would happen when I wasn't here tomorrow, and the days that followed? Only Kayan would remain, and how much longer would it be before he was arrested and interrogated and sent on his way?

That evening I went to say my goodbyes to Dr Salih, the Zaghawa doctor I'd first worked under in obstetrics and gynaecology. When I told him that I was leaving he was dumbfounded. Why was I being sent to such a remote area when I hadn't completed half my training? I told him that I didn't know, but those were my orders. Next I spoke to Kayan. He was so surprised and so sad to hear that I was leaving. I told him to keep up the good work, but not to trust anyone. Otherwise, they might do the same to him.

Last, I said farewell to Dr Rashid, the man in charge of the accident and emergency ward. I'd enjoyed working under him, and as I looked into his smiling face I believed in my heart that he was a good man. He was speechless at my news, and then he became angry. No way could I be transferred so early, and to such a place. I should refuse to go. He would go himself and raise it with the hospital manager. I told him that if I stayed, it would only make problems for the rest of the staff. I told him that I would survive. I'd be okay.

I went to the dorm and packed my things into my green metal trunk, and then made my way to my uncle's house and told him about the transfer. He and his wife were uneasy about it. Surely it was better to remain close to my family, they objected. Why had I decided to go? It wasn't my choice, I told them. I had been ordered to by the Ministry. I promised that once I reached Mazkhabad village I would get word through that I was all right. But I did ask them to send word to my father about what was happening. And there was one thing that reassured me a little about the move: Mazkhabad is a Zaghawa area, so at least I would be among my people.

I stayed the night at their house and early the next morning I left to catch my transport.

The journey to Mazkhabad was by truck. This time I would be riding in the back, as I'd had no time to book myself a seat up front. The rear of the truck was full to overflowing. There were women with little children trying to sleep in their laps. There were men gripping the sides and keeping an eye on their sacks of sorghum flour and maize. And there were scores of nervous sheep and goats crammed in alongside the passengers.

Beyond the city outskirts the road became rough and difficult, the truck bouncing through potholes, throwing people off their feet. The wheels coughed up a thick cloud of dust, and soon it was everywhere: in our hair, in our eyes and even up our nostrils. But in spite of the discomfort, people were smiling and friendly.

I got talking with some of the women. They asked me where I was going and what I planned to do there. I told them my destination, and they introduced me to some of the women from Mazkhabad. I shared with them my mother and father's family names, and some of our ancestor history. I asked whether they knew of any relatives that I might have in their village. But no one could think of any.

An old man standing nearby bent to talk to me.

'I overheard you, sister,' he remarked, with a toothy grin. 'Welcome. Welcome. Welcome to our village. My name is Bushara. Tell me again your family names – I think I may know someone.'

I repeated our family lineage.

He smiled. 'Yes. Yes, I think there is someone. In fact, I'm sure. Once we get there I'll take you to his house.'

I thanked him. I was so grateful. Just the thought that I might have family there was a real comfort to me.

The truck pulled over for a mid-morning breakfast stop, and Bushara invited me to eat with him. There were roadside stalls selling roasted corn on the cob, boiled sweet potato, trays of salted and spiced peanuts, and boiled eggs sliced onto a slab of flat bread. As we ate, Bushara asked me what was bringing me to Mazkhabad. I hesitated for a second, but my instinct told me that I could trust him. I told him that I was a doctor being sent to work in the village clinic. As soon as I had said this his face lit up.

'A doctor! A real doctor!' he enthused. 'Allah – we are blessed. You must first come to my house, to meet my wife and children.'

'I'm honoured, Bushara,' I told him. 'But first let me see my own people – this family that you know of. Then I'll come to visit you.'

He smiled. 'Ah, this is better, this is just right. This is the correct way to do things. But a real doctor for the village! I can still hardly believe it . . .'

As we resumed our journey I remembered a story Grandma had told us when we were kids. One day a stranger arrived in a Zaghawa village, and asked to be taken to a certain man's house. By the time he got to the right house it was very late. Even so, he was invited in and given food and drink and somewhere to sleep. In the morning the host went to waken the visitor for breakfast. But it turned out that he had died in the night.

The whole village was called together to discuss what to do. No one knew the visitor's name or even where he was from. But the village elders decided that he still should have a proper village funeral. So that day they buried the man in the graveyard and mourned his passing, just as if he had been a family member. After that the host decided to try to find out the stranger's identity. He travelled far and wide, and eventually discovered that the visitor was his long-lost half-brother, someone who he had been trying to find for years.

The moral of the story was that no Zaghawa should ever refuse a stranger hospitality. We should ask how their journey had been, whether they were tired, and whether they needed food and drink. For we never knew – they might even be our close family. Likewise, I knew that I could rely on my relatives in Mazkhabad, no matter how distantly we were related.

It was late at night by the time we reached the village. I could see tiny dirt streets with flickering oil lanterns scattered among the shadows. It was just like a scene from my own village, and I felt strangely at home here and homesick, all at the same time. Bushara helped me down from the truck, grabbed my trunk, and set off into the darkness. As he walked he talked, showing me what was what, and all the while welcoming me to my new home.

'Welcome. Welcome,' he enthused. 'I'll send my wife and children tomorrow, just to say hello. Then you'll have some friends. And maybe if they have something – just a small headache or something – then you can help them. We haven't had a real doctor here for so long. We're so lucky to have you come.'

I murmured my thanks. I didn't feel like a real doctor yet. I hadn't even completed my training.

'The house of your relatives is just here,' Bushara indicated. 'The man has three wives, so I'm hoping he's here tonight. If not, we'll have to check the others. But don't worry – they're just nearby, so it's no trouble.'

We stopped at the fence. '*Assalam alaikum* – peace be unto you!' Bushara called into the darkened house. 'Are you there? Are you in? I have a special visitor for you!'

There was a moment's silence, followed by the wood-on-wood creak of an unlatching door.

'Welcome! Welcome!' a sleepy voice cried out. 'Welcome my visitors.'

The gate was dragged open and a head popped around the side. The man had a smiling face, topped off by a head of pepper-grey hair. He beckoned us inside, closed the gate and took us to his living area.

'Welcome,' he repeated. 'Welcome. Please – sit. Tea? You've travelled far? You must have some tea. Wait, my wife is asleep. I will wake her.'

Before we could object he bustled off into the darkness. He returned, bent to the hearth and blew hard on the embers, adding a few wisps of dry straw. In no time a merry flame was dancing among the shadows.

'So, my name is Abakher,' he remarked. 'Welcome again. I am always so pleased to have visitors.'

'This young lady is a medical doctor,' Bushara began. 'I found her travelling on the truck. She is also a Bashir, from the Coube clan, from Hadurah village. I think you know her people? I thought I should bring her straight to your house.'

'Aha! She is my relative – my daughter,' Abakher declared happily. 'Welcome my daughter. I'm so happy to have another daughter, and this one a doctor daughter!'

I couldn't help but laugh. 'Thank you, Abakher, thank you. And I'm so happy to have another father!'

Abakher's age certainly made him a 'fatherly' figure for me – he had to be in his mid-sixties, at least. He introduced his wife, Safia, who was the youngest of the three. She tried to insist on making me a meal, but I told her that I'd eaten along the way. She brought me some warm milk, and showed me a place in her hut where I could sleep, while Abakher went to spend the night in the men's hut.

In the morning, Safia cooked a delicious breakfast of *acidah* mash, and while we ate I told Abakher some more about our family. It turned out we were most closely related on the Coube side. Abakher knew he had relatives down south in Darfur, but he rarely if ever had news of them. He told me something of his life. He was a farmer, and he had a donkey that he rode to the fields each day. He ran through the children he had with each of his wives.

I asked Abakher if he would take me to the village clinic so that I could introduce myself. Once I had finished my breakfast and my tea, he would gladly do so, he said. He knew the man who ran the clinic, so he could introduce me personally.

Abakher's house was near the centre of the village, and a short stroll took us to the clinic. It was a squat brick building with a galvanised iron roof, built in the shade of some acacia trees. At the front was a porch with a grass thatch roof, which was where the patients would queue for treatment. The porch led into the one treatment room. There were half a dozen iron beds on either side, each with a vinyl-covered mattress worn smooth and shiny with use. There was precious little equipment, but at least the place looked clean, and it smelled of bleach and disinfectant.

To one side was a cramped office, where Abakher introduced me to Sayed, the man who was in charge.

'So, this is my daughter,' he announced, with a wide smile. 'She is a doctor, and she has come to work at the clinic.'

'I had no idea . . .' Sayed began, as he rose from his desk to welcome me. 'Welcome. Welcome. I didn't know you were coming. But we are so pleased to see you.'

I shook his hand and mumbled something about being honoured to be there.

'Come. Come and meet the others,' he announced. 'We've had no doctor here for so long. You know, all the bad cases have to go to Hashma, and it's a terrible journey. Sometimes, the worst die on the way. But now we have you here . . .'

As I followed Sayed into the treatment room I felt the heavy burden of responsibility settling upon me. It was daunting. How would I cope? I'd read my books and studied and studied, but I had little hands-on experience, which counted for so much in a place like this. I tried to put a brave face on things as I was introduced to Sayed's team of four.

First I met the nurses, Sumah and Makka. I told them that one had my grandma's name, and the other had the name of my mother's sister, Makka. I asked them where they had studied. It turned out that they had only completed basic first-aid courses, Makka's in midwifery and Sumah's in general medicine. Then there was an orderly, a young man whose job it was to register the patients and ensure they formed an orderly line. Out the back of the clinic was a dispensary, where the fourth team member worked, keeping an eye on supplies and dispensing the prescription drugs.

Sayed explained that his job was both to run the place and to make diagnoses and write prescriptions. Now that I was here, he could concentrate more on the former. Before I could object he asked me to take a look at an old woman who was the sole patient resident in the treatment room. She was lying on a bed with sheets provided by her relatives, as the clinic had no means to provide such basic luxuries. Her problem, Sayed explained, was that she could keep no food down at all.

The old lady was as thin as a skeleton. I took her arm, checked her pulse and had a good look in her eyes. They were yellowish, and I reckoned she might have a liver problem. I checked her hands, and sure enough she had 'club finger' – with nails that were curved over like animal claws. This is a sure sign of chronic liver failure. Her family had tried to treat her using the tradi-tional burning cure, but the burns had become infected. She was unable to eat anything much. I told Sayed my diagnosis, and that she had to go to hospital in Hashma.

Sayed nodded. 'I thought as much. We've tried to get her to go, but she refuses. See if you can persuade her, Doctor. She's a bit deaf, so you'll have to speak up.'

I bent close to her ear. 'Auntie, you have something wrong with your insides – your liver. You'll have to go to the big town, for tests at the hospital.'

She fixed me with a suspicious eye. 'I've heard all that before. Who are you?'

'I'm the new doctor. I've been sent here from the big town.'

She snorted. 'You – a doctor! A young girl like you . . . I don't believe it. A real doctor is an old man with grey hair and glasses.'

'No, really, I am a doctor.'

'You're not! You're just a student, sent here to experiment with us! I won't hear a word more. Go away! Don't talk to me!'

I was at a loss for words. Makka grabbed my hand and gave it an encouraging squeeze.

'Ah, Dr Halima, don't worry – this lady is very old. And you know what old people are like. She's always picking fights with us, then the next minute she's laughing. Just pay no attention.'

I gave her a squeeze back. 'It's okay, sister, I'm not worried.'

Just then the old lady's daughter arrived with her breakfast.

'You can't speak to the lady doctor like that!' she scolded, once she'd heard what her mother had been saying. 'You're so rude. She's only trying to help.'

'*You* may believe she's a doctor,' the old lady retorted. 'But *I* don't. I'm not going anywhere. If I'm to die, I'll do so in my own village. And what's so wrong with that?'

Part of me was annoyed, but part of me saw in her just an older version of Grandma Sumah. She had the same stubborn spirit and refusal to be told that we all adored in Grandma.

I gave her daughter a smile. 'Don't worry. I'll leave her alone if that's what she wants. But she does need to get to a hospital. Maybe you can talk to her . . .'

By the end of that first day we'd had just a handful of people through the clinic. But word had gone round the village that a real doctor had arrived, and Sayed was expecting a flood of new patients. I made my way back to Abakher's third wife's house – my temporary home until something more permanent could be found for me – following a little path that snaked between tall stands of maize.

As I walked I reflected upon my day. I had come to this place fearing that dark powers had set a trap for me. I had come here fearing that the security services were after me, and that somehow Mazkhabad was going to be a place of fear and vengeance. Whatever the truth of why I had been sent here, I had found a simple village where people were in need of help. Far from it being a 'punishment posting', I realised that I might actually enjoy my time here.

The next morning Sayed's predictions seemed to have come true: the trickle of patients had become a flood. A queue of mostly elderly people snaked out of the veranda and across the open ground in front of the clinic. More kept arriving. Sayed took the strain alongside me, and as I diagnosed he suggested what drugs to prescribe.

Pretty quickly I realised that half of the patients had nothing much wrong with them. But if I tried sending them away empty handed it looked as if I'd have a full-scale riot on my hands, so I tried prescribing a full course of aspirin. Eventually, Sayed took charge. He took two aspirin tablets, cut them in half and popped them into a plastic bag. Unless we rationed, we'd quickly be out of drugs, he warned me.

Once the patients had their bags of half-pills they were happy. Each wanted to return home with something they could show off as being from the new doctor. In most cases they wouldn't even take the pills: they'd hoard them for the future, in case they really *did* get ill.

It was an exhausting day but one that I really enjoyed. I returned to Abakher's house that evening and fell into a deep sleep.

I awoke later to the sound of a voice calling me. It was Sayed, and I could tell by his tone that it was urgent. He was sorry for waking me, but there was an emergency at the clinic, he explained. Would I come? I was surprised at how much faith he had placed in me already, and I was determined not to let him down.

As we hurried down to the clinic Sayed briefed me on what had happened. A local man had been opening a big can of cooking oil, his six-year-old son helping hold it steady. A shard of tin had sheared off and sliced into the boy's thigh. Sayed hadn't inspected the wound yet, but there was a lot of blood and it looked serious. We lit the clinic's oil lamps and quickly got the man and his son into the treatment room.

The boy had blood oozing down his leg, and he was clearly frightened and in shock. I inspected the wound, probing around with my fingers, the child crying out in agony as I did so. I could tell that the boy's father was close to tears. Could I help his son, he pleaded. He'd been torn between trying to get to the hospital in town or bringing his boy here. The fact that we now had a proper doctor had decided it for him. But could I do anything to help?

The first priority was to stop the bleeding, I told him. With Sayed's help I tied a tourniquet tight around the boy's leg, just below the wound. Blood was coming up the leg and pumping out through ruptured veins, but at least the tourniquet lessened the flow. I asked Sayed to boil some water and sterilise a needle and thread. He lit the charcoal stove and put a pan on to boil. Sayed was unflappable in his actions, and he inspired me with confidence for what lay ahead.

I had never in my life sutured up something as serious as this. The tin had cut right through the little boy's muscle. I could see his thighbone gleaming ghostly white in the bloody depths of the wound. My main worry was the loss of blood. We had no painkillers, and I knew that I had to work fast, for the long journey to hospital in Hashma would be the death of him, of that I was certain.

Sayed handed me the sterilised needle and thread. I asked the boy's father to hold his son down, for this was going to hurt. With the little boy screaming in agony, Sayed pulled each side of the ragged wound together as I began to sew. By the time I had finished I was sweating and weak with nervous exhaustion. But at least the gaping wound was clamped tightly shut. We cleaned and bandaged the wound and then we were done.

I turned to the little boy's parents – by now the mother had joined us – and I could see fear and gratitude shining in their eyes. I told them that their son had to remain in the clinic so that I could keep an eye on him. Early the next morning I wanted them back again, so we could start him on a course of antibiotics to fight any infection.

Before leaving, the father insisted on making some proper introductions. His name was Osman, and his wife was Mounah. They had four children. The little boy I had treated was their youngest, and he was called Ibrahim. They were from the Berti tribe, a black African people whose lands border those of the Zaghawa. Mounah was about my age, and I sensed a great warmth from her. I had a feeling that she, Osman and I were going to become good friends.

Little Ibrahim slept well during the night and by morning he had strengthened. For all of that first week I forbade him to leave his bed or go out to play. After that, I figured the worst of the danger was over. Mounah and Osman made a point of inviting me to their house to eat and drink, and to chat and relax. They were affluent by village standards, for Osman was a trader with high connections among the Zaghawa chiefs of the area. I enjoyed their company and their friendship so very much. And no matter what I might say to the contrary, they were convinced that I had saved their son's life.

Who knows, perhaps I had. Either way, they were soon going to be called upon to save my own.

18

Rebel Doctor

Abakher's first wife – the eldest – lived close by the clinic. Her children were grown up and had left home, so she had a hut free. As I was now his 'daughter', Abakher wouldn't hear of me staying anywhere else. His first wife's name was Asia – the same as my little sister's. She was in her fifties, so closer to Grandma Sumah's age than my mother's. Asia quickly took me under her wing, becoming like my mother and my best friend all rolled into one. She would do my washing, and cook my favourite foods of an evening.

During the day Asia did a little trade in the village marketplace. She sold *ghou* – the flour used to make *acidah* – spices and *mousarran* – dried bundles of animal intestines that are used in a traditional Zaghawa stew. Every third night Abakher would come to visit her. She would cook his favourite food and chat with him, and once he'd finished she'd tell him to go and stay with one of his younger wives. She was old and infertile, she'd say, so he might as well go and try his stuff with one of the young ones.

Abakher was in his mid-sixties, yet already he had four children with his youngest wife. He wanted to keep on having children until he couldn't do so any more or until he died. If he died, his youngest children would grow up as part of his big, extended family, being looked after by their older brothers and sisters. Abakher started bringing people to the house at all hours to meet his new 'daughter'. She was a real live medical doctor, he'd tell them proudly. I didn't mind, and I was happy to treat any ills they might have.

Each evening Asia and I would finish our dinner and sit out under the stars. Sometimes she detected a deep sadness within me. I was still worried for what the future might hold. I hadn't forgotten the secret police in Hashma, or their dark threats. But most of all I was scared for my village. War might come at any time, and if it did I would know nothing about it, stuck out here in Mazkhabad.

But no matter how close I felt to Asia, I couldn't share my problems with her. I kept my worries bottled up inside. I didn't want anyone here to know my real story. If I told Asia, I feared she might decide that it was too dangerous for me here. I feared she would tell me to stop doing my work and bringing trouble on myself, and to go back to my village. I didn't want that. I still felt my work was important. I still felt there was scope for serving my people, and a way that I might truly help in the struggle.

I thought about what my father would want me to do. I felt certain that he would want me to continue playing a role if I possibly could. He'd want me to use my medical skills to help the cause. In any case, I felt as if I had crossed a line in Hashma, and that I was now a part of this war. Of course, Asia put my unhappiness down to my lifestyle. How could I hope to be happy, she asked, if I was alone and childless?

Asia had a gentle way of saying such things. 'Why aren't you married, my daughter? You should be having children, not travelling and living alone.'

'Ah, it's just not my time,' I'd reply. 'Anyhow, you should stop asking questions and let me get on with my life.'

Asia would chuckle softly at my teasing. 'You should have three or four children by now, like Abakher's youngest wife. What d'you think will come of this strange life of yours?'

'All this criticising,' I'd counter playfully. 'You should show me some respect. Don't you know I'm a medical doctor?'

'All that education, it's confused your mind. I'm going to have to find you a man. There must be one free man somewhere in this village . . .'

———— ✦ ————

One evening, a month or so after my arrival in Mazkhabad, Abakher brought a visitor to see me. I was used to this by now, but the young man had a very odd appearance. His head was almost completely covered in a scarf, only his eyes left showing. After chatting for a while I asked if he was sick. He told me that he wasn't, but his friend was injured. He needed dressings, bandages, antiseptic ointment and antibiotics. I told him that his friend should come to the clinic. I couldn't just hand out medicines to anyone who came and asked.

I saw the young man glance at Abakher. Abakher nodded. 'You'd better show her. She's like my daughter. You can trust her.'

The young man lifted up his robes to reveal a dirtied, bloodied bandage. For a second he gazed at me, then indicated the wound.

'So it's *you* who's injured!' I exclaimed. 'But why did you say . . .?'

I let my words tail off. I had a good idea why he might have been hesitant to tell me. It was best if I didn't know. At least then I could claim ignorance if anything happened to me as a result of helping him.

'D'you mind?' I asked. I reached to inspect his injured leg. I saw him flinch and glance again at Abakher. 'I have to see the wound. I'm a doctor. I can help.'

By the light of an oil lantern I unwrapped the dirty bandage. He was lucky. The bullet had passed clean through the calf muscle, just missing the bone. But it was still nasty and in danger of going septic.

'When did this happen?' I asked.

'Three days ago,' he replied. 'I heard there was a Zaghawa doctor here, a sister who would help.'

I turned to Abakher. 'I need to get him to the clinic. I need to clean and dress the wound, and I can't do that here.'

Abakher smiled. 'Anything, my doctor daughter.'

I made the young man comfortable on one of the clinic beds. I got Abakher to boil some water and sterilise the instruments. I told the young man to watch carefully what I was doing and learn to do it himself, for I guessed he wouldn't be coming back again any time soon. I removed the dressing, swabbed down the wound, cleared away the dead skin and applied antiseptic cream. Then I packed out the wound with fresh dressing and bandaged it up again.

'Can you stay for a day or so?' I asked. 'I want to keep an eye on it, in case there's any infection.'

He shook his head. 'No, sister. But thank you for what you've done . . .'

'Well, d'you think you can manage all of that on your own?' I asked.

He smiled. 'I'm no doctor, but I think so.'

'I'll get you enough materials so you can clean and dress the wound yourself, okay?'

He reached out a hand. 'Sister, there's one more thing. I have a friend in the bush with bad gunshot wounds. He can't risk coming to the village. Can you give me medicine for him?'

'Tell me about his injuries,' I said. 'I'll prepare a package for him also.'

It was past midnight by the time the injured fighter left. As Abakher and I made our way back to Asia's house, not a word was spoken between us about what had happened. There was an unspoken understanding that it was best left that way. I knew by now that Abakher was helping the Zaghawa fighters, and he knew for sure now that as a doctor I was willing to help. Today, I had well and truly crossed the line.

Word must have spread rapidly among the fighters in the bush. Two days later another came to see me, and this one came directly to the clinic. He was dressed in a long robe that completely covered his wounds. He spoke to me in Zaghawa, a language that none of the others would understand. Sayed was from the Berti tribe, and the nurses were Massalit. I made up a package of dressings, ointments and antibiotics and sent him on his way.

Gunshot wounds are nearly always recognisable for exactly what they are, but he had kept his injuries hidden. More wounded fighters started coming. They either came to see me at home if I needed to examine them, or they came to the clinic. Those at the clinic explained what was wrong, and I sent them on their way with a package of medicines and instructions on how to treat themselves.

One day I asked Sayed to fetch me a parcel of medications from the store. The clinic had no budget as such, but it did have a certain monthly allocation of medicines. We charged patients a little for prescription medicines, and that money was used to buy charcoal for the stoves, oil for the lanterns and any other supplies that we might need. The parcel that I'd asked Sayed to prepare chiefly consisted of dressings for gunshot wounds.

For a moment he gazed at me, quizzically, before asking me what it was for. I told him that my family were sick, and I was sending it to my home village. I was sure he knew what I was doing, as did the rest of the staff, but none of them had raised any objections. If any of them had felt that I was putting them in danger by my activities, I hoped they would have said so.

Once a week I went to have dinner with Mounah and Osman. It was their way of saying thank you for saving their son's life. I instinctively felt that I could trust them. We would talk long into the night, and of course our main topic of conversation was the war. There had been some minor incidents in our area, but the village itself still felt secure. We spoke about how peaceful people's lives had been, before the Arab tribes started attacking villages and killing people. Who could comprehend where the hatred had sprung from?

I confessed that I didn't really feel at home in the village. But I felt as if I was doing good work there, which was the main thing. Sometimes, though, I wondered why I didn't run a similar clinic in my home village. At least there I would have my family around me, in case of any trouble. Here, I felt as if I was on my own. Mounah and Osman tried to reassure me. I was far from alone, they said. I had saved their son's life and I was like a sister to them. If anything happened, I was to come to them for help.

Dinner with Mounah and Osman invariably got me thinking about home again. I decided to try to get a call through to Uncle Ahmed. What I dreaded most was the thought that my village could be attacked and that I would never know. In Mazkhabad market-place was a radio, with a big cable aerial strung up in a tree. People called it a 'radio-telephone', and in return for a small charge it was possible to place a call to a telephone number anywhere in the country.

Or at least that was the theory. In practice it mostly didn't seem to work. Once or twice I had tried to call Uncle Ahmed, but his words had come through all distorted, with lots of other voices talking over him, and fragments of other conversations bleeding through. As the radiophone was in the open market I had to be careful what I said, for I never knew who might be listening.

This time, I managed to get through to Uncle Ahmed on a reasonably clear line. My family were fine, he told me. There had been sporadic fighting in our area, but no trouble in the village itself. But how much longer this could go on was anyone's guess. Here in Mazkhabad I had a steady stream of injured fighters coming to the clinic, so surely there had to be fighting going on. My greatest fear was that either here or at home, one day soon an attack would come.

I left the market-place and made my way back home, lost in my thoughts. All of a sudden there was the snarl of an engine behind me and I jumped to one side. The Mazkhabad police Land Rover thundered by. As it disappeared in a cloud of dust I saw a row of faces staring out at me. At least they were the regular police, and not the dreaded security men. But still I had this horrible feeling that they were watching me, and that sooner or later they would discover what I was up to at the clinic.

A week later I was just finishing dealing with the last of my patients when I heard a car pull up outside. This was in itself a rare thing, as few people in the village owned vehicles. I looked up to see the police Land Rover. For a moment I hoped that it might be an entirely innocent visit. Sayed had already warned me that the police dropped by now and then, to check how our work was going. Or perhaps one of the policemen was sick or injured.

Three Arab-looking men got down from the vehicle. I watched them squaring their shoulders, so as to make themselves look fierce, and with a swaggering posture they headed my way. This was no community visit, and none of them looked particularly unwell. I noticed Sayed dart out of the treatment room, so as to greet the policemen on the veranda. I didn't know exactly why they had come but I had a bad feeling already.

'Hello, Commander. Welcome. Come in, come in,' Sayed fawned. 'What a pleasant surprise. Welcome. Everything is fine. Everything is good. How can we help?'

The Police Commander parked himself in the doorway, a cold and silent presence. He swept the room with his eyes, as if he owned the place.

'Ahem, so this is the new doctor,' Sayed continued. 'Dr Halima

Bashir, just recently qualified in Khartoum. You know her? She's doing great work . . .'

The Commander held up his hand to silence Sayed. 'Enough! Yes, we *know* her. We know all about her. We've heard many, many things.'

I did my best to ignore them. My patient was a young woman in the advanced stages of pregnancy. I was trying to figure out exactly how her baby was situated, and whether she was going to have an easy birth. If not, she might have to go to Hashma to deliver. I felt along her tummy, trying to locate the baby's head. As I did so, I could feel the Commander's eyes on me, boring into my back.

I heard boots scuffing across the floor. The three men came and stood next to me – one on either side, the Commander facing me across the bed. Sayed had made himself scarce, but I knew he was listening at the window. I could see his shadow. The Commander hooked his thumbs into his belt, over which bulged the fat of his belly. He squared his shoulders as he waited for me to acknowledge his presence.

'So, you are the new doctor,' he sneered. 'We hear you've come here to serve your people – the Zaghawa. Is it true?'

I glanced up at him. There was no warmth: just a dark, hostile stare. 'I'm a medical doctor. I treat all people. It doesn't matter who they are.'

'Is that right? How noble of you. Trouble is, that's not what we've heard. Not at all. It's said you are the Zaghawa doctor who's come to treat the Zaghawa people.'

'I've already told you – I treat everyone, regardless.'

The Commander leant forward, bringing his face close to mine. 'Listen, Doctor, we know what you're up to.' His breath was rancid, suffocating. 'We know it all . . . Now, there's something we want from you. A list of names. A list of names of all the Zaghawa men who come here. You keep that list, and maybe we won't have to trouble you any more.'

I shook my head. 'I can't. I'm a doctor. I came here to treat people, not to keep watch on them. That's not my business.'

His eyes widened. 'Not your business? *Not your business?* You think you decide what is your *business*? Ha! Doctor, I'm telling you – you will give us that list of names.'

'No, I am a medical doctor,' I replied, quietly. 'I am not here to compile lists for the police.'

His hands twitched, his face twisting into a mask of rage. 'No one ever says "no" to us. *No one, you hear me?* Who do you think you are? Be careful, Doctor, be very, very careful . . .'

There was silence for a second. I folded my arms and tried to stare the Commander down. His eyes narrowed to piggy little slits, his voice dropping to a menacing whisper.

'Better learn to obey my commands. I expect that list. I command you to prepare it. *So do it.* Or you'll see what happens.'

They left, the Commander first, the two others turning after him. I followed them with my eyes to the door and out to their car. As soon as it was gone, Sayed came in. He had been subservient and fearful when they were here, but now he feigned a relaxed indifference.

'Don't worry, Doctor,' he said. 'They're always like this – stupid policemen. Threatening people and throwing their weight around. Just ignore them.'

I nodded. 'Thanks. That's what I was intending to do.'

Someone in the clinic had reported me, of that I was certain. I didn't believe it was Sayed. He was weak and ineffectual, but he had a good heart and he wasn't anyone's spy. I had no idea which of the others it might be. I would just have to be more careful. But I was worried now, and my fears about the security men in Hashma had returned.

That evening I went to see Osman and Mounah. I explained what had happened. No way was I keeping any lists for the police. But I was worried what would happen next. Osman's cousin was a senior tribal chief in Hashma, so he had power and influence. I wanted him to know what had happened, just in case things got any worse for me.

'They poke their noses in and order me around,' I told them. 'I'm not doing it. I'm a doctor, not a spy.'

'Just ignore them,' Osman counselled. 'If they ask for the list, just say it's not ready yet. But don't openly defy them.'

I glanced at Osman, scrutinising his face. 'What happens if they make trouble for me? Can you do anything to help?'

'I can have words with certain people, yes. But it's far better to stay out of trouble. You're a woman – you don't want to end up fighting those policemen.'

I decided to take Osman's advice and avoid any open confrontation. I had been at Mazkhabad for three months now, and I reckoned twenty Zaghawa fighters had been through the clinic. Often, I had cleaned and bandaged their wounds. More importantly I had sent them back to the bush with consignments of medical supplies. I wasn't about to stop doing this: it was too important. But I would have to be more secretive about it.

I decided that in future wounded fighters should only ever come at night, and always to Abakher and Asia's house. I would set up a makeshift clinic, and have medical supplies on hand. In that way I could keep what I was doing hidden from whoever it was reporting on me. I felt certain it wasn't Sayed. He was a good friend of Abakher. Both of them knew about – and were complicit in – my activities. But someone was spying on me, and I had to find a way to thwart them. Using the house as my base might just work.

Two weeks later I was sitting out at the front of the clinic with Sayed having a mid-morning cup of tea. The village seemed to be strangely, eerily quiet – almost as if it were holding its breath, *awaiting something*. I was just discussing with Sayed what supplies we needed for the clinic when I heard a distant commotion down at the market-place. There were faint cries and the pounding of running feet, as if lots of people were on the move. For a second I wondered, fearfully, if it was an attack, but surely there would have been gunfire.

Suddenly, I caught sight of a crowd of people surging out of the market-place. They turned as one and started running in our direction. Among them were figures carrying heavy burdens in their arms. I couldn't quite tell what, at this distance, but it looked as if they were human forms. As the crowd drew closer, I realised what they were carrying: it was the girls from the village school. I could see heads lolling and beige *nyangours* – a long dress that is standard girl's school uniform – flapping in the breeze.

Sayed and I glanced at each other in dismay. *What on earth was going on?* The onrush of bodies approached in a heaving, panicked mass. Sayed and I went forward to meet them. I caught the look of pain and rage on the faces of the adults, and I could hear the pitiful cries of the girls. I caught sight of one of the women teachers, but she seemed to be clawing at her face and hair, as if driven out of her mind. As the crowd enveloped us, I realised that the schoolgirls' *nyangours* were ripped and dirtied, and streaked with blood.

My God, what had happened? *What had happened? What in God's name had happened?*

The cries were all around me now, confusing and deafening. I tried to make sense of the words.

'. . . beasts . . .'

'. . . attacked the school . . .'

'. . . monsters . . .'

'. . . the devil himself . . .'

'. . . children . . .'

'. . . raped . . .'

'. . . ruined . . .'

'The Janjaweed! The Janjaweed!'

Desperate hands clawed at me, and I was dragged back towards the treatment room. As I took the first of the little girls and laid her bloodied form on the bed, I felt as if I was drowning.

19

Black Dogs and Slaves

Come here my child,
I have a heart for you.
Come here my child,
I have my tears for you ...

Never, not even in my darkest, blackest nightmare, had I imagined that I would ever witness such horror. What was happening to my country? Where had all the love gone, the goodness, the humanity? Who had let the devil in and given him free reign? How could people be so evil? They were adults and these were little children ... Did they have no children of their own? Had they never been children themselves? Did they have no heart, no innocence, no adult's love for a child? Were they really even *human*?

These were the thoughts that were firing through my mind as I helped lift that first little girl onto the bed, so that I could inspect what the Arabs, the Janjaweed, had done to her. As I gazed in horror at her limp form a keening, empty wail kept coming from somewhere deep within her throat – over and over and over again. It was a sound such as I had never heard before – a hollow cry of brutalised innocence, of innocence forever lost. It is a sound that I shall never forget no matter how long I live.

In spite of everything – the shock, the confusion, the trauma – my medical training took over now. I reached for the little girl's face, one side of which was swollen and bloody. I probed around the wound. She'd been hit with a blunt instrument – probably a rifle butt – and it needed stitches. But there were other, more urgent priorities. I checked her eyes: they were dead and glazed with shock. *Unseeing*. But at least she was still conscious. I felt for her pulse: it was racing and fearful. Yet it was strong, and I knew then that she was going to live. She would live – as long as I could stop the bleeding.

I lifted up her *nyangour*. It was slick with congealed blood. As gently as I could I tried to prise apart her shaking, bloodied knees. The soft child's skin of her thighs was criss-crossed with cut marks, as if a pack of wild animals had been clawing at her. I felt her body stiffen, her leg muscles tightening and resisting, as that chilling, empty wailing in her throat rose to a terrified screaming. I felt wave after wave of panic sweeping through her now – *no, no, no, no, not again, not again, not again*.

I tried to talk to her. 'I'm sorry, little sister, but I have to look. It's Doctor Halima, from the medical clinic. I have to look, I have to . . . But I won't hurt you or do anything nasty, I promise.'

She turned her head towards me, but her eyes remained a glazed mask and the cries kept coming. She had withdrawn to some inner place, a fairytale landscape of childhood innocence where the horrors had no way of reaching her. But by my very actions I was threatening to drag her back to the terrible present. Yet I had to examine her, for she was bleeding heavily and I had to decide how best to treat her. I knew in my head what must have happened, although my heart refused to accept it. I had a good idea what I had to do – and I was dreading it.

I glanced across at her parents. Her father's face was a slick of tears, as he wept openly and uncontrollably – a young Zaghawa man paralysed by heartache and anguish for his little eight-year-old girl. I reached for his arm and gestured with my eyes to his daughter.

'Talk to her. You have to talk to her. Tell her you're here. Tell her it's okay. Tell her I need to see, she has to let me. I'm going to help her. We all are. *Talk to her.*'

The man nodded, and I saw him visibly try to pull himself together. He wiped his face with the sleeve of his robes, then bent towards his daughter's face.

'It's Daddy,' he whispered. 'Daddy's here. Daddy's here. Daddy's here. I'm holding your hand, little Aisha, and I'm going to protect you. Forever and ever I'll be here with you. No one can hurt you now. But you have to let the doctor look. You have to let her see . . .'

I felt the tears running down my own face. I couldn't hide it. I wept openly. Everyone else was crying – why shouldn't I? Who was I to be so strong? Yes, I was a medical doctor, but I was also a woman – and with every one of these little girls I felt as if they were my own daughters, each my own child.

I eased little Aisha's legs open, to reveal a red, bloodied rawness. She had been circumcised, just as I had been. When that first Arab had forced himself into her, he had ripped her apart. I felt a wave of nausea and revulsion rush over me, followed by a hot panicked dread. It was exactly as I had expected, exactly what I had been fearing. I would have to clean the wound and sew her up again, and I knew that I had no anaesthetic with which to do so.

I glanced around the room. It was a seething mass of crying, traumatised schoolgirls and shocked and grieving parents. How many girls were there here? A dozen? Two dozen? Three dozen? Maybe more? We didn't have enough beds for them all. More worrying still, did we even have enough medical supplies to treat them all?

'I need boiling water!' I cried, calling for Sayed. 'Boiling water. And needle and thread – as much as you can find.

'Sumah and Makka – two girls to a bed!' I cried to the nurses. 'Give them paracetamol – half a tablet each. Bathe their wounds with boiled water and antiseptic lotion. I'll follow to do the stitching . . .

'And Sayed – get Malik from the dispensary to assist you. Just as soon as you can leave him, come and help me with the stitching.'

Nothing in my medical training could have prepared me for what lay ahead. By the time I had cleaned and sewn up Aisha's torn womanhood, her cries of agony were forever burned into my mind. And she was the first of many. I knew by then that we didn't have enough supplies to treat them all, and that we would have to improvise.

I also knew that everyone – parents, teachers and clinic staff alike – was looking to me for leadership. But what could I do? How were we going to treat the girls without enough supplies? At no stage in my years of study had I been taught how to deal with eight-year-old victims of gang rape in a rural clinic without enough sutures to go round.

As I stitched up a second girl's ragged, bloody wound an image from my childhood flashed into my mind. It was of my mother and Grandma Sumah binding up my own womanhood, following the cutting time. They had bound my thighs tight with a rope – so tight, in fact, that I'd been unable to move. Maybe we could do the same with the injured girls here. I called Sayed and explained what I had in mind. We would need the parents to fetch the rope, as we had none at the clinic, but there was plenty in the market.

I finished stitching up that second little girl and stepped back unsteadily. She grabbed my hand and held it tight. Her eyes were wide with fear and agony, her face wet with tears. Her mother was at her side, but her father was out in their fields and would have no idea yet what had happened to his daughter. The little girl tried to say something, her lips moving, but no sound seemed to come. I bent closer. She tried again, her words a fearful whisper.

'The Janjaweed . . . the Janjaweed . . .'

I nodded, and tried to force a smile. 'I know, I know. Don't worry . . .'

'Why . . . Why . . . Why did they do this to us?'

'I don't know, little sister. I don't know. They are bad people, evil people . . .'

'But why? Why did this happen? What wrong did we do to them?'

'I don't know. But we'll stop them. Don't worry. We will never let this happen to you again . . .'

I turned away from the little girl and wiped a hand, exhaustedly, across my face. It was slick with blood, but I was too far gone to care. There was a thumping pain inside my head, as if it was about to explode. I felt the little girl's mother beside me, her arms around my shoulders. She held me and hugged me tight. I rested for a moment on her. I knew most of the parents in the village by name, and their children. They were like my family, and we were united in the pain and the horror of what had happened.

'God give you strength,' she whispered. 'God give you strength. God give you the strength to help them. And God willing, it will be all right. It will be all right.'

I held onto her, gathering my strength for the next little girl. I steeled myself to go on, to deal with the pain of it all. I looked at her. Nodded. I was ready.

Her dark eyes met mine. They were pools of incomprehension and pain. She shook her head in disbelief. 'How could they? How could anyone do this to little children?'

I shrugged. 'Only God knows. Only God knows.'

'The Janjaweed . . . the Janjaweed . . .' she whispered. 'They want to drive our children insane, *our children* . . .'

'God is stronger than they are,' I told her. 'They are like the devil, but they are weak. God is strong. He will destroy them. They attack children, like the cowards they are. But one day God will finish them all . . .'

As I went to treat the next little girl I told myself that I had to be strong. I had to be strong for them all. For everyone. All of them were relying on me, and if any of the little girls failed to survive I would blame myself for not having saved them. But I didn't know if I could be strong. I felt the anger and rage rising up inside me, hot and bitter and corrosive like acid, threatening to overwhelm me. I wanted to fight. I wanted to fight them all. I wanted to fight and kill every Arab, to slaughter them, to drive them out of our country.

I felt hatred like a furnace blasting its fire and rage inside me, burning, burning for revenge. I tried to channel that hatred, to use it to give me the strength to go on. I picked up the needle and thread and turned to the next little girl . . .

As the morning wore on one trauma merged into the next, until it became like one long terrible vision of hell. It was as if evil itself had come to our village, as if the devil himself had come to do his very worst.

The youngest of the girls was just seven years old, the oldest thirteen. All of them had been circumcised. They had been repeatedly attacked in an unimaginably brutal bout of sexual violence. Of the two teachers, I knew that one at least had also been raped. I could see the pain in Miss Sumiah's face, the fear and revulsion in her eyes.

Miss Sumiah was about the same age as me. She was a tall, elegant, beautiful black African woman from the Massalit tribe. And she was a lovely, gentle person. In Sudanese culture a teacher was someone who should always be respected, so this made the rape even more of a violation. It was as if the Janjaweed had targeted the school to show they could do exactly what they wanted with us – as if that was the way to instil the worst possible terror.

Sumiah told me not a word of what had happened to her. I knew that she was trying to hide it, and I understood why. Sumiah was married, and she didn't want her husband to know. She was feeling guilty: guilty that she hadn't resisted her attackers, fought them off, or died trying to do so. Better to have died and preserved one's dignity, than to have suffered the soul death of rape – that's what the Massalit, and the Zaghawa, believed.

But I was having none of that. As far as I was concerned, every single woman and child in that room was a victim. For what could they possibly have done to resist? I had heard rumours of rape. We all had. It was part of the dark and evil texture of this war. But I'd never quite believed them. And not for one moment had I conceived that grown men could be capable of doing such things to little children. Yet now I had seen it with my own eyes, and I knew that the unthinkable was true.

It was early evening by the time I had finished stitching up the last of the girls. Sayed and I had been doing the suturing, with Makka – the nurse with midwifery training – lending a hand. Nurse Sumah had been cleaning the wounds, with the store man keeping the charcoal stoves running and boiling potful after potful of water. There was one saving grace to the horrors of the day: nearly all of the girls were too young to have been made pregnant by their attackers. But this was something that would be lost on the traumatised victims.

More than forty girls had been brought to the clinic, but I knew there were more rape victims than that. In some cases their parents were so ashamed that they had taken their daughters home, and would be treating them privately with traditional cures. In that way they hoped to keep the violation of their loved ones secret. It was a sad fact in our culture that rape victims were somehow seen as being damaged goods, their lives destroyed by the evil that had happened to them.

By the time the day was done most of the girls were able to return home. Eight of the worst victims – the smallest, youngest, most serious cases – remained. They were in deep shock and unable to stop crying. Among the eight was little Aisha, the first victim I had treated. I kept each of them on their beds, with a drip of saline solution mixed with glucose going into their arm. This would help with both the blood loss and the shock.

I told the parents of the eight to go and fetch their daughters a little food. They had to try to eat. A little soup would be best – maybe chicken or lamb broth, something easy to digest. I'd had no time to eat myself, but the last thing on my mind was food. I was too shocked and sickened by all that I had seen to even think about eating.

Once the girls had tried to eat a little, I gave each half a sleeping tablet, so that they might find the sweet forgetfulness of sleep. Each of the girls drifted off into the land of their dreams. I just hoped and prayed that their dreamland would remain free from dark and evil nightmares.

I went and sat at my desk, burying my head in my hands. I closed my eyes and laid my face down on the smooth wooden surface. Apart from the girls' parents I was alone now; Sayed, Makka and the other staff had gone home to get some rest. Shortly, I felt a presence at my side. I looked up. It was Sumiah, the teacher rape victim.

She gestured towards the girls. 'I just came back to see how they are.'

'They're sleeping, which is good. I hope they'll be better in the morning.'

'You look finished . . .'

I shrugged. 'I don't think I'll be able to sleep much, not after today . . .'

'Still, you need to get some rest.'

'Sumiah, tell me what happened . . . I mean, if you don't feel able to, it's okay . . . But I just feel I need to know . . .'

'You really want to hear?'

I nodded. I did. For some reason that I couldn't quite explain, I needed to know. Perhaps the knowing might help me deal with my burning anger and pain. I might start to begin to understand the full horror, and so come to terms with it . . .

'It was around nine o'clock,' Sumiah began. 'Lessons had just started. All of a sudden, I heard the pounding of hooves and wild yelling. Doors were smashed in and the windows too. We didn't even have time to cry for help. Suddenly they were inside . . .'

Sumiah paused, her face downcast, her eyes looking inwards as she relived it all.

I touched her arm gently. 'Don't if you can't. Don't go on.'

Sumiah shrugged. 'It's better to talk . . . *I need to* . . . It was like a band of wild animals just jumping on us and forcing us to the floor. All around me girls were being raped, regardless of their age. The Janjaweed carried guns, knives, heavy sticks – the ones they use to beat their horses. If any girl tried to resist they beat her with those sticks . . .'

Sumiah glanced at me. 'They were shouting and screaming at us. You know what they were saying? "We have come here to kill you! To finish you all! You are black slaves! You are worse than dogs! Either we kill you or we give you Arab children. Then there will be no more black slaves in this country." But you know the worst? The worst was that they were laughing and yelping with joy as they did those terrible things. Those grown men were enjoying it, as they passed the little girls around . . .

'In all the confusion one or two of the girls managed to escape. They ran to their homes and raised the alarm. But when the parents rushed to the school they found a cordon of government soldiers had surrounded it and were letting nobody in. If anyone came too close, the soldiers shot at them with their guns. Parents could hear their daughters screaming, but there was no way they could help.

'For two hours they held the school. They abused the girls in front of their friends, forcing them to watch what they were doing. Any girls who tried to resist were beaten about the head with sticks or rifle butts.

'Before they left, they spat on us and urinated on us,' Sumiah whispered. 'They said: "We will let you live so you can tell your mothers and fathers and brothers what we did to you. Tell them from us: if you stay, the same and worse will happen to you all. Next time, we will show no mercy. Leave this land. Sudan is for the Arabs. It is not for black dogs and slaves.'''

I stayed at the clinic late into the night, my mind a whirl of exhausted thoughts. I kept replaying Sumiah's words in my mind. *Sudan is for the Arabs. It is not for black dogs and slaves.* Where had such blind, unreasoning hatred come from? Who but the evil and the insane could be capable of such bestial behaviour towards innocent children? It was *inhuman*. And where would it ever end? *Where would it end?*

I had no reason to stay any longer at the clinic now. The girls were fast asleep, and even their parents were dropping. I was staying for one reason only: I was scared, so scared, of being alone. I forced myself to my feet. I told the parents that if there was anything – anything at all – then they must come to fetch me. The place where I stayed was just nearby, and it was unlikely that I would be sleeping.

As I walked home through the darkened village I tried to face my fear. I was scared of the night itself, but still I stuck to the shadows so as not to be seen. I was scared that the Janjaweed would come again. When I reached home I found that Asia had waited up for me. She had been in the market that morning, selling her wares, and so she had seen the crowd. When I told her the details of what had happened she was sickened beyond words.

'Even the children? *Even the children?* Even those little girls?'

'Even the children,' I confirmed. 'They targeted the school, deliberately, to destroy our very souls.'

'We have to fight them,' Asia declared. 'We have to kill them all. They are like a dark evil, spreading throughout this land . . . We have to kill them all.'

I was silent. Asia glanced at me. In the firelight she could see that I was crying. She reached out and held me, rocking me in her arms. With the children, I had tried to be strong. With them I had tried to hide my emotions, to hold back my tears. Now I could let them flow.

When we retired to our huts I took a stick with me and hid it under the bed. I lay there all night long, straining my ears in the darkness. If I heard them coming I would run and try to escape. But if they caught me, I would take up my stick and fight. Terrible images crowded into my mind: images from the school that morning; images of pain and lost innocence from the clinic that day.

As I tossed and turned those images turned into ones of my own village under assault, of my family fleeing from the screaming hordes of the Janjaweed. I wondered how far this evil madness had spread. Maybe all of the schools were being attacked. Maybe this evil and darkness was everywhere across our land. Here I was so far from home, so far from my family and my people.

As soon as it was light I hurried down to the clinic to check on the girls. Most were still fast asleep. The ones who were awake were in pain, and they were afraid even to go to the loo, as it was such agony to do so. I prepared hot water so they could wash. It would be soothing, and it might make it easier to go to the loo. Aisha's mother and father were there, and they kept on thanking me for helping their daughter.

'If it weren't for you, Doctor, we don't know what we would have done,' her father said. 'But d'you think our daughter will go crazed in the head because of this? That's our greatest fear . . .'

'She didn't sleep well at all,' her mother added. 'She was crying, thrashing about, waking up with horrible screams. She said she could still see those men, even in her sleep.'

'You know, time is a great healer,' I said. 'With time they will forget. And with time they will heal physically, too. Everything will all go back to normal, you'll see.'

I did my rounds, checking on the girls. When I came to little Aisha she grabbed hold of my arm.

'I don't want those bad people to come again,' she whispered. 'Don't let them. You'll stop them, won't you? Please, don't let the Janjaweed get me . . .'

'Don't worry, don't cry, little sister,' I comforted her. 'Don't worry, we'll protect you. You're safe now. You're safe here with us.'

If only it were true. If only it were true.

I spent the day with the girls, trying to comfort them. By mid-afternoon there was little more that we could do at the clinic. They needed to eat and sleep, so that their bodies and minds could recover. And they needed to try to forget. The best place to do so was at home. One by one girls and parents left the clinic. As they did so I wondered just where the fat Commander of Police had been on the morning of the attack. Not a thing went on in the village without him knowing, yet strangely he was nowhere to be seen.

Sayed and I were just clearing up the treatment room when I heard a vehicle stopping outside. Maybe it was the Police Commander. Maybe he'd decided that he did exist, after all. Instead, two smartly dressed men came and introduced themselves to me. They were from the United Nations, they told me, and they had come to the village to investigate reports of an attack on the school. Did I know anything about it? Had I heard anything? Seen anything? Could the terrible reports that they had heard be true?

I agreed to tell them all that I knew, on one condition – that my name wasn't used. I told them that I was scared. I had already been in trouble with the authorities, and I didn't want to be again. Two of the girls had still to leave the clinic, and as long as their parents were happy then the UN workers could also speak with them. That way, they could hear for themselves exactly what had happened, and from two of the victims.

As they listened to the accounts of the attack on the school the UN men were visibly shaken. They took notes of everything, and they even took some photos of the two little girls. Eventually they left, promising to lodge immediate reports of the attack via their organisation. They also pledged to return to the clinic in the next few days with extra medical supplies.

During the days that followed I made a point of visiting the homes of the rape victims, so that I could check on them personally and dress their wounds. But fear stalked the village now, and as I walked from place to place I could feel its dark presence lurking around every corner. Talk of the war and the horrors it was bringing was on everyone's lips.

The school remained closed, its smashed doors and broken windows staring out like dark and empty eye sockets. What was the point in it reopening? Parents were fearful of their children returning – for what was to stop the same horrors happening all over again? It was government soldiers who had surrounded the school as the Janjaweed had done their work. This horror was the government's doing; it had been sanctioned by the rulers in Khartoum.

What had the inhabitants of Mazkhabad village done to deserve such treatment? What had they possibly done? What had the schoolgirls done to deserve such treatment from their own government? As the village talked in fearful whispers, no one could understand what had happened. What was it designed to achieve? It was pure madness, senseless evil. What in God's name had the village done to deserve such things?

And what could any child ever have done to deserve to be treated in this way?

20

They Come for Me

A week after the attack on the village school they came for me. Around midday I heard a car pull up outside the clinic. For a moment I hoped it might be the UN men returning with the promised medical supplies. But instead three men dressed in scruffy khaki uniforms strode into the clinic. With barely a break in their stride they hauled me to my feet by the scruff of my white medical tunic, knocking over my desk things as they did so.

'Move!' a soldier ordered. 'Move! You're coming with us!'

For a moment I tried to resist. 'What d'you want? What d'you want? Get your hands off me!'

A face was thrust into mine, hatred burning in bloodshot eyes, a savage mouth flecked with spittle: 'Shut up! Shut up! Shut up! Shut up! SHUT UP!'

As they dragged me out of the clinic, my eyes momentarily met those of Sayed. For a second he looked as if he might say something, and then his fearful gaze was cast down to the floor. They marched me across to the waiting jeep and threw me into the rear. One got in on either side of me and the doors were slammed shut. The third soldier got into the driver's seat and gunned the engine.

There was a dark, terrifying silence in that vehicle as we drove away from the clinic. No one spoke a word. I didn't even try to ask where they were taking me. I knew that, this time, it was deadly serious. My heart was pounding, pain drilling like a jack-hammer inside my skull. I knew they were going to kill me. A voice kept yelling inside my head: *today they're going to kill you; they're going to kill you; they're going to kill you today.*

I didn't know exactly why they were going to kill me. Was it my help for the injured fighters? My help for the rape victims? Who else had I helped that might mean that I had to die? Or was it my failure to keep the list of names? In a way I was past caring. Sooner or later, we all of us knew that the darkness was going to come down. Everyone in Mazkhabad knew in their hearts that the horror was coming.

So they had come for me early. *So what?* The country was burning. Children were being gang-raped. Evil stalked the land. Sooner or later all of us Zaghawa, Fur, Massalit – all of us black dogs and slaves – were going to get some. You might be lucky, and live. You might be luckless, and die. It looked as if my luck had run out. So be it. *At least, God, let me die quickly. Please, God, let it be painless. Please, God, don't let them torture my soul.*

They took me to the far side of the village, to a military camp. We stopped at three huts, with a wire fence running around the outside. The soldiers dragged me out and marched me into the nearest one. It had a hard concrete floor and bare brick walls. The windows were barred, and closed with metal shutters. A single light bulb revealed dark, blotchy stains on the floor. I didn't want to imagine what they might be.

I stepped into the room, and without warning the beating began. I was kicked hard in the stomach. As I bent double with the pain, further kicks and blows rained down on my legs, hips and shoulders. I fell to the floor, and tried to cover my head with my arms. A boot made contact with my face, a searing white light shooting through my eye socket. Another kick to the head, this one smashing into the fingers of my hand with a crunch of breaking bone.

The scrunch of soles turning on the bare concrete floor. The dull thump of booted feet slamming into my soft, fleshy parts. Then silence. Tensing myself for the next blow, but none coming.

Just silence, as I lie there huddled into a ball on the cold hard floor. Silence, and the sound of their breathless, excited animal breathing. Silence – is it for a second, or a minute, or an hour? I am in too much pain to register such things. Why does killing me have to start with so much pain?

'You are the Zaghawa doctor!' a voice screams at me. 'The Zaghawa doctor! We know who you are!'

'You speak to the foreigners!' Another voice screaming. 'You tell them lies. LIES! Why do you tell them lies?'

A hand gripping my hair, dragging my head upwards. A series of savage blows to the face, whipping my head from side to side. A soldier crouches down, his face a mask of loathing, his putrid breath rank in my nostrils. His dead eyes are staring into mine, as he twists his fingers into my hair and drags my head higher off the floor.

'Listen – we know you gave information to the foreign people,' he rasps, his voice cold and laden with hatred. 'Why did you do this? You signed a declaration. Or did you forget? You signed a declaration to keep quiet. You promised to. Why did you break your promise?'

'This time we will deal with you!' A voice off to one side, screaming again. 'This time we will teach you a lesson you will never forget!'

The crouching man glances upwards. He smiles thinly at his colleague, the Screamer. 'Zenil wants to deal with you. In his own, particular way. Shall I let him? Would you like me to?'

'She speaks about rape!' The Screamer again. 'This dirty talking! About rape! Lying to the foreigners! About little girls … She knows nothing of rape! Nothing …'

'Zenil wants to be your teacher,' the Croucher again, his voice slick with menace. 'He's offering to teach you. Would you like him to? Would you like him to teach you all that he knows?'

'We will teach you to shut your mouth!' A kick to the small of my back, a bolt of agony shooting up my spine. 'To shut your mouth! Forever!'

'We have the power to make you do anything,' the Croucher hisses, his fingers still locked in my hair. 'Anything, Doctor. Anything we want. Don't you know this?'

I feel the Croucher get to his feet, releasing his hold on my hair. My head drops to the hard floor. He turns and speaks to the third man, the Driver, the man who's taken no part in the interrogation so far.

'Ali, fetch some rope and tie her. Tie her firmly. I don't want her going anywhere before we've dealt with her.' The Croucher turns to stare at me. 'Put her in the detention hut. Let's give her some time to think. Some time to consider her crimes, before we punish her.'

The Driver and the Screamer haul me to my feet and march me out. They shove open the door of another hut and fling me inside. With the Screamer kneeling his weight on me, the Driver binds my wrists together. He gets my arms and forces them up behind my back – up, up until I'm burning in agony. It feels as if they are being torn from their sockets. He binds them tight in that position, so tight that my joints are burning with pain. I can't help myself now. For the first time since the assault began I start crying.

'Bring some rags,' the Screamer orders. 'We need to stop up this black bitch's mouth. No one wants to hear her dumb crying.'

A dirty piece of cloth is jammed into my mouth and tied tight around my head. The Screamer gets off me now. I see the two of them make for the door. The Screamer turns.

'Don't go away now,' he sneers. 'We'll be back later. For your first lesson.' He turns to the Driver and leers. 'They don't call me Zenil the Teacher for nothing . . .'

The Driver sniggers. The door is slammed shut. I hear a key turning in the lock, boots crunching away. Then silence. It is dark in the hut. Pitch dark. I am alone in there – apart from the mice and the rats. I can't see them, but I can hear them. Up in the rafters and scrabbling across the floor. They can smell my blood and my fear. I crab myself backwards in an awkward, agonising motion until I am tight against one wall. I face outwards. I kick with my legs to let the vermin know that I'm still conscious and alive, that I can still hurt them. I'm not a corpse yet. Not yet for the eating.

I know what is coming now. It is rape and death, rape and death. Death I can accept. It is the violation by these devils that I cannot face, that I cannot allow. Is there a way out – a way that I can kill myself? There must be a way. There must be something in that room with which I can end my life. My body is a mass of cuts and bruises, and I am racked with pain. But if I can only get free of these ropes, there must be some way in which I can kill myself. *If I untie the ropes, perhaps I can hang myself from the rafters.*

I try. I struggle to free my hands. I twist my arms and strain my muscles, but each time I try to break free it just causes me more pain. Eventually, I am too exhausted to continue. I lie there, the fight gone out of me. I lie there with my face on the dirty concrete floor, and I cry. I cry and I pray. I pray that God may save me from the Driver, the Croucher and the Screamer. I pray to God to give me sweet release, to give me death, to take me away from this life of pain and hurt. I pray for sweet release.

My God, release me. My God, release me. My God, release me.

That night they come for me. It is dark outside. I can see this when the shadowy figures unlock the door. One of them lights a lantern. But it is not the Screamer, the Croucher and the Driver any more. It is three strangers, all in dirty army uniforms. As they approach me, I see the evil and the lust burning in their eyes. One of them grabs a handful of my hair and kneels his weight on me, crushing my chest into the floor, forcing my arms further behind my back. I can see him laughing as he reads the agony and the terror in my eyes.

The second one grabs me by the legs. I see the flash of a knife blade. I feel the rending of material as he starts to slice my trousers off me. But my legs are unbound and free, and with all my might I kick out at him, slamming him back against the wall. A cry of rage issues from his unshaven, brutish, idiot features. He lunges forward and drives the knife blade deep into my thigh. I cry out in agony, but the cloth stuffed deep into my throat chokes my cries. I try to kick out again, but the third man pins my free leg to the floor.

'Hold her legs! Hold the black bitch's legs!' the knife man urges, as he slices my trousers to the waistline. 'She's a strong one, is this one. Real strong . . .'

'Strong enough for all of us?' the one kneeling on my chest calls.

'For sure! For the whole damn regiment maybe!'

The kneeling man laughs. 'Here, this'll make the black dog keep still.'

He pulls something out of his pocket. It is a cut-throat razor. He flicks open the gleaming blade, holding it up to the light so that I can see it properly. He reaches out and slices open my blouse. He smiles. Slowly, very slowly, he brings the blade down, and then slashes at my exposed flesh. I feel a searing stab of pain in my breast, followed by a warm gush of blood. He moves the blade across and places the cold steel against my other breast. I close my eyes and pray and pray and pray and pray.

'That's it, relax,' he sneers. 'Fight it, and you'll get more. Pity to spoil them both, isn't it? Lie back and take it like the black slave you are . . .'

Below, the knife man is astride me now. I tense my muscles and try to resist, but the two of them are down there, forcing my legs to open. I feel a searing agony as the knife man thrusts himself inside me, ripping me apart as he does so.

'My God, she's tight!' the knife man cries. 'Real tight! They make these Zaghawa ones tighter than the others . . .'

'Well, loosen her up for the rest of us,' the kneeling one calls over his shoulder. He turns back to face me. 'So, now you know what rape is, you black dog. Now you know.'

The three of them took turns to rape me, one after the other. Once the third had finished, they started over again. And while doing so they burned me with their cigarettes, and cut me with their blades. They raped me until I lost consciousness. When I came to my senses I was alone in the hut. I was curled into a ball in one corner. I wished I was dead. There was nothing more that anyone could do to me. My life was over.

The second day they came for me again. This time it was the Driver and the Screamer. They raped me until I fainted, they raped me until one animal assault merged into the next. On the third day the door of the hut opened once more. Light flooded in from the bright outside. *Please, God, please – not again, not again, not again.* The Croucher came in. He was alone. He walked over to where I was curled in a foetal position against one wall. He sank down on his haunches and stared at me in silence.

'You know what we've decided to do with you?' he announced quietly. 'We're going to let you live. We're not going to kill you. Get it? Not die. Not die. Live.'

I said nothing. I barely responded. I was in a place where no one could reach me. I was beyond words.

'You know why we're going to let you live?' he added. 'We're going to let you live because we know you'd prefer to die. Isn't that clever of us? Aren't we clever, Doctor? We may not have your education, but we're damn smart, wouldn't you agree?'

I stared at him with dull, unseeing eyes. I saw nothing. I was in a faraway place where my God had taken me, a place where they couldn't reach me any more. I was safe there. It wasn't death, which is what I'd asked for and begged for and prayed for. But it was the next best thing – the next best thing that my God could do for me in the circumstances.

The Croucher shrugged. 'Anyway, go. Go. It's over, for now. You know what rape is, so go. The Teacher and the others – they've shown you. As for me, I wouldn't touch a black dog like you if my life depended on it. Anyway, go. Go and tell the world. For the rest of your life you're going to have to live with it. Go and tell whoever you want what rape is.'

Some time later I found myself at Osman and Mounah's place. I had no idea how I had got there. As soon as Mounah clapped eyes on me, she knew that something terrible had happened. My clothes were ripped and dirtied, my face a bloodied mess, my trousers and blouse horribly stained. She took me inside and tried to make me wash and eat and drink. I hadn't eaten for days, but I had no hunger. All I could do was sit and stare into the fire, rocking myself backwards and forwards as I cried and cried.

Eventually, Mounah managed to get the story out of me. Once I'd finished talking she warned me never to go back to Asia's house, or the clinic. If I did they might be waiting for me, and they might take me again. I had to go back to my village. It was the only place where I might be safe from them. I was to wait here until Osman came home. He was away on business, but expected back shortly. Osman would help me escape.

Late that night Osman reached home. As quickly as she could, Mounah explained what had happened. Osman agreed that I had to disappear. Those who had attacked me would never forget or forgive, and it would never be over, not until they said it was. Osman told me that he owed me a debt of life. I had saved his son, Ibrahim. He would repay that debt by saving my life. He needed twenty-four hours to prepare my escape. We would leave the following night. In the meantime I was to remain hidden in the house.

The following evening, as darkness descended over Mazkhabad village, Osman saddled up his camel. He'd got Abakher and Asia to pack my green metal trunk with my clothes, sleeping blanket and some other possessions. He slung it onto the camel's back, along with some provisions for the journey. Osman planned to stick to the remote desert tracks and the mountains, and we would need to be able to feed ourselves and bed down along the way.

Osman mounted the camel and helped me to climb up behind him. It was difficult and painful, and I needed Mounah and Asia's help. Just sitting on the hard saddle was agony. God only knew how I was going to survive the journey. But I didn't care. If I died along the way, so be it. I just had to get away from Mazkhabad – to get away from my tormentors. With a few whispered good-byes, we threaded our way silently through the sleeping village and out into the desert and the bush lands.

All that night we pushed onwards, crossing flat desert plains and dry riverbeds. Just before dawn the route climbed into the rocky mountains. Osman knew all of the secret ways, for his life as a trader had taken him along each and every one of them at some point. Now and then we passed by a sleeping village, but Osman gave them a wide berth.

Dawn showed in the east, the sky shot through with rods of burning steel. Osman looked for a hiding place. He found what he wanted high among some tumbled rocks. There was a patch of trees with a commanding view, somewhere where the camel could graze and we could keep watch without being seen by others. We dismounted and took cover in the bush. Osman handed me some dry bread and dates and told me to eat. I should sleep as well, for I needed my strength for the journey. He would keep watch.

I knew that Osman was right, and I lay down and tried to rest. But there was a raw and burning ache in my pelvic region, and I didn't doubt that I was infected down there. The pain was made all the worst by the hard, jolting camel ride. I knew that Osman was worried about being followed, and that was why he was taking the most difficult, least travelled ways. He was a brave man, and whatever happened I would be forever in his debt. I slept fitfully, a sleep menaced by dark nightmares. I woke often in tears.

Two days later we reached my village. The pain in my pelvis was worse now, but all I cared about was seeing my family. In any case, the physical pain was nothing compared to the pain deep inside me – the pain of loss and defilement. Life as I knew it, the life that I had dreamed of, was pretty much over. I couldn't hide what had happened. And no Zaghawa man would want a woman who had been gang-raped by Arab soldiers. I had my education, and that would enable me to survive – but as to having a husband and a family . . .

We had travelled through the night and we rode into the village just as dawn was breaking. As we approached my house the first person I spotted was my mother. She glanced up, did a double take, and then realised it was me. She knew immediately that something was wrong, and she came running out to meet me. I came down from the camel and dissolved into her arms. The tears just poured down my face as grief engulfed me.

My mother kept asking what was wrong, but I could find no words to tell her. My father came and hugged me tight, his face a mask of worry. Finally, Osman suggested that they let me rest. He needed to leave almost immediately. But he could stay for a short while to speak with my father. My mother led me across to Grandma's hut, showed me to my old bed and bade me rest.

Osman spoke to my father. He told him that I had been helping my people at the clinic, and I had been targeted by the police and the military for doing so. I had been beaten and interrogated. He, Osman, had taken it upon himself to help me escape, riding through the secret and unknown places to reach our village. My father thanked him from the heart. What he had done for me they would never forget. Osman told my father that he had owed me a debt of life. I had saved his son's life. Now that debt had been repaid.

Osman said his farewells, mounted his camel and rode into the bush. He had omitted telling my father about the rape, because so many women would try to keep such things secret. But I couldn't do so. Later that morning my mother came to talk to me and I broke down. I confessed all. I asked her to tell my father, for I was too embarrassed to do so. My mother tried to comfort me, but at the same time she was so very angry. The war had finally come home. Before now it had been all around, but now it was in our home.

Later, my father came and joined me in the hut. Upon hearing from my mother what had happened he'd been possessed by a terrible rage. Now, he was ashen-faced with shock. I had never seen him looking so shaken or so careworn. He took my hand gently in his and told me not to worry. I was home now, and I was safe. It didn't matter what had happened. Nothing mattered. All that he cared about was that I was home.

He looked me in the eyes then and promised to find the people who had done this to me. He would find them and kill them all. I felt so guilty. I felt as if I should have fought those men off, or died trying. But the one thing that was keeping me alive was the knowledge that I knew the faces of those who had attacked me. They were burned forever into my mind. I knew them and I could try to find them and kill them. I imagined plunging a knife into them – and that was the hope that was keeping me alive.

'Where's Grandma?' I asked my father. I hadn't seen her anywhere, and I felt as if I needed her strong spirit by my side.

My father shook his head. 'Didn't you know? We sent a message via Uncle Ahmed. Grandma's gone. She's passed away. She's dead. Grandma Sumah's dead.'

Grandma had passed away barely a week prior to my reaching home. My father had tried to get a message to me, via Uncle Ahmed and the radiophone in Mazkhabad. They had wanted me here for the funeral, but the message hadn't got through. Her death had been quick and painless, my father told me, and it sounded like a stroke. It had happened in the middle of the night, and by early morning she had passed to the other side.

Just when I most needed her fighting spirit and strength, Grandma Sumah was gone.

21

A Long-distance Wedding

For days on end I stayed in Grandma's hut, hiding from the world. I tried to mourn for her, but my own state of mind was such that I had little energy left to grieve for anyone other than myself. Yet I missed her terribly, and especially now. If Grandma had been alive, I felt certain she would have done something dramatic to avenge what had happened. She would have taken her revenge on any Arab that she could get her hands on, with no thoughts for the consequences. That was just how she was.

As for the rest of my family, each reacted in their own way. My mother's response to what had happened was one of emotional collapse. My 'little' brother, nineteen-year-old Omer, stomped around looking enraged and fiery. But what could he do? Who could he fight? How could he strike back at them? He and Mo would need my father's leadership to carry them, and my father's intentions lay in a more long-term, considered approach. My father's hopes lay in contacting the Zaghawa rebels.

It was on the day of my return that my father decided to join them. It was clear to him now that we had no choice. We had to fight, or die. No one could avoid the truth any more. He had seen what they had done to me, and from Osman he had heard of the attack on the village school. He shared his plans with my brothers, and there was lots of fighting talk. Just as soon as they could, he, Mo and Omer would join the rebels.

The only people who knew what had happened to me were my family, and they were determined to keep it that way. When people asked why I had come home, they said that I'd sought safety in the village from the war. Because I didn't want to see anyone, they told visitors that I was resting after a long and difficult journey. I lay in Grandma's hut, hiding myself away and consumed by grief. The void of a deep depression swallowed me, where the loneliness and darkness seized hold of my soul.

After a month or so I started showing my face around the home. I helped my mother with the chores. This was as much as I could manage. I felt like a child again – a child at home, doing childish things and protected by my family. My favourite job was washing the clothes. It would take me the whole day to complete a basket of washing, and somehow I felt that with each one I was making myself clean again. Sometimes I would catch myself scrubbing and scrubbing at my own skin – as if by doing so I might rid myself of what those men had done to me.

My father started being absent from the home for several days at a time, far longer than we were used to. No one talked openly about it, but I presumed that he had to be off making contact with the rebels. I still didn't have the energy or the will to be interested. My daily interaction was limited to passing the time of day. A quiet 'hello, how are you?' and that was about it. Then I would go and busy myself with the daily chores.

In reality I was still in hiding: I was hiding away from my family, from my friends and from life in its entirety. The more it became obvious that I had stopped wanting to be part of my family, the more it hurt them. My father in particular was consumed by worry.

Four months after my return he came to find me in Grandma's hut. He sat down next to me and held my hand. He knew that I was isolating myself, he told me gently, and he understood why. He knew that I feared rejection, rejection from all those who loved me. He knew that I was trying to protect myself, by rejecting them first. I was a victim, and nothing would ever alter his love for me. He would always love me dearly. He just wanted me back again.

My father said that I needed something to live for, something to bring me out of the darkness. And so he had taken the liberty of asking the parents of my cousin Sharif if they would agree to a marriage. If I was happy, Sharif had accepted the match. He had fond memories of me, and we were both university-educated, so it would be a union of equals. Sharif was an educated, liberal man, one deeply involved in the struggle. Did I think I could accept him, my father asked. Would I agree to the match? If so, there was much to organise . . .

I embraced my father, burying my head in his shoulder. He was so full of love for me: he was trying to drag me back from death to life. Most of the time that he had been away he hadn't been meeting the rebels at all. He'd actually been trying to match-make for me. He'd been trying to find a man who might understand that I'd been horribly victimised, and who would not see me as the guilty party to some unspeakable, heinous act.

As terrible as it might seem, a victim of rape is likely to be treated as an outcast by her community, and even her family. And this had been preying so much on my mind. Who would want me now, I wondered. I should have been dead. *I was dead.* At least, inside I was. But I didn't want anyone marrying me out of charity, either. Rather death than that.

'Did you tell him?' I whispered. 'Did you tell him the truth? Does he know? What did he say?'

'Don't worry,' my father comforted me. 'Don't worry. You know Sharif. He works for the cause, the struggle. He has seen so much suffering, all across our country. He understands suffering. He knew that it would come to Darfur, that it was our inescapable fate. Don't worry – he can accept you for who you are.'

It wasn't an answer to my question, but it was enough for me. I hoped my father was right. I hoped Sharif was a good man, a man of enlightened understanding, a man who might understand that no woman ever invites rape. A man who might understand the unspeakable pain and trauma that I had been through, and who would care.

'So, Rathebe, is that a "yes"?' my father prompted. 'Can I tell his family you agree?'

I nodded. I gave a tearful half-smile. I felt my face crack as I did so. It was the first time that I had smiled since those men had done those things to me. My father had brought a smile to my face at last. I loved him so dearly. My father went on to explain that there was one complication with the marriage: Sharif was no longer in Sudan. He had fled to safety in England, because the security services were after him, too. He and I were both survivors – survivors of the madness and evil that was burning up our country.

'You are a rebel yourself, Rathebe,' my father said. 'Whether you like it or not, it is in your blood. Sharif is just the same. You are both born rebels.'

I smiled again. That name again – *Rathebe*. It was so long since I had heard it. My father had been right to give me that nick-name – for it embodied the person that I had become. And he had been so right to give me my birth name, Halima, after the medicine woman of the village. Both names defined me now: I was the Zaghawa doctor, the doctor rebel.

My father left to deliver the good news to Sharif's parents. I tried to imagine what he would be like. My last memory of him was the thirteen-year-old farm boy driving us home in his ratty old donkey cart. I had an image in my mind of the man that I'd always wanted to marry. Yet my right to choose the man of my dreams had been taken from me by rape, and now I was to wed a near-stranger. Yet in spite of this, my father's news was like a rebirth for me. I was a phoenix rising from the ashes of my shattered dreams.

The following morning my uncles and aunts came to visit. They sat with my father and agreed upon the date when we would make the special readings from the Holy Koran so that Sharif and I could be declared man and wife. After that we would have a modest celebratory feast. My groom would be absent, of course, but once it was safe for him to return to Sudan I would have a proper traditional Zaghawa wedding.

The day of my marriage was a low-key affair. I sat with Sharif's relatives and received their congratulations. They told me that they were proud their son was marrying a medical doctor. It was such an honour for their family. Sharif's mother gave me the gift of a cow, so that I could drink its milk and grow strong while I waited for his return. It was very different from my childhood dreams of my wedding. But I didn't mind. I just hoped that my marriage to a distant Sharif might give me the will to go on.

I decided that my days of hiding away were over, and that I wanted to do something again. A health clinic had been started in the village. A charity run by some *khawajat* had been to check what medical facilities the village had. The traditional medicine women had each been given a few days' medical training and a stock of basic medicines. Each day one of these women would staff the clinic, and they were paid out of a community fund that had been raised by the village elders. I went and offered my services.

The clinic was a shelter made of wooden uprights with a grass thatch roof, and a couple of tables inside. It was basic, but it served its purpose well. The medicine women were my fellow villagers and friends of friends, and I was able to chat and laugh with them as we worked. They appreciated having a doctor around to handle some of the load.

An old woman came, complaining of headaches and weakness. I checked her over. She had swollen hands and feet and alarmingly high blood pressure. I told her there was nothing we could do for her at the clinic. She would have to go to hospital, where they would give her tablets to control her blood pressure.

The woman glared at me. 'You give me a pill to make it better! I saw you give one to our neighbour – what about me?'

'You need a different sort of pill,' I explained. 'We don't have them here. Plus you need some proper tests.'

She shook her head in disgust. 'Ah, this doctor – anything you say, even a headache, she just tells you to go to hospital.'

Many of the women who came to see us were expectant mothers, and they wanted to know when they were going to give birth. This I could help with. I'd feel their tummy, have a listen with the stethoscope, and tell them what I thought. I loved this side of the work. Gradually, I grew more contented. I was helping my people, and I could laugh with them and feel at home. I felt happier here, and I felt as if nothing could harm me.

Of course, there were lingering fears in the back of my mind. I had fled from Mazkhabad and I had effectively disappeared. It wouldn't take much for someone to work out where I had gone – a brief scan of my hospital records would reveal the location of my village. But I didn't dwell on this. I was desperate to put my troubles and horrors behind me. And it was the marriage that had been the key to me breaking my self-imposed isolation.

I now know that marriage is not the end – it is simply another beginning. But at this stage of my life I was deeply immersed in my culture, and I felt as though it was everything. After the horror and the guilt of the rape, my marriage was like a rebirth. Yet at the same time it was as if a death sentence was hanging over me. I didn't know if Sharif knew the full truth – so there was always a chance that my new life might be taken from me again.

For a while I considered keeping the darkness a secret from him, but I knew that it wasn't something that I could ever hide. I knew in my heart that I had to tell him. I would await his return to Sudan, and then I would ask him to accept me as I was – a damaged woman and a victim of rape, but a woman all the same.

In the meantime I would hope and pray that he and I could build a life together in our country. I dreamed of a family, of children, of the type of life that had seemed lost to me after the terrible things that had happened. I dreamed of happiness, of the love of my husband and my children. I dreamed of my parents becoming grandparents, and of the joy that would bring. I dreamed a dream that my loving father had made possible for me.

Unfortunately, my dreams were about to be irrevocably shattered.

22

The Devil Horsemen

It was five months after my return from Mazkhabad when they came to attack our village. It was the morning of 23 December, just two days prior to what I now know and celebrate as Christmas Day. I was helping my mother prepare a breakfast of *acidah* mash. My father, my brothers and my little sister were sitting nearby, waiting to eat before spending their day in the fields or, in my sister Asia's case, attending the school.

I stirred the *acidah* mash, peering into the pot to check on its consistency. Too thick and it would stick to the bottom; too thin, and it wasn't possible to scoop it up with one's hand and throw it into one's mouth. In the far distance I caught an odd sound – a faint thrumming in the air. I listened hard, as the strange thwoop-thwoop-thwooping grew louder. It had to be some sort of aeroplane, but it was unlike any that I had heard before.

Little children ran out into the streets, jumping up and down excitedly and pointing in the direction the noise was coming from.

'Khawajat! Khawajat! Khawajat!' I heard them singing. They clapped and danced about in time to thwoop-thwoop-thwooping. 'Plane Number 3! Plane Number 3! Plane Number 3!'

I smiled, reflecting on how they were still singing the same songs that I had sung as a child. 'Plane Number 3. Plane Number 3.' Why did we say that, I wondered. And why was it that we always presumed aircraft had to be full of *khawajat* – of white people?

I turned back to the pot and started to dish out the mash. I had a tray set before me from which we would eat communally, scooping up the maize mash with our fingers. I saw my father get to his feet. He stood, gazing into the distance, shading his eyes against the rising sun. The strange noise grew louder – the thwoop-thwoop-thwooping sounding as though it was going to pass somewhere close by the village.

I could hear the children calling out to each other: 'Aeroplane with a fan! Aeroplane with a fan! Aeroplane with a fan!' That is the phrase that we used for helicopters.

My father could see the aircraft now. A fleet of five helicopters were coming speeding out of the sun. He tried to make them out more clearly. He couldn't be certain, but each seemed to be painted in the dull khaki of military green. The atmosphere in the village began to change, as all around us people started to sense that this wasn't right somehow. I glanced up from the breakfast tray, feeling a growing tension and panic. I jumped to my feet. We gazed at the onrushing air armada, trying to work out exactly where they were heading.

Suddenly, the lead helicopter banked low over the village and there were a series of bright flashes and puffs of smoke from under its stubby wings. An instant later, the huts beneath it exploded, mud and thatch and branches and bodies being thrown into the air. I couldn't believe what I was seeing. I told myself that my eyes had to be playing tricks, that it couldn't be happening. But while my heart refused to believe it, my head knew that it was all too real.

They were attacking the village! They were attacking the village! They were attacking the village!

All around us people were waking up to the fact of the attack, and crying out in alarm.

'*Kewoh! Kewoh!* – Run! Run!'

'*Souf! Souf!* – Hide! Hide!'

For an instant I was frozen with fear, before my father grabbed me by the shoulders.

'Run!' he cried. 'Run! Take your brothers and sister and run! To the forest! Hide! And don't come out until we come for you. Run! Run! There's not a moment to lose . . .'

'I'm not going!' Omer yelled. 'I'm staying! I'm staying to fight!'

'Don't you dare disobey me!' my father thundered. 'I'm your father and you do as I say! Go with your mother and sisters, to protect them. Now – do as I say! GO!'

Mo and Omer were wide-eyed with fear, but my father's face was calm and stern as he prepared to face the enemy. He seemed so resolute and so in control, gripping his dagger as he ordered us to flee for our lives. My brothers' fear – and especially Omer's – terrified me. It was as if the village had become a vision of hell so terrible that even my warlike little brother was petrified. But my father – my father was firm like a rock, and I drew strength from him being so.

I took one last look at his face, then tore my eyes away. I grabbed my sister and my mother by the hand and we turned and ran. We raced out of the gate, joining a mass of people scurrying through the village. They were screaming wildly, as they ran and ran as fast as their legs would carry them. My brothers ran after us, leaving my father standing firm and alone.

In the distance beneath the helicopters a massed rank of horsemen swept forward, firing their guns and screaming as they smashed into the village.

The Janjaweed! The Janjaweed were coming!

Asia, my mother and I ran. The village women were all around us, little babies clutched in their arms; older brothers ran with their younger siblings slung across their shoulders. Everyone was screaming in terror, and racing to get ahead of the person in front of them.

'Run! Run!'

'Run! Don't let the Janjaweed catch us!'

'Don't let them kill us!'

'God save us! God save us!'

The Janjaweed urged their horses forward, tossing blazing torches onto the huts, the dry thatch roofs bursting into flames. I kept glancing behind in fear at the flashes of gunfire and the flames that were sweeping through the village like a wave of fiery death. I could hear the devil horsemen screaming like animals, a howling wave of evil and hatred tearing our village asunder. As they got closer and closer I could make out the individual Arabic phrases that they were chanting, over and over and over again.

'We're coming for you! To kill you all!'

'Kill the black slaves! Kill the black slaves!'

'Kill the black donkeys!'

'Kill the black dogs!'

'Kill the black monkeys!'

'No one will escape! We will kill you all!'

'Kill them all! Kill them all! Kill them all!'

Up ahead I could see the helicopters circling, turning for another attack run, and then there were further flashes and smoke, and bullets and rockets were tearing into the fleeing women and children, ripping bodies apart. Omer grabbed my hand, and dragged my mother, my sister and me to one side, out of the murderous path of their onslaught.

We weaved and dodged and raced ahead for the safety of the forest, passing bloodied heaps that had once been our village neighbours and our friends. Their bodies had been torn apart by the bullets from above. Some of them were still alive, crawling and staggering on. They cried out to us, holding out their hands and pleading for help. But if we stopped the Janjaweed would be upon us and we all would die. So we ran, abandoning the wounded and the old and the slow and the infants to the terror of the Janjaweed.

My mother was slower than the rest of us, and I could tell that she was tiring. She urged us to leave her – she would run at her own pace and catch us up in the forest. But we refused to do so. Together with Mo and Omer I half-carried and half-dragged her forward. I cried out for God to help us, to help save us all.

We ran and ran, each step taking us further from the hell of the village. I was terrified for all of us, but half of my mind was back in the village with my father. With no weapon but his dagger he had chosen to stand and face this terrible onslaught. I knew why he had done so. Those who had chosen to stay and fight did so to stop the Janjaweed from reaching the women and children – *to buy us some time*. They stayed to save their families, not to defend the village. They did so to save us from the Janjaweed.

Finally we reached the safety of the deep forest, where the helicopters could no longer hunt us down from the air. We hid within the cover of the trees. Everywhere I looked there were scattered groups of villagers. Mo, Omer, Asia, my mother and I were breathless and fearful. We crouched in the shadows and listened to the noise of the battle raging on – trying to work out if it was coming closer, and whether we had to run once more.

The noise of the helicopters faded into the distance. From the village I could hear gunfire and yelling and the booming echo of the odd explosion. All around me was the wailing of little children. Tiny voices were crying and crying. Why had these men attacked us and destroyed our village, they sobbed. What wrong had we done to them? Desperate mothers sought news of their children. Many had lost little ones in the mad rush of the flight from the village.

Mothers began beating themselves and wailing hysterically, so guilty were they at having left little ones behind. We tried to quieten them, in case their cries betrayed our hiding place to the Janjaweed. Some wanted to return and search for their missing loved ones, but we had to hold them back – for to do so would mean death, of that we were certain.

Hour upon terrible hour we waited. The atmosphere was hellish. Exhausted from weeping, women and children stared ahead, their faces blank with shock. Now and then the dull hush of the fearful quiet was torn by the crackle of gunfire. With each gunshot children jumped, wailed, eyes searching in terror for the enemy. Had they somehow found us, and were we all about to be killed? But mostly my mind was back in the village, on my father. I prayed to God to protect him, and to keep him alive.

An hour or so before sunset the noise of battle died to a deathly quiet. A thick column of smoke rose in the distance, where the village was burning. No one had come to the forest to fetch us, and my father had ordered us to stay here until he did. But we just had to hope that he and the other men were busy in the village with the injured. If they were, it was my duty as a doctor to be there with them. Fearful eyes met fearful eyes, as we wondered what was best to do. Should we stay in the forest, or risk returning to the village?

There was a murmur of fevered whispering. Could anyone hear anything? No, it was all quiet. What did that mean? Did it mean that the enemy had gone? Maybe it did and maybe it didn't, who could tell? Maybe the Janjaweed were hiding, ready to ambush us. The only way to find out was to sneak back to the village. Finally, a collective decision was reached. Slowly, carefully, stopping every minute to listen, we retraced our way through the darkening forest until we reached the outskirts of the village.

As the first huts came into view, people couldn't hold back any longer. They ran towards their homes to seek out their loved ones. I raced through the choking smoke, my mother and brothers and sisters at my side. Fires glowed red all around us, the crackle of the flames thick in the air. At every turn I could smell burning and death. Bodies were everywhere. Somehow, I navigated my way through this scene from hell to our house. The fence had been smashed down and our possessions lay scattered all around. But I didn't care. I cared only for one thing – *my father*. My father! *Where was my father?*

I rushed to my neighbour's house. Perhaps my father was there, helping Kadiga's relatives. One of her sisters had just given birth to a little baby girl, and I had helped with the delivery. I pushed aside the door of her hut, only to find a body slumped on the floor, the ground around it soaked in blood. Beside the dead mother was a smoking fire, a tiny charred body lying among the ashes. The Janjaweed had shot the mother in the stomach and thrown her baby daughter onto the fire. The smell in the hut was sickening.

I turned away and sank to my knees, the nausea rising and gagging in my throat. As I bent to vomit, I heard a chorus of cries coming from the centre of the village, a wailing crescendo of gut-wrenching grief. Women were screaming that they had found the men of the village! The men of the village were there! Together with my mother and my brothers I rushed towards the source of those grief-stricken cries. We reached the open area at the market-place with the darkness of night settling over the burning village.

The ground was littered with shadowy corpses, women kneeling and keening over their loved ones. They were crying out the names of the fallen, beating their heads on the bloodied ground in their grief. But among the bodies were one or two who were still alive. I searched frantically, my mind screaming. Where was my father? Where was my father? *My father! My father! My father!* Where was he? God, let him be alive. Let him be injured, but let him have lived. *Let him be alive! Let him be alive! Let him be alive!*

I saw my brother Omer stop. His features collapsed in on themselves as he sank to his knees, his hands grasping at his head and tearing at his hair. He bent to embrace a fallen figure, his arms locking around the body, his face buried in the face and hair. He was sobbing and wailing and shaking like a wounded animal. I fell to the ground myself.

I knew it was my father. I knew it was my father. I knew it was my father. I knew it was . . .

286

I came to some time later. I was lying on my back with my mother beside me. Her face was tear-stained, her expression glazed and empty. I glanced about me at the crowd of wailing women, and suddenly I remembered the image of Omer bent low over my fallen father. My mother glanced down at me, her eyes pools of shock and loss. I went as if to question her, but she shook her head, and fresh tears began to fall. As she did so, I vented my pain and my loss in a guttural howl of agony and emptiness that went on and on and on. I would never stop crying for my fallen father, no matter how long I might live.

There were many villagers who were injured but still alive. There were gunshot victims, burn victims, victims of shrapnel from the explosions and victims of stabbings. I should have been trying to help them, but I was in such a state of shock that I could do nothing, absolutely nothing. The surviving women and children had gathered together in a group. The crying and wailing and the calling of the names of the dead would have been terrible to behold, had I not been so bound up in my own unspeakable loss.

We were bundled heaps of misery, unable to comprehend what had happened to our lives. As we mourned, the men – my brothers included – went and checked on the fallen, trying to work out who was dead and who might be saved. The majority of those killed were the men who had stayed to fight. And then there were those too slow to run and save themselves – the old people, children. Pregnant women had been cut down as they ran. Village elders had been burned alive in their huts. Babies had been flung into the fires.

All through that dark, hellish night the men collected up the bodies of the dead. By dawn they were ready to bury them. The first of the donkey carts creaked out of the village, its load a pile of stiff, bloodied corpses. I was in such shock that I was living in the memory of my dead father, his face before me in my mind's eye, still talking to me and hugging me and laughing and smiling.

If I tried to drag myself back to the present, all I could see was a film of red mist that obscured everything. It would take a new level of horror to shock me out of my stupor.

A living woman had been mistaken for one of the dead. As the cart moved off towards the graveyard, someone noticed her arm twitching. They called out in alarm and the cart stopped. She was separated from the corpses and laid on the ground. It was the sight of that dead woman living that dragged me back to my senses. The woman's name was Miriam. She had lost her husband, her father and two of her children. Her third child had survived, and he desperately needed his mother to live, for he had no one else in the world.

I bent over her prostrate form. I felt for her pulse. It was faint and she was barely breathing. I checked for any sign of injury, but there was none that I could see. It must have been simply the shock and the trauma that was killing her. I put my head close to hers, and started to give mouth-to-mouth resuscitation. After each breath I pressed my weight hard onto her chest. I did this for half an hour or so, her little boy holding his mother's hand and willing her to live. *I had to save her!* For his sake alone, I had to . . .

Suddenly, her eyes opened. She gazed around herself, as if she was coming back from the dead. As soon as she realised that she was still alive, she started to scream and scream and scream. She was screaming out the names of the dead. Why hadn't death taken her, she wailed. Where was the sweet release of death? I tried showing her that her little boy was still alive, but she was beyond reason, in a place where no one could reach her. The one person whose life I had saved actually wished that she was dead.

Some time later that day three young Zaghawa men turned up in the village. They wore traditional white robes, and they had their heads swathed in a white headscarf, with only their eyes showing. Each carried a machine-gun. They introduced themselves as being from the Sudan Liberation Army, the SLA – one of the main rebel groups. They had heard about the attack, and so they had left their secret base in the mountains and come to investigate. It was the first time that we had seen rebel fighters openly in the village.

We gathered round and told them about the attack. As we talked, the surviving men of the village – my brothers included – were angry and tearful. All they wanted now was to fight. All other interests were gone. Mo and Omer were among the first to volunteer, but scores more followed. I tried to volunteer myself, but I was told that women were not allowed to fight. I tried to offer myself as a rebel doctor, but I was told that there was work enough for me here with the injured.

We gathered as a family and tried to decide what we should do next. But there was an aching void where my father should have been. As the eldest child I knew that I had to take a lead now, alongside my mother. There was nothing in the village to stay for, I argued. Most of the livestock was gone. The crops had been burned, as the Janjaweed had turned our beautiful village into a place of scorched and bloodied earth. They had ridden over our fields, smashing open the irrigation ditches. Even the fruit trees were blackened with fire.

Mo and Omer's minds were made up. The rebels would be leaving by nightfall, and they would be going with them. They would kill the Arabs and avenge our father's death. Nothing else mattered. There was talk of fleeing to Tchad, or of going to stay with relatives in the big towns. But many of the injured villagers were too sick to travel, and part of me felt as if it was my duty to stay with them. If I couldn't be a rebel soldier, I could at least use my medical skills to try to save as many lives as possible here in my dying village.

'Perhaps we should stay,' I told my mother. 'People in the village need us. We can stay until they are well again. Then, God willing, we will leave this place.'

My mother shook her head. 'We should go to Tchad. We have

relatives there. We can go and stay with them. We can take our gold, so if anything happens on the way we have something to bargain with.'

'We still have our gold?' I asked. I'd presumed it had all been stolen.

'We do. Grandma had it well hidden. We could even try to hire some camels in a neighbouring village. That might make it easier for us to find our relatives.'

Grandma's husband had a second wife in Tchad, so her children were my mother's half-brothers and sisters. My mother knew their names, although she had never met them. If their village had been attacked and they had come to us for help, we would have welcomed them in. My mother knew they would do the same for us. The problem was how to reach Tchad safely. We might run into the Janjaweed en route, and then we would be finished.

'It's a long journey,' I remarked. 'And we could be attacked on the way. I doubt if the enemy will return to the village. There's nothing worth coming back for. So perhaps we're safer staying here for now. Maybe it's best to stay.'

My mother shrugged. 'Sooner or later we have to go. Everything's gone. There's nothing to eat. And this is a place of death now. What's to stay for?'

'There are people here who have nothing. They've got no home, no money and no relatives to go to. We can't just abandon them. Plus there are the injured. We should stay for a while, to help.'

We finally decided to stay. In that way, my brothers would still know where to find us. Once they were trained as rebel fighters, they could return to protect us. At least, that was the theory. That evening the men of fighting age prepared to leave. I bade farewell to Mo and Omer, but there were no tears left to cry and little energy for real sadness. And then they were gone.

All that now remained were the old, the women and the children in our dying village.

23

A Time of Fear

This was the beginning of the time of fear. Every waking moment we tried to remain alert, keeping our eyes and ears open. And whenever we slept it was only ever a half-sleep, in case they returned in the night to attack us. We were living like hunted animals, and like animals we feared the air above and the earth at our feet. And like frightened animals we herded together, as if there was safety in numbers.

The huts in our compound had survived largely intact. My mother, my sister and I moved into one, while our neighbours took the others. We pooled what little food and bedding we had left. Each evening we would call together the survivors in our area, and we would eat as one big family. As we ate we listened to each other's stories, and lamented each other's terrible loss. This was a process of collective mourning, as people shared their pain and their hurt with others who had suffered.

Mariam – the woman I had brought back from the dead – stayed with us, along with her little boy. Each evening she would cry and cry, and everyone would cry with her. Her pain forced us all to remember, to return to that terrible day again and again. But no one resented her for doing this. She was living inside her pain, and our greatest fear was that she would never get out. She had to – for the sake of her little boy, if not for herself.

As for me, I had changed overnight. Before the attack on our village I was still a victim, still a woman trying to come to terms with my own horrors. Now all that had been replaced by a burning rage. I wanted to fight. I longed to fight and to kill the Arabs – those who had done this evil. Those who had stolen my father away, my wonderful, wonderful father. Those who had burned and desecrated our village.

The village had been utterly laid to waste. What they couldn't carry off the Janjaweed had smashed, burned and destroyed. Even the village water pump had been torn to pieces. Corpses had been dumped into the well, to poison the water. We realised that they must have planned it like this. In this way, anyone left alive after the attack would die from starvation or thirst. They came not only to kill us, but to destroy our ability to live.

The little children kept asking why the Janjaweed had done this, why they wanted us all to die. How were we supposed to answer such questions? What could we possibly say? When the children were sleeping we talked among ourselves. The Arab tribes had always been poorer than us: they had no settled villages, no crops and few animals. So where had they got the powerful weapons that they had used to attack us?

We knew that there had to be the hand of the government in this. There had to be a driving force that had ordered them to do what they had done. If they had simply come to loot our homes, why destroy the village? It didn't benefit them at all. They must have done this with orders from on high. As this realisation set in even the simplest villager realised that this government of Arabs had decided to back their own, and to wipe us off the face of the earth.

We knew now where the lines were drawn. We knew that this government was our bitter enemy. For me, this was hardly a blinding realisation. I had long suspected it. I had witnessed the rape of the children of Mazkhabad. I had witnessed that horror, and then the soldiers had come for me. My eyes had been forcibly opened. Together with my father I had railed against the Arab government that kept us down in our own country. But many in our village had lived in naive hope until the very day of the attack.

For three whole weeks we lived like this, suspended in a limbo somewhere between life and death. I spent my time either scavenging for food in the ruined village or tending to people's injuries, boiling water and binding up their wounds with whatever came to hand. I gathered the forest plants to make the burns ointments that Grandma had used. I burned the leaves to a fine ash and mixed that with sesame oil. Each day I would apply the paste afresh to people's burns, and with many it did seem to help.

But some of the little children had burns covering their entire body. It was a miracle that they were still alive. They had been thrown into burning huts, and somehow survived the inferno. But they were in total agony. Their skin blistered and peeled off, the burns becoming infected and pustulous. I had so much training and knowledge, but there was little that I could do without proper medical supplies. It broke my heart. It would have been better if they had died, and each day another passed into the merciful release of death.

But it was the mental injuries that I was least able to treat. In the worst cases women had lost their entire families – husbands, children and parents, all dead. Many of these women had also lost their minds. They sat and muttered and cried and laughed aloud. They hugged themselves and rocked backwards and forwards, gazing at nothing for hours on end. They refused to eat and had no idea of day or night. And I could do nothing to help them.

As I did my rounds everyone was talking about the same thing. What would we do if they came to attack again? How would we escape this time, with no men to defend us? Some were considering going to join their relatives in other villages, but what was there to prevent those from being attacked, just as ours had been? Others were planning to head south, all the way to the Nuba

Mountains, where we hoped that our black African brothers would offer us sanctuary. Was it in those mountains that we could find safety?

Or was it better to flee across the border, to Tchad? Our fellow Zaghawa lived there, as that was also the land of our tribe. But was the border guarded? Would the government soldiers or the Janjaweed catch us as we tried to cross to safety? Or was it better to try for the big towns? There was little fighting in the towns, so maybe they offered the best chance of escape.

The village was dying all around us. We knew that it was finished. It was about to be scattered to the four corners of the desert, like so much chaff on the wind. People were preparing themselves for that eventuality: remembering how a burnt hut had once been so-and-so's family home; remembering what a wonderful wedding we had had in so-and-so's yard; remembering how as children we had played in that field, stolen fruit from that orchard, and fought with our clay warrior horsemen in the dust by that fence.

There was an old woman whose only child had been killed. Her husband was already dead, so now she was all alone. She would sit by herself and cry: 'No family . . . Nobody at all . . . All of them gone . . .' One evening I found her wandering in her burnt hut and singing tearfully to herself. She had composed a lament for the death of the village.

> *The raiders took the young men,*
> *And cut them down.*
> *The raiders took the old men,*
> *And cut them down.*
> *The raiders took the women,*
> *And cut them down.*
> *The raiders took the children,*
> *And cut them down.*

We have no home,
It was cut down.
We have no crops,
They were cut down.
We have no milk,
It was cut down,
Now our children have gone to fight,
They will be cut down.

Villagers gathered round to hear her sing. As they listened, people started to cry once more. When she had finished, the old woman said that she would never leave the village. She would die here. She had no family, so where could she go? We tried to persuade her to make some plans to leave, but she refused. Why would she even want to save her life? Everyone was leaving and the village was finished, so she just wanted to die. Others had their children, and something to live for. But she had nothing.

I felt as if I was taking over the role of head of the family. My little sister, Asia, was crying the whole time. As for my mother, mostly she tried to be strong. I may have felt like death inside, but I knew that I had to think and use my head, and find a way to escape. Now and then I reached a place where I just wanted to give up, but I held on.

I kept telling myself that what we needed now was Grandma Sumah's fire and anger, not lamentations and tears. I tried to imagine what Grandma would have done in the present situation. I tried to put myself into her mindset. What would she have done? I felt certain that she would have chosen to move. She would have led us out of this hell into a place of survival. She would have opted for the journey to Tchad.

We will survive it, Grandma would have said. *We are Zaghawa, we are Zaghawa, and we are strong . . .*

By now we were nearing starvation point, so we had little

choice but to leave. And, like it or not, that decision was about to be thrust upon us. In the middle of a searing hot afternoon we heard that hateful sound again – the thud-thud-thud of rotor blades clawing through the air. This time no one hesitated for an instant: we turned as one and ran to the forest. The pounding of explosions followed us, as the helicopters tore into the village.

We were terrified, fearing that this time there was no one left to defend us and that we would all be overrun and killed. But the three helicopters seemed content to loop around in lazy circles, blasting the last remnants of the village into fire and dust and oblivion.

The noise of the attack helicopters pounding the village faded away. For hours we waited in trembling fear, crouched in the dappled shadows and straining our ears to hear the blood-curdling cries and gunfire as the dreaded Janjaweed swept in to attack. A pall of smoke drifted above the village, but there was only an eerie silence. If anything, this was more frightening, and we wondered if they were sneaking up on us to attack.

With the setting of the sun we crept back into the village. The huts that had escaped the first attack were burning, but there was no sign of the enemy. It was as if the helicopters had been sent to finish off the village, and that was all. With the fiery glow all around us and the acrid smoke thick in our lungs, we camped out in huddled groups wherever we could. It was clear what we had to do now. Tomorrow we would leave. Tomorrow we would leave. Tomorrow we would all leave and the village would be no more.

Early the next morning I decided to make one last round of my patients. I was their doctor still and I owed them this much. I set off, telling my mother and my little sister to be ready to leave on my return. I went around checking injuries, dressing burns and doing what I could for my patients. With each I talked about where they would go. I feared that some of them – especially the children – would never survive the journey. But what more could I do for them?

By midday I was back, but there was no sign of my mother or my sister. I went next door, to speak with Kadiga's uncle. Like us he was readying himself to leave. I found him in his yard, stuffing a few possessions into an old sack in preparation for the journey.

'Where's my family, Uncle?' I asked.

He glanced at me and shook his head. 'They're gone . . . A group of soldiers came in a vehicle right to your house. They were wearing uniforms and carrying guns. They asked your mother many questions. "Where is this Zaghawa doctor who escaped from Mazkhabad?" they asked. Your mother told them that she had no daughter other than Asia. She told them that she didn't know what they were talking about.'

'Oh my God . . . Oh my God! But where are they now?'

'The soldiers left a message with your mother. "We know she is your daughter. We know you are lying," they said. "Tell her from us – we are searching for her and one day soon we will find her. Tell your daughter she will never escape from us. Never." That was the message. Your mother and Asia were too afraid to stay any longer. They're gone.'

'But where . . .?'

'They're heading to Hashma, to your Uncle Ahmed's place. They couldn't face the journey to Tchad without you. Your mum says you must escape. But don't go anywhere that the soldiers might find you. They said they knew eventually you would find each other again, and be reunited.'

'But did my mum say where I should go?' I asked in bewilderment.

Kadiga's uncle shrugged. 'She didn't know. Somewhere safe. Maybe south to the Nuba Mountains. Somewhere far away so those men cannot trace you and get you. And your mother told me to tell you this: "She knows where we have hidden the valuable things, the gold. Tell her to take it all, and use it to help her find her way.'"

As if I was in a dream I returned to our yard. I dug up the valuables from where I knew they were hidden, and stuffed them into my pocket. I took a black plastic carrier bag, loaded into it a handful of dried dates, a spare *tope* and a thick robe. Then I said my goodbyes to Kadiga's uncle. I took one last look at my childhood home, turned away and started walking. I knew in my heart that I would never be returning to this place again.

I said nothing to Kadiga's uncle about where I was going. I didn't know for sure, and I wanted to leave no trail that the soldiers might follow. All I knew was that I would go south. Possibly I would try for the Nuba Mountains. It was a long way, but perhaps that was the only choice left open to me. Staying with family was impossible: it would bring the wrath of those who were hunting me down on the heads of those I loved. I set off alone walking south into the sun-baked bush and the desert.

When I was young, I'd seen how the government was trying to recruit Zaghawa men to fight in a 'jihad' against the 'unbelievers' of the south, including the Nuba. I knew that many Nuba were Christian, and others were moderate Muslims. Now I knew that religion was irrelevant in our country. All that mattered was the colour of one's skin. If someone had an Arab skin, they were my enemy; if they had a black skin, they were my friend. I would seek safety among black Africans, no matter what belief system they followed.

I walked all afternoon and into the night. I prayed to God to guide me. By the morning I knew what I would do. I was close to the railway line. It ran south to the district of Kordofan, which in turn borders the Nuba Mountains. I would walk the whole way, using the railway tracks to guide me. If a train came I would hide myself in the bush, for a train might mean danger. At the main stops police would board the train, searching for guns or other contraband, and checking people's identity papers. I would be far safer walking.

An hour or so after sunrise I reached the railway tracks. I turned southeast and started my journey. Now and then I passed small groups of people. Like me, they were following the tracks to some place, somewhere. It was a common enough practice, for it was a sure method of finding one's way. I kept my head down and pushed onward. By midday I was hot and parched. I decided to sleep through the heat and continue my journey that night. It would be cooler then, and I would be less visible to any Arabs who might be on the prowl.

I spread my cloak under a tree where some travellers were gathered, and lay down to rest. They were black Africans like me, but they were Fur, Massalit and some other tribes. They asked me where I was going, and I told them I was visiting family in Kordofan. I shut my eyes and tried to sleep. I could hear them talking among themselves. From the odd Arabic word I realised they were talking about attacks on the villages in their area. It seemed that the madness and killing was everywhere.

At dusk I set off once more. At first the darkened railway line frightened me, but I soon realised that it was easy to follow the polished metal tracks that glinted in the moonlight. I walked and walked, alone in the vast emptiness of the desert night, with only my thoughts to keep me company. I traced the tungsten blue of the moonlit rails, and I was reminded for an instant of happier times – of the fun and laughter of the moon-bone game.

Around midnight I paused to eat the last of my dates. I was out of food now, and I would have to buy some more from the stalls that lined the way. I walked until I could see the glow of dawn to the east. I still felt strong and so I decided to push on until I reached El Dein town. The tribes around there were Kordofani, a black African people, and I felt I would be safe among them.

I reached El Dein station by sunrise, and looked around me. Crowds of people were sleeping on the ground – men, women and children huddled together. Were they all, like me, refugees? I lay down with my carrier bag under my head, wrapped myself in my robe and fell asleep.

I awoke hours later with the sun high in the sky. A woman was firing up a charcoal stove, preparing to sell coffee. Seeing that I was alone, she offered me a cup. It was hot, black and sweet, and it was hugely energising.

'Where are you headed, my sister?' she asked me.

I shrugged the sleepiness out of myself. 'I'm not sure. Where can I get to from here?'

She pointed behind her. 'Trucks leave from there going to all places. You can even go to Khartoum – not that you'd want to.'

'I was thinking of further into Kordofan – maybe towards the Nuba area.'

She nodded. 'Then you'll have to take the truck for Khartoum, and change at one of the stops along the way. That's the easiest.'

I thanked the woman for her kindness, and waited in the truck stop as a driver warmed his engine. He was a black African in his early forties, and he had a young assistant with him. I told the driver I wanted a ticket to ride in his cab. Did he have any seats available? He did, the driver confirmed. But he was curious as to who I might be – a young, smartly dressed woman travelling on her own, many, many miles from home. He was especially curious as my one item of luggage was a half-empty, dusty carrier bag.

'So, it's just the one of you, is it?' he asked.

'It is.'

'And where are you headed, sister? Khartoum?'

I told him that I was going all the way to Khartoum. I said this because I was worried that he might not agree to take me if I would soon be changing trucks.

'It's a long way.' He grinned. He had an engaging smile. 'It'll be expensive. I'm just warning you, because I don't want you thinking I'm taking you for a ride or anything.'

We negotiated a price, I paid him the money and soon we were on our way. He stopped every now and then to pick up passengers. The rear of the truck was loaded with timber, so there were only so many he could carry. With an engaging frankness he explained that the more passengers he could carry, the more money he would earn. It was his little sideline, and without it he could never make ends meet. He had a wife and children and life was expensive. School fees to pay, uniforms to buy, a wife who spent too much on clothes ... In no time he seemed to have told me his whole life story.

He glanced across at me. 'So you know about me: how about you? Where are you from and why are you off to Khartoum?'

'I'm Zaghawa,' I replied. Then a small lie. 'I've got relatives in Khartoum.'

'So you're Zaghawa? But where's the rest of your family? It's not so good to be travelling alone, and so far from home.'

'I don't mind. I've done a lot of it.'

'But why? Is it to do with your work or something?'

The questions went on and on until at last I decided to tell him a little of the truth, in the hope of shutting him up.

'Look, I don't want to have to explain everything, okay? I'm just going away, that's all. I need to get away. If you can help me, that's good. If you can't, I'll get off at the next stop and take another truck.'

'No, no, no,' he objected, taking his hands from the steering wheel and gesturing in alarm. 'I'm happy to help. Happy to. And you've paid for your journey ... Are you from Darfur? Is that it?'

'I'm from Darfur. And things are not good there right now. I just need to get away, that's all.'

'Sister, I'm happy to help,' the driver repeated. 'My name is Abdul Rasul. You can trust me ... I have children almost as old as you are. You're like my daughter. When you need help you have to trust someone, don't you?'

I sneaked a look at Abdul's face. He had roundish, kindly features, and my instinct told me that I *could* trust him. But most of all, there was something about him that reminded me of my father. Something warm and open and likeable. He even had the same name as my father. On my long walk through the desert I had prayed to God to give me guidance.

Maybe this man, Abdul, was an answer to my prayers.

PART FOUR

Desert of No Return

24

Escape from Darfur

We drove all day on rough desert tracks. Just before nightfall there was a nasty metallic crunch from underneath the truck and we ground to a halt. Abdul got down from the cab and checked the underside of the vehicle. It wasn't good news. The road was rough and the load heavy, and the piece of machinery that drives the wheels had snapped. We would have to wait for another truck, and ask them to take the part to the nearest town for repairs.

As luck would have it another truck came by shortly. All the passengers decamped to that vehicle, and Abdul's young assistant left with the metal shaft to see to the repair job. Since I had decided to put my faith in Abdul, I stayed with him and the crippled truck. We had broken down in the middle of the bush, and so he offered me the cab to sleep in, while he took the ground. It would be warmer in there, he said, and I would feel more secure.

'You know, my whole life is one bad luck story,' I remarked. 'And now this. You should never have agreed to take me.'

Abdul grinned. 'Ah, don't worry. We're always having problems with this old truck. We'll get it sorted. We always do.'

The following morning we sat out under a tree. Abdul brewed some tea on a charcoal stove that he carried with him. He had a tin kettle, some glasses, a pot of sugar and fresh mint leaves. We might be here some time, he warned me, as we sipped the delicious mint tea. We should decide on a story to tell, just in case anyone asked any questions.

A man and woman travelling together who were unrelated and who weren't married – it would immediately arouse suspicion. We should pretend to be man and wife, Abdul suggested. I knew that he was right. If anyone asked, I was to be Mrs Rasul.

That day I really warmed to Abdul. He was a kind man. He walked to the nearest village to fetch food, which he heated over his charcoal stove. He urged me to eat and be strong, as I had a long journey ahead of me. He let me sit in his cab and listen to music on his radio. He urged me not to dwell on the past, but to try to be happy again. He told me funny stories and made me laugh. And bit by bit I started to reveal more about my myself.

He didn't believe that I was simply trying to escape from the war. What had I done, he asked. What was I running from? Had I killed someone? I told him that I had to escape from the military men, the security people. I was a target. If they found me they would kill me. I didn't want to go into any more detail. It was too horrible and too private.

'Are you certain they're after you?' Abdul asked.

I nodded. I was certain.

'If you're really certain then you'll have to leave the country. If you stay in Sudan, they'll find you. The danger will never pass.'

I shrugged. 'I know. But where would I go?'

Abdul glanced at me. 'Listen, I *have* to ask you this, but it is *not* the reason I'm helping you. You understand?'

I told him that I did.

'Right – do you have any money? I know people who can get you out of Sudan. But it'll be costly. That's why I'm asking . . .'

Part of me feared to answer Abdul truthfully. Part of me feared that if I told him, he might rob me and hand me over to the government. After all that I had seen and experienced it was hard to trust anyone.

'Where could you send me?' I asked, trying to avoid the money question. 'Which country?'

'Honestly, I don't know. It's not up to me. There are agents who handle these things. They'd arrange everything. But they'd charge for doing so, obviously.'

'How much?'

Abdul shrugged. 'I'm not sure. It wouldn't be cheap. Millions of Sudanese pounds probably. So it's whether you have that sort of money . . .'

'How would we organise it?'

Abdul thought for a moment. 'You could come to Khartoum and stay with my family. I have a wife and four children. You don't look so different from us – we could say you're a relative. And when we're all set, you leave the country.'

It took four days to fix the truck. By the time it was done I had decided to go with Abdul to Khartoum. I had tried to think things through rationally, but at the end of the day it all boiled down to a feeling. Abdul was like my father. That's how it felt to me. And because of that, I felt I could trust him to be my guide. As we set off again, I hoped and prayed that I was not mistaken.

A day's drive later we reached the town of Khosti, from where it was smooth tarmac all the way to Khartoum. It was evening by the time we reached the city outskirts. I was worried to be back here, for now I was a wanted person and I was in the heart of the Arab regime that wanted to kill me. We drove directly to Abdul's house. It was a low, concrete block building, with a yard where he parked the truck. His children came running out to greet him.

'Daddy! Daddy! Daddy!' they cried. 'Daddy's home!'

Then they spotted me. 'Who's this?' they demanded, all curiosity now. 'Who's this person in Daddy's truck?'

Abdul's wife came out to greet him. She was even more surprised to see me, although she did her best to hide it. Her name was Malaika, and she was tall and slim and quite beautiful. She invited me into the house for tea. Shortly, Abdul and Malaika excused themselves and disappeared into their bedroom. I guessed that Abdul wanted a private moment so he could explain who I was and why I was there.

Meanwhile, of course, I was surrounded by their curious children. I tried my best to smile and answer all of their questions. As I did so, I glanced around the house. Apart from the kitchen–dining room, there was Abdul and Malaika's bedroom and one other room that had to be for the children. The kitchen itself was well equipped, having an electric cooker, a fridge and a TV set. The house seemed crowded but comfortable. There was a happy feel to the place, as if Abdul's was a happy family.

When they reappeared from the bedroom Malaika gave me a big smile and a hug. She showed me where the children slept, and apologised that they had no guest room. I would share a bed with their oldest daughter, while the other kids shared the second bed. One of Abdul's kids went to fetch the neighbours' children, and they came rushing round to stare at the new arrival and ask yet more questions. Malaika was quick to tell them that I was her younger sister, and that I had come to help look after the children.

After dinner, I helped Abdul's kids with their homework. As I checked their sums and corrected their spelling and their grammar, I noticed that Malaika was watching me closely. Once the children were in bed, Abdul, Malaika and I sat down to watch TV. All that was on was some sports programme. Abdul was glued to it, but Malaika and I were bored. Malaika turned to me and I could tell that she wanted to talk.

'You're so clever,' she remarked. 'I saw you with the children . . . Where did you learn such things? Did you go to university?'

'Not really,' I replied. 'I just did well at school.'

'Were you a teacher then? I can tell you're educated. No one learns all that just at school.'

I shook my head. 'No, I wasn't a teacher. I'm just good at maths, that's all. I got it from my grandma.'

Malaika grinned at me. 'I *know* you're educated. Why does an educated person like you have to run away?'

'Ah, sometimes you just have to get away because trouble follows you ...'

Malaika gripped my hand excitedly. 'Are you running from your family, is that it? Did they try to marry you to some horrible old man? Tell me!'

'No, it's not that. I just have to get out of Sudan, that's all.'

Malaika sat back, disappointed. I didn't blame her for her curiosity. I could tell that she wanted to be friends. She wanted to have some excitement in her life, which the story of a woman on the run was sure to deliver. But I wasn't about to confide in her. I'd told her husband as much as I was willing to. My greatest fear was that if I revealed the truth, then they would be so afraid that they would hand me in to the authorities. Abdul may have been a good man and brave, but I didn't know his wife well enough to judge.

For eight weeks I stayed in their house, rarely if ever leaving. I was fearful myself, and I felt safer remaining hidden. Abdul said the fewer people who knew that I was there, the better. I spent my time helping Malaika clean the house and looking after little Mayay, their five-year-old daughter. I could tell that Malaika liked having me around. I was friendly and useful and someone for her to talk to. But I hated it. I was bored and lonely and my life was in limbo. And every day I had to cope with my fear.

Every other day Malaika would go out to do the shopping. Alone in the house, my mind drifted to thoughts of my family, of my dead father and our desecrated village. I would think of my mother and sister, and try to imagine where they might be now and if they were safe, and of my brothers fighting with the rebels. Our family had been torn apart and scattered across Sudan. We no longer knew where each of us was, or even if we were still alive. How had it come to this, I wondered. How was it possible?

Malaika would return to find me in tears. She'd put her arms around me and beg me to tell her what was wrong. She'd beg me to open my heart and treat her like a true sister. But I couldn't. She and her husband had been good to me, but I couldn't tell her my story. I was worried that if I revealed my tale of war, torture, rape and being hunted by the police and the military, then they might desert me. I couldn't take that risk, and so I let Malaika remain convinced that I was running from a forced marriage.

Some two months after I had arrived in their house, Abdul brought home an Arab-looking man in his early thirties. This was the agent who would organise my escape. From the very first I instinctively disliked him. He told me that his services would cost eight million Sudanese pounds. I told him that I only had two million in cash, but I had some gold. His eyes lit up at the mention of gold. He would happily sell my gold for me, he said, and then we would see how much money I had.

I knew that he was only in this for the money. But what had I expected – another good man, like Abdul? I showed him what I had, the wealth of our family. It was Grandma's gold, my mother's gold, my sister's and my own. There was Grandma's big gold bracelet and her three rings with rubies in them. There was her beautiful *agadi* – a traditional Zaghawa chain made of ancient tribal gold. The agent stared at it in glee.

He needed it all, he said. *All of it.* And even then there still might not be enough. For a moment I resisted. So many memories, so much of my family, was bound up in its glittering beauty. But then I reflected on what it was worth to me here in Sudan, here where I was a dead woman walking. There was one big ring that had been Grandma's favourite. I said he could take the rest, but that I wanted to keep that one. But he told me that he needed it all. Eventually, I gave in. I even gave away the four beautiful gold bracelets that my father had brought me as my wedding present.

Every day after that I kept asking Abdul what had happened to the agent. What was to stop him running off with all my worldly wealth? If he did so, then I was finished. But Abdul told me not to worry. He knew where this man lived. He couldn't simply disappear. Abdul promised he wouldn't let me down. I had to stay calm and trust him.

One month later the agent reappeared. He announced that everything was ready for my escape. The next day he would come with a car to take me to the airport. I asked him where I was going. All he would tell me was that it was a safe place where there were good people who would help me. We would travel together, posing as man and wife. My role was to follow him and do exactly as he said. It was a condition of his work that at no stage was I to ask him any more questions. Like it or not, those were the rules.

I didn't even know his full name. I presumed he would tell me no more in case we were stopped. The less I knew, the less I could reveal to the authorities. Now that I was going I was happy and fearful, all at the same time. I kept asking myself where I was going and what would happen when I got there. And what if he just abandoned me halfway? But the time for worrying was over. It was in the hands of God now. If God willed it, I would make it through safely.

I couldn't sleep that night. No matter how much I prayed to God to calm my fears, my mind remained a whirl of troubled thoughts. Would I be caught? Or was this the end of my terrible journey, to leave like this? Would I ever return to my country? Would I ever see my family again? How would I see them, if I was far away in a foreign land?

The next morning Malaika gave me a little handbag in which I might carry my few possessions. All that I had was a spare *tope*, my travel cloak, a shawl and a toothbrush. I had nothing with me that spoke of home – not a rock or a branch nor even a grain of sand. All I had were my memories. Malaika wished me luck. She smiled. She would never forget me, she said, and maybe one day I would tell her my story. As for Abdul, he told me not to worry. It was going to be all right, he could feel it in his bones.

At three o'clock my agent turned up with a driver at the wheel of his car. We sat in the back and drove in silence through the city. I was worried, and I tried to sink down in my seat so as not to be seen from outside. But the agent just told me to sit up and act normally. Then I started worrying that he was taking me directly to the police himself. Why wouldn't he? If would be far easier than undertaking the journey that now lay ahead of us. I knew that I would only feel safe when I was finally sitting aboard that plane.

As we approached the airport my agent started to issue me with instructions again. 'Do as I tell you, never say a word or do anything without my permission. Behave like this and we will be all right.' But if I forgot what he had said and did something stupid, then I would be found out. Remember that we were supposed to be married. I should at all times be obedient and walk a few paces behind him, like a good Muslim wife.

The driver pulled up at the airport. He glanced in his mirror. 'When are you back?'

The agent shrugged. 'Not sure exactly. I have nothing to do when I get there apart from getting her sorted. So, if all goes well, tomorrow.'

'Shall I be here to collect you?'

'Yeah, at the usual time. Unless I call.'

There was a crowd milling around in the departure area. Gradually it thinned out, as people were checked in for their flights. The agent deliberately held back, and he only approached passport control when everyone else had gone. He reached over and shook the hand of the uniformed official before handing him two passports. I stood back, acting like his obedient wife. I saw the official glance at me, and then he smiled at my agent. It was a knowing smile. They chatted away for a minute or so, and then our passports were stamped and we were waved through.

'Goodbye and safe journey,' the official remarked to my agent. 'We'll see you again soon, eh?'

He smiled. 'You will. And thanks.'

We reached a second set of officials. This time, we had our bags searched before being allowed to pass. We walked through the airport and down some steps. We waited on the tarmac with the rest of the passengers for a bus to appear. A short drive across the tarmac, and we were delivered to the aeroplane. It sat on the runway, squat and gleaming bright.

A group of white people in smart blue uniforms were standing beside it. One of the white women gave the agent a smile of welcome as she ushered us onto the plane. I climbed up the steps, my heart in my mouth. With barely a backward glance I stepped inside the aeroplane. *I was safe. I was safe.* I was safely inside this machine that would fly me away to safety.

I was on my way out of Sudan, to a place where the hunters couldn't find me. God only knew which country I was headed for, but all that was ahead of me. What mattered now was that I was getting out of my country, a country that was eating up my homeland and my people. I leant back in my seat and felt a wave of exhaustion wash over me. I was so tired. So tired. So tired. I had never felt so tired . . .

As the aircraft clawed its way into the sky, I guess I should have been scared. I had never flown before and it should have been a terrifying experience. But after all that I had been through I didn't care any more. What could touch me? What could really hurt me or scare me? If we exploded in a fireball, what would I have lost? I had begged for death so many times, and death had failed to find me. What was there to fear if it did so now?

I'd only ever seen aircraft from the ground, and now here I was high above the earth and speeding through the sky. As we climbed higher I saw the clouds shooting past the window. I gazed out right into the middle of a bank of puffy whiteness. We were inside the clouds, and I wondered what was keeping us up here. For a moment I was lost in wonder at the magic of it all, as the soft hush of the sky rushed past the window.

I gazed around at the passengers. Might there be a clue there as to where I was going? Most were dressed in the traditional robes of the Gulf Arabs, so it looked as if I might be going to one of those countries. Which could it be? I tried to remember my geography lessons from school. Might it be Dubai, Saudi Arabia or one of the smaller Arab Emirates? One of the ladies in the smart blue uniforms came up to us. She had snowy white hair and a smile in her eyes.

'Madam? Tea? Coffee?' she asked. 'Or perhaps a soft drink?'

I shook my head. 'No, thank you.'

I was too excited and too worried to think about drink or food. And I had no money, as my agent had taken everything, and I presumed I would have to pay. My agent asked for a tea, and as the lady leant across me I caught its fragrance. It smelled simply delicious. I noticed that she asked for no money, so I changed my mind.

'D'you mind?' I asked. 'Could I actually have a tea?'

Two hours later we started our descent. The sun had set during the flight and I felt the aircraft falling through the darkening sky towards the earth. Where were we landing, I wondered. In which country was I to try to make my new home? And how would I ever survive there? We hit the runway with a gentle thud and taxied across to the airport building. I rose to my feet with the other passengers, only to feel a hand gripping my arm. It was my agent, and he was gesturing at me to sit down.

He shook his head. 'Not yet. There's a second flight. Wait on board the aircraft.'

For an hour we sat on the runway. My agent slept. More people boarded the aircraft. Most of them were Gulf Arabs, with a handful of white Europeans. A middle-aged white man took the seat next to me, with a friendly smile. I tapped him on the arm and asked how long the flight would take. It was six hours, he said. In six hours' time we would be in London.

So that was where I was going! I was going to London, in England, the country that I had learnt about during my school days.

I was going to the land of the *khawajat* – the white man.

25

The Hostel of Despair

I awoke in the early hours. One of the air stewardesses was handing me a plastic tray of breakfast things. The airline staff were so helpful and friendly. My agent had said that I was going to a country where people would help me, and I wondered whether everyone in England would be like this. I pulled off the tinfoil cover and inspected my breakfast. It wasn't *acidah* mash, that was for sure!

My agent prodded the food around on his plate. 'Pork!' he muttered. 'You're going to a place where they love eating pig. You've been warned.'

With that he pushed his tray away and stared out of the window. Getting me out of Sudan had seemed so easy, but I wondered how he was intending to spirit me into England. He had two passports, so one presumably bore the name of his supposed wife – me. I hadn't managed to get a close look at the passport, and the agent had warned me not to ask any questions. But he had taken a photo of me back in Khartoum – for the travel papers, he'd said – so maybe that passport actually bore my real photo.

I was worried again now. If my agent did get me into England, what was I to do then? All he had told me was that I should follow him and he would take me to a safe place. For a while I thought about my husband, Sharif, and whether I might be able to find him. As far as I knew he was still in England, but it was months since there had been any contact. I concluded that my first priority had to be to get into England – for that meant I was safely out of Sudan. Sharif, how I would live, my future – all of that could wait.

As the plane flew across the dawn skies, I gazed at what I presumed must be London. I could see lights twinkling below, but they were veiled by what looked like cloud low on the ground. We landed so smoothly I hardly felt a bump. How could the plane do that, I wondered, when it had just fallen out of the sky? I grabbed my handbag and got up to follow my agent out of the aircraft. We joined a crowd of people surging into the building, and followed a series of corridors that took us to a line of booths.

We stopped. There were two queues. One was for those carrying purple passports, the other for everyone else. Most of the people with the purple passports were *khawajat* – so I presumed this was the queue for the British. I was surprised when my agent joined that queue. I lined up with him and we inched forward until we were at the desk. The official reached out and took the two passports from my agent. He pushed them into some sort of machine, gazed at it for a few seconds, glanced at my agent and me, and then waved us through.

I couldn't believe it. How had my agent managed it? How had he got us into England using the British queue? We had no luggage to collect, so as quickly as he could my agent led me through the terminal and into the cold outside. A weak sun was trying to trickle though, but the terminal building was shrouded in the thick fog that I'd seen from the aeroplane. Beads of moisture covered everything: car windows, people's clothing, even their hair. And it was freezing cold.

I pulled my cloak from my bag and tugged it around my shoulders. Still I was cold. We joined a queue, and a black vehicle stopped in front of us. It had a yellow light on top, which illuminated the English word 'TAXI'. My English was pretty basic. It consisted of what I had learned at school, refreshed now and then by watching English TV programmes. I recognised 'taxi' from some of those. My agent spoke to the driver through his open window, and then motioned for me to get in.

'Right, my job's done,' he announced. 'This man will take you to the safe place. I've paid him, so he'll deliver you. I'm done. Goodbye.' And with that he turned and was gone.

The taxi pulled away from the airport. I tried to relax: at least it was warm in there. I glanced around me at the city. It looked right; it looked like the pictures of London that I had seen in my schoolbooks. But I didn't trust my agent one bit. The taxi driver was a white man and he had seemed friendly enough. I leaned forward and tapped the glass.

'Is this London?' I asked. 'Is this really London?'

He glanced at me in his mirror. 'It is, love. It's rainy, foggy old London Town. A real dump, innit?'

We drove for an age, on and on through this sprawling city. I couldn't believe that a city could be so large. There were so many houses and cars and people and the tower blocks did go high into the sky, just as our schoolbooks had shown us. Eventually, the taxi driver pulled over to the side of the road. He pointed at two men in dark uniforms.

'Police. Tell 'em you need asylum, love, okay? *Asylum.*'

'Aslum,' I tried saying the word. 'Aslum. What does it mean?'

'Don't worry about it, love. Just say it and that's enough. Now off you go. Chop-chop.'

I dodged across the busy road and approached the two policemen. But I was worried. My experiences with the police in Sudan had hardly been pleasant ones.

'Good morning. Aslum,' I said nervously. 'Do you know aslum?'

The nearest policeman smiled. 'New here are you, love? Here for the first time?

I nodded. 'I come from the airport.'

'You're seeking *asylum*, is it?'

'Yes. Asylum.'

'All right, follow me.'

He led me over to a grey concrete tower block. There were two queues of people outside, and he showed me to one of them. There were people of all differing nationalities, speaking many different languages. At school the English teacher had told us that in London you would find all the nationalities on earth. She hadn't been joking. It was early still, but already the queue was long. Many of the people had suitcases with them.

A black man smiled at me from his place in the queue. 'Somalia?'

I shook my head. 'Sudan.'

I scrabbled in my bag for my shawl. It was so cold that I had started to shiver. A white man was checking people in at the door of the building. He was middle-aged and he had a kindly face. He came across to me.

'Where from?' he asked. 'Sudan? Darfur?'

I nodded. 'Darfur.'

He smiled, sympathetically. 'Are you okay?'

I shook my head. 'Freezing.'

'I thought as much.' He took off his big black jacket and handed it to me. 'Here – try this for size. Go on – wrap yourself up. I'm used to the cold.'

I smiled shyly. 'Thank you. Very kind . . .'

'Come on, let's get you inside before you catch your death.'

He took me to the front of the queue, gave me a little ticket and showed me to a side room.

'Wait here,' he said. 'I'll find people to see you. Wait here, okay?'

I nodded again. I was feeling happier already. This man had been so kind to me. I curled up in the chair and tried to get warm. I started to feel sleepy. Two Indian-looking ladies came in and asked me if I was hungry. I was too shy and embarrassed to say yes, so I said that I was just tired. They told me to wait until the number on my ticket was called.

I dozed fitfully. But suddenly I was wide awake. There was

screaming coming from the main hall. I peeped out through the glass door. I spotted the Somali man who had greeted me in the queue with a policeman on either side of him. As I watched they started to drag him out of the building.

'No, my brothers! No!' the Somali man cried. 'Don't kill me! Don't take me away! Don't take me!' I was shocked and confused. I wondered what he had done to be dragged away like that.

Three hours later my number came up on the screen. I was shown to a window and sat down against the glass. Next to me was an Arabic-looking lady. She introduced herself, telling me that she was my interpreter. I should speak to the man behind the glass and answer all of his questions.

A young white man arrived on the other side. He had a very strange appearance. He was rather fat, and his hair was pushed up into jagged spikes. I had never seen anything like it before. Why did this man make himself look like *Shaitan* – like Satan – I wondered. Beneath his spiky hair he didn't seem to have a very friendly face, either.

'Answer only what I ask,' the spiky man announced. 'And tell the truth. If you tell us any lies, we'll punish you by putting you in prison. D'you understand?'

I nodded. 'Yes.' I was worried again now.

'What is your name?'

I told him.

'How did you come here?'

I told him about my two flights.

'What was the name of the airline?'

I told him that I didn't know.

'Of course you know the name of the airline,' he objected. 'What was it?'

'I was with an agent. He brought me. I've no idea . . .'

'Come on! You're trying to say you didn't see the name on the aeroplane? Or inside it?'

I nodded. 'Yes. I didn't see it.'

'I don't believe you! I don't believe you for one moment!'

I glanced at the Arabic interpreter lady in bewilderment. 'Why is he getting so angry? Why would I lie about something like that?'

'What's she saying?' he demanded, from behind the glass.

'She's just checking that she understands the question,' the Arabic lady lied. 'Look, he's getting upset, so try to remember. Is there anything you can remember about the inside of the aeroplane? Letters? Numbers? Pictures? Anything?'

I thought for a second. There had been some letters on the breakfast things, but it was the last thing on my mind.

I shook my head. 'I don't remember. I don't remember. I'm sorry.'

I saw the spiky man's face redden. He glanced at his watch. He was taking a tea break, he declared, and when he came back he wanted some answers. My interpreter told me that she had to go, as it was the end of her shift.

I sat and waited. A replacement interpreter arrived. She told me that she was called Alicia, and that she came from the Lebanon. The spiky man returned, and I was relieved to see that he had calmed down a little.

'So, let's cover some basics. Where exactly are you from?'

I told him the name of my village and the big towns that were near it. He was looking at a map. He asked me for the names of my schools, and I told him.

'Why have you come to the UK?' he asked.

'There is war in my area. I had a problem with the government. They wanted to kill me. My village was attacked and my family too. I had to flee the country.'

'Are you married?' he asked. 'Any children?'

'I am married. But we have no children yet.'

'Where is your marriage certificate?'

'I don't know. It may have been with my father, but he was killed.'

'Look, are you married or not?' The angry scowl was back again. 'There's no marriage without a certificate.'

'Yes, I am married.'

'Well, you can't prove you're married without a certificate. Where is your husband?'

'I think he's here in England. But I'm not sure.'

The spiky man stared at me in disbelief. 'Okay, so let's get this straight. You claim to be married, but there's no certificate. You claim to have a husband, but you don't know where he is. He might be in England or he might not. Is that it?'

'Yes. That's it.'

'Was it your husband who paid the agent to bring you here?'

'No. I sold the family gold to pay the agent. Even my grandma's rings.'

'Yeah. Right.' He rolled his eyes. 'So where is your husband? Which European country is he in?'

'I told you, I don't know. He's probably in England, but I don't know.'

'How can you not know which country your husband is in? It's impossible.'

I kept silent. I was trying to be helpful. I was telling the truth. What more did he want of me? He asked me for Sharif's full name, and for the date and place of his birth. Then he glanced at me.

'So, is he your *only* husband, or are there any more?'

'Why is he asking me such a question?' I demanded of the interpreter. 'Do women have many husbands here in England?'

She shrugged. 'Sorry. They're always like this.'

'Well, ask him from me how many wives he has. None, I bet. Who would want to marry such a horrible man?'

The interpreter tried not to laugh. 'What's she saying?' the spiky man demanded. 'What's she saying?'

'She's saying that she only has the one husband,' the interpreter lied. 'Just the one.'

The spiky man sent me off to the 'next stage'. I sat to have my fingerprints taken. Then I was photographed and given a card, which was my photo ID. I was returned to the same booth, and now there was a third interpreter. This time it was an old black man with pepper-grey hair. He was dressed smartly with a jacket and tie, and he had a warm, kindly expression. I could tell immediately that he was Sudanese.

As we waited for the spiky man to reappear he told me that he was from Kordofan, the area that I had walked through on my escape from Darfur. He even had a daughter studying at the same university that I had attended. The spiky man returned, but he seemed in a hurry now. I guessed he was keen to get home. He gave me the name of a place where I could stay for the night, and handed me a map.

'It's marked on the map. See? If you get lost ask. Someone will show you the way.'

I stared at the map in confusion. Of course, we didn't have maps back in the village, and I had no idea how to use one.

'But I don't know anywhere in this big city. How can I find my way?'

'I told you – just use the map and ask. Go on! Go and find your own way.'

'But if you came to my country and I told you to find your way across Khartoum, you'd be lost. It's the same here with me.'

The spiky man sighed. 'Look, it's late. We're about to close. You're no longer my responsibility. I told you – you need to get on your way.'

The interpreter placed a restraining hand on my arm. 'Don't worry. Wait for me outside. I'll help you.'

It was nine o'clock by the time we left. The old man led me on a short walk to another building.

323

'These people will organise somewhere for you to stay,' he told me, as he ushered me inside. 'I came here as an asylum seeker, so I know what it's like . . .'

I smiled at him. 'Thank you. You've been so kind.'

'Here,' he said, handing me a £10 note. 'Take it. It's not much, but I can't afford much. It's something, at least . . .'

That night I was sent to an asylum hostel in Croydon. I was put in a room with two other women – one from Eritrea and another from Burkina Faso. The Eritrean woman was heavily pregnant, and so she took the lower bunk and I took the one above. There was a horrible air of desperation about the asylum hostel. I could sense the pain, the dislocation and the burning frustration that was squeezed between its walls. I lay awake that night thinking of home, and about the love and warmth of my family, and I started to cry.

My first impressions of the asylum hostel were entirely correct: it was a place of real despair. I quickly learned the rules. Every morning we had to sign a book to show that we were there. Then we had to queue for a breakfast of tea and bread. Apart from our small room, there was a canteen that smelled of frying fat, and a reception area with two TV sets in it. There was little to do, and the only way to pass the time was to sleep.

If you failed to sign the register once, you were warned. Twice, and they would threaten to throw you out. At least that was the theory. In practice, it didn't work that way at all. There was an Iraqi writer in the hostel whose entire family had been murdered. He was still obsessed with writing, and every morning he'd get up early and go and sign the entire register. He'd even make beautiful copies of people's signatures. He had lost his mind, but he was harmless – and we didn't object to him signing the register!

My Eritrean roommate, Sarah, quickly took me under her wing. There was a war in her country, and women were being forced to fight. She had left behind four children and a husband when she had fled the country. I couldn't believe it when she told me that she had been living at the hostel for almost a year. The Home Office had lost her file, and so she had been forced to make a whole new asylum claim. She had been there for so long that she was an expert on the place, and all the new arrivals came to her for advice.

When I couldn't work the laundry machines Sarah showed me how to put my clothes in, and how to dry them afterwards. I had little desire to eat, so I skipped most meals and stayed in my room. But Sarah tried to persuade me to eat something. I didn't want to mix with the others much, because so many seemed to have lost themselves. Even after everything that I had been through, I still had my sense of self, my pride in my identity. But there were people there who would fight with each other for no reason, or break down in the corridors, rolling around and screaming.

Whatever horrors those people had suffered in their home countries, it had broken them. There was one Iraqi woman who had been forced to abandon her ten-year-old daughter. Every time she thought about it she would break down in fits of hysterics. She spent whole nights screaming and wailing, and her cries would echo down the corridors. It was so horrible. Lying there unable to sleep and hearing her screams was enough to drive anyone mad. I knew that she had suffered, I could see it in her eyes. But so had we all.

Every day it seemed that the hostel staff would have to call the police to restrain someone, or take them away. Everyone had their problems, and no one was alone in their suffering. I knew that these people had been through hell, but I didn't want to be like them. I didn't want to end up like that, to be one of them. Having survived the hell of Darfur, and my flight from those who hunted me, I didn't want this to be the place that finished me.

But I wasn't coping so well. With no exercise and little food I became ill. Yet my sickness was as much in my head and my heart as it was in my body. I was depressed. I was deeply depressed and lonely as I had never been before. My family were either dead or scattered far and wide. My village was gone. My tribe was being wiped off the face of the earth. What was there left to live for?

I stayed in the hostel for four months, yet it felt like a lifetime. I kept wondering why I had come. For this? For this terrible limbo, this madhouse, this nothingness? Perhaps I should have taken my chances in Sudan. Here I was alive. I had saved my life. But other than that, what did I have to live for? I knew that I had to get out of this place. I just had to.

Sarah alerted the hostel staff to my ill health and they sent me to see a local GP. He was a middle-aged Englishman, and he listened to me with real sympathy. As a fellow doctor I felt I could trust him, and because of his age he was something of a father figure. I told him everything. I told him about my frustration and my darkness. I was a medical doctor, just like him. I wanted to do something, to contribute, to feel that I had a reason for living. I didn't want to sit round doing nothing in that hostel of despair.

The GP was very understanding, but there was only so much he could do. He gave me some anti-depressants and sent me to hospital. After all that I had been through he wanted me to have a full medical check-up, and he wanted me to eat properly and get well. It turned out that I had a raging ear infection, from where the soldiers in Mazkhabad had beaten me around the head. And there were other things wrong with me too.

I stayed in that hospital for three weeks, and I grew strong again. But eventually they had no excuse to keep me any longer, and I had to return to the asylum hostel. I hated being back there. Sarah, my Eritrean friend, told me that if I really wanted to get out of that place I would need a solicitor. I asked why. I had done nothing wrong. Why did I need a lawyer? My lawyer would argue my case with the Home Office, Sarah explained, which should move things along more quickly.

Sarah took me to visit a firm of solicitors. I was allocated a lawyer, a middle-aged Englishwoman. I had to relate my whole story all over again, so that she could produce a witness statement. She would use this to argue my case with the Home Office, she explained. When we'd finished she looked over my interview notes.

She glanced at me and smiled. 'I've rarely seen such a strong case. You're from Darfur, and after all that's happened it's a miracle you're alive. You should be granted immediate asylum.'

My mood brightened. Maybe things were about to change.

Two weeks later, Sarah gave birth to a beautiful baby girl. She called her Tashana. As Sarah was now a mother with a newborn baby, she was allocated a room of her own. A friend of hers discovered an old TV set dumped on the street, and she brought it back to the hostel. We installed it in Sarah's room and got it working. Now we had a little oasis of calm where we could gather together in private, watch the TV and chat.

For a few weeks it made life that tiny bit more bearable. But it couldn't last.

26

In London, in Love

Two weeks later Sarah's name came up for resettlement. Each morning people would check the hostel notice board, to see if there were any new announcements concerning accommodation. A flat or a room could be allocated to you at any location across the country, and at least it meant getting out of the hostel of despair. I was overjoyed for Sarah and her little baby girl. But at the same time I was saddened, for it meant losing my best friend and mentor -- not to mention the room we had made our sanctuary.

Just as soon as Sarah heard the news she burst into tears. A string of people came to congratulate her, the hostel staff included. Sarah had been there so long that everyone knew and loved her. But once Sarah and little Tashana were gone, my spirits sank again. I went to see my kindly GP, and he arranged for me to see the Medical Foundation for the care of the Victims of Torture. He was confident that they would be able to help me.

On the way back from the GP's office I stopped in a little park. It was a sunny day, the park was beautiful, and it was free. I lay on the grass and stared at the sky, dreaming of home. I must have fallen asleep. When I awoke there were a man and a women quite close by. They were sitting on the grass with their arms wrapped around each other, and they were kissing and kissing and fumbling with each other's clothing.

At first I couldn't even look at them, but then I couldn't stop myself from staring. Why didn't they do this in the privacy of their own home, I wondered. Didn't they have any shame? What sort of country was this, where people did such things in public? There were many strange habits and traditions here that I just didn't understand.

—— ——

The lady who saw me at the Medical Foundation was very kind and gentle with me. I had to tell her my story in the finest detail. She asked to see my scarring, and I showed her where the soldiers had cut me and burned me. She was so visibly moved that I didn't mind doing so. She told me that she would be my caseworker, and that I should start coming to see her every other week. We would talk through my problems and she would try to help me.

She assured me that I could tell her anything I wanted to. On a practical level, she would talk to my GP about the anti-depressants I was taking. She would also look into college courses for me – to get me out and about once more. I needed to meet people and to start using my mind again. I needed to rebuild my self-confidence and I needed to discover a reason for living. She was right, of course, and I knew it. If only it was that easy.

I started a course in English at a college local to the hostel. I had my bi-weekly visit to the Medical Foundation. And occasionally I would go to see my solicitor. Each time I went out London struck me as being such a strange place. No one ever said 'hello'. People didn't even seem to speak with their neighbours. They just went around with a face like a closed mask. There was none of the spontaneous warmth that I was used to in my village.

Whenever I lost my way, which was often, I would try to find an old person from whom to ask directions. At least they generally had time for you. Younger people just seemed to be forever in a hurry – running, running, running. More often than not the old people seemed to want to stop and talk for as long as the words lasted. I realised that many of them were lonely – lonelier even than I was. I had no family here, but at least I had others in the asylum hostel to talk to.

One day I found an old lady sitting on a park bench. She and I got chatting and she told me her story. She lived alone in a big house. She had four children, but they were grown up and gone away. Now and again they would phone, but she only ever saw them at Christmas and birthdays. I told her that in our culture you would never leave your parents to live out their old age in isolation. Your mother had carried you for nine months, and nourished you as a child. Your father had protected you. You had to cherish and respect them when they were old. By the time I had finished speaking the old lady had tears in her eyes.

I had been at the hostel for four months when my name finally came up for resettlement. I was being sent to Newcastle, a city that I was told was in the north of England. I was sent from the hostel of despair to a dispersal hostel, in Crystal Palace. But on the day of my scheduled departure I was too ill to be moved. I had developed an infection in my stomach. I still wasn't eating properly, and now I was vomiting up everything.

I stayed in that dispersal hostel for two weeks. During the weekdays it was deserted, as everyone had been bussed off to their various destinations. At the weekends it was full to bursting with the next batch for dispersal. The only other person staying there was another girl who was, like me, too ill to travel. Together we nicknamed that place 'the ghost hostel'.

At the end of my second week another batch arrived. Among them was a man I recognised as being Zaghawa. We got talking, and his story was a heartbreaking one. At every opportunity I had sought news of Sharif, but as yet there had been nothing. I asked this man if he had heard of a Zaghawa man whose doctor wife was looking for him. He hadn't heard anything, he said, but he did offer to call the Zaghawa community support group, which was based in Coventry. Perhaps they might know something.

I gave him my full name and that of Sharif, and he made the call. He spoke for a few moments, and then his face broke into a wide smile. He nodded and smiled again, and grabbed a piece of paper to scribble something down. It was the number of Sharif's mobile phone. The Coventry group knew all about Sharif and me. They just hadn't been able to find out where I was, or how to put the two of us in touch.

With a shaking hand and a trembling heart I called Sharif's number. I heard a voice answer. 'Hello. Hello.'

'Sharif? Sharif? Is that you? It's me, Halima. It's your . . . wife calling.'

I felt so strange using that word – 'wife'. I didn't feel I was married really. I knew that I *was* – it was just that there had been no sign of it in my life to date.

'Wow! Halima! Welcome. Welcome. When did you come? How did you find me? I'm so happy – I've been looking everywhere for you.'

'I'm happy to hear your voice,' I told him shyly. 'Where are you?'

'I'm in a place called Southampton.' He laughed. 'It doesn't matter where it is. You'll see it soon enough. Where are you? I want to come and see you!'

Sharif told me he would travel up to London the following morning. We would meet at the asylum hostel, and then go out for the day. It was late September, and if we were lucky we might even get a sunny day.

The following morning I stood nervously at the hostel entrance, waiting to meet my husband. There was a crisp blue sky above, so I felt as if my prayers for a fine day had been answered. But I was worried, so worried. Would he know, I wondered? Would

Sharif know? Would he see right through me and see the scars of the rape? Would he sense my fear, my shame and my guilt?

I caught sight of a figure walking towards the hostel. I knew instantly that it was him. I recognised my childhood cousin, but he had changed so much from the adolescent village farm boy. Here was a tall, dark, dashingly handsome man, dressed in a smart sheepskin coat, with dark trousers and shoes. We smiled shyly and greeted each other.

He whisked me off on a red London bus to Shepherd's Bush market. It was a meeting place for Sudanese of all ethnicities, he told me, and we could eat real Sudanese food there. On the journey we caught up on news from home. I asked Sharif if he had heard from my family, but he shook his head. He had heard nothing. He told me not to worry, though: by now they were certain to be safely in refugee camps in Tchad.

Shepherd's Bush market is a sprawl of stalls and little shops clustered among the archways of a raised railway line. It was crowded and chaotic, and it reminded me immediately of markets back at home. We stopped at one stall and Sharif brought me a pay-as-you-go mobile phone, so we could stay in touch. Then we found a stall selling *foul* – the bean stew mixed with fresh tomato and sesame oil that I used to love eating.

We wandered around the market-place, eating our *foul*. I couldn't believe that I was here at last by my husband's side. Sharif had a quiet way of speaking, and most of the time a shy half-smile played across his handsome features. He was studying hard to complete his degree, he told me. His time at university in Khartoum had ended abruptly, when he was forced to flee the country. He worked nights as a security guard, and he shared a small flat in Southampton with three Zaghawa friends. It was crowded, but it was home.

'Why don't you come and live with me?' Sharif suggested. 'Southampton is a nice place. We'd have to share with my friends, but we're all Zaghawa and we'd make it work.'

'But where would we sleep?' I asked. It was a lovely idea, but was it practical?

'Don't worry. I've spoken with my friends about it. They'd give us the bedroom, and they'd sleep in the living room. Like I said, we'd make it work.'

I couldn't get out of that asylum hostel quickly enough. A week after Sharif's visit I moved into his home. The one-bedroomed flat was tiny, but I didn't care. At least I had escaped from the hostel of despair.

Sharif seemed to know every Zaghawa person in Southampton, and we had a stream of visitors. In their eyes I was new to England, new to their community, and I was Sharif's new bride. I was treated as if I was just married. I had so many lovely wedding gifts: a new dress, beautiful jewellery, some things for the kitchen.

I was happy to be living among Zaghawa people again. It wasn't a trial with so many of us being there: it was like a tiny version of the village. Some worked nights and some days, so we developed a system of hot-bedding. But we always tried to eat at least one daily meal together, as a 'family'. Food was communal, and at meal times people pooled whatever they had. Between Sharif and his friends, even clothing seemed to be shared. It was as if we had brought the traditions of the village into our English home.

But my greatest relief was to be out of *the system*. There were no threats here, no rules and no regulations. I still had to travel to London to see my solicitor and the Medical Foundation, but at least now I was independent and free. My health and my mood improved no end, and as it did so I gradually plucked up courage to tell Sharif something of what had happened to me. I couldn't bear to think that my happy new life was based upon a lie. Sharif was my husband and he had to know.

I told him about my arrest by the security men in Hashma; about the rape of the schoolgirls in Mazkhabad village; and little by little I revealed the rest of the dark horrors that had befallen me. Sharif listened quietly, and with pain in his eyes. Eventually, there was nothing left to tell. I could see that he was angry, but none of his anger was directed towards me. He was burning up inside at those who had done these things to me. His immediate reaction was that he wanted to go and fight and kill them all.

Sharif told me that he had seen so much suffering in Sudan, especially during his visits to the south of the country. He had realised then that men are capable of doing the most inhuman things imaginable to women, and even to little children. Just like so many others in Sudan, I was a victim of a monstrous crime. I bore no blame and no shame fell upon my shoulders, Sharif reassured me. Those who had done such things were worse than animals. His only desire was for vengeance.

As I had confessed my secrets to Sharif, so now it seemed that it was his turn to confess his 'failings' and his 'insecurities' to me. He told me that the flat we were living in was on short-term rental only, and we could be thrown out at any time. Worse, his claim for asylum in the UK had run into the sand, and he'd lost track of his exact status. His Zaghawa pride prevented him from throwing himself on the mercy of the benefits system – so he was trying to work to pay his way and study hard to finish his degree, all at the same time.

Sharif was determined to work and hold his head up high, but there were many asylum seekers who were just abusing the system. The Somalis were the worst: they seemed to know every trick in the book. They would get allocated a flat, then rent it out and live with their relatives. They would cheat the system, bringing their entire family to London with false tales of abuse in their home country. They just didn't seem to care.

It was going to be tough making a life for ourselves here in Britain, Sharif said, but he promised me we would make it work. In fact, we were going to have to. It was all the more vital that we did – because by now I knew that I was going to have a baby.

Of course, physical intimacy had been difficult at first. After the horrors I had suffered at the hands of the Croucher, the Screamer and the Driver, I didn't know if I could ever trust another man. But with Sharif I was so lucky and so blessed. Somehow he managed to combine the strength and bearing of a Zaghawa warrior with softness, and a gentle hand. And because he himself had suffered, and seen much of the suffering, he was able to give me his patience and his understanding.

Over time, I grew comfortable with him, and I grew accepting of our intimacy.

It was early January by the time my bump was really starting to show. Sharif and I were so happy. In our culture, a marriage means nothing without children. Exiled many thousands of miles from home, Sharif and I were the only family we had. But soon there would be a third member of our 'clan', all being well.

At the end of January two women came to visit the Zaghawa community in Southampton. They were from an organisation called the Aegis Trust, and they were gathering evidence of war crimes in Darfur. They were especially keen to talk to women. A Zaghawa friend came to our flat and introduced the two women. Was I willing to tell them my story, he asked. No names would be used. Six Zaghawa men had already spoken, but no women. There were precious few Zaghawa women in the exile community, in any case.

But was I willing to be the one to break the silence?

27

Breaking the Silence

At first I was reluctant. Sharif and I had agreed that the horrors that had happened to me were our own secret. I called Sharif and asked him what he thought. He told me that if it was in private, and if I wanted to, then I should go ahead. I asked the women what the information would be used for. They told me it would be given to powerful governments to expose the terrible abuses in Darfur. And the women's voice was a vital one.

For a moment I thought about my father. I knew what he would have wanted me to do. He would want me to be like my namesake, Dolly Rathebe, and to speak out. I told the women my story, but leaving out some of the worst private horrors. They didn't pry. I told them about the attacks, what I had seen and how I had escaped. Once I'd started talking, I began to feel better about it. It was good to be doing this, knowing that my words might have an effect. Perhaps it gave some meaning to all that I had suffered.

After speaking with these women life quickly went back to normal. I had lots to deal with, of course, like preparing for the birth of my baby. I was convinced that I was going to have a little girl. I went shopping and brought girly clothes in girly colours, all flowery and pink. But as the pregnancy progressed I started to feel horribly weak and tired.

I was hospitalised, and after various tests I was diagnosed with chronic anaemia. I had bleeding in the womb, which was very serious. I was pregnant and I was constantly losing blood. I was sent to London to see a specialist, but still they couldn't work out exactly what was wrong. I had to keep going back and forth to see that specialist, but deep inside I still felt as if it was going to be all right. And then the bombshell hit.

It was early May and I was seven months pregnant. I was still weak and the bleeding hadn't stopped, but at least I still had my baby. I had a call from my lawyer. She didn't quite know how to break the news to me, but my case for asylum had been refused. She couldn't even begin to explain why, but I would have to go to London to prepare an immediate appeal. We had five days in which to do so. If we failed to lodge the appeal, then they would deport me. They would send me back to Sudan.

I have no words to express how I felt upon hearing this news. I was in such physical discomfort that I knew I wouldn't be able to manage the bus journey to London. My pregnancy had made me hypersensitive to smells, and I couldn't bear the thought of being cooped up on a stuffy, airless bus for hours on end. So Sharif forked out the expense of a train ticket for me – which we could ill afford – and I set off for London.

I sat on the train and stared out at the pretty English country-side. Spring flowers were pushing through the grass, trees were in bud, but there was winter in my heart. Almost a year had passed since I had lodged my asylum claim. What had that year been for? *For this?* To be told that my story was untrue and be sent back to Sudan? My village had been destroyed, my father killed, and my family were scattered to God only knew where. My people were being hunted down like animals, as I had fled from those who hunted me.

Yet I was to be sent back to Sudan?

I wondered what that spiky-haired man had written about me on the day that I arrived in London. What could he possibly have said that might warrant such a decision?

Upon arrival at my lawyer's, my refusal letter was read out to me. As far as I could understand, the main argument seemed to be that it was safe to return me to Khartoum. There was no fighting in Khartoum, so why would I be in any danger there? How could they say such things? Had they even read my file? This was madness – blind, stupid lunacy.

I was allocated a new lawyer who dealt specifically with asylum appeals. He was a kindly young Englishman called Albert Harwood, and we met in a cramped office that was piled high with files. We had to prepare a whole new witness statement for my appeal. I had to repeat my story, only this time adding in the new developments: finding my husband, my pregnancy, talking to the Aegis Trust people. Albert wrote down everything, and my trust grew in him as we worked. He really seemed to care. He told me not to worry. Once the appeal was lodged I would be safe – it would then be illegal to deport me to Sudan.

After I had finished talking to Albert I went to see my GP. He examined me, and told me that I was going back into hospital right away. I was so weak that he doubted I would be allowed out again before the birth. There was certainly no way that I could return to Southampton. And he was going to try to get me housed as an emergency case, in London.

Sure enough, I was told that I would have to stay in hospital. I was around thirty-seven weeks by now, and soon I could be induced. I spent a few days there, bored and fed up and alone. I wanted to give birth in Southampton, so that Sharif and my friends could be there. I told my consultant that I wanted to go home. She begged me to stay. One more week of eating well and building up my strength and then she would induce me, she promised. I agreed to stay.

On the day of the inducement Sharif travelled up to London. But the birth was difficult from the very start. I started bleeding heavily, and my Australian midwife pressed the emergency button. A team of doctors came running. They used ultrasound to check, and it seemed that the placenta was stuck to the baby. I would have to give birth by caesarean. Sharif donned a medical gown so he could be with me in the operating theatre. But all of a sudden the baby just started to come, and the room went into total panic.

My baby was born naturally, but by that time I knew nothing of it. I came to some time later in a dark and shadowy place. I was surrounded by lights that peeped and flashed with every beat of my heart. I was cold, so cold. I felt as if I might be dead. I saw a white face appear above me, floating among a sea of muted lights. It was one of the nurses.

I was in the Intensive Care Unit, she explained. My body was bound in bandages, and I had drips going into either arm.

'How are you feeling?' she asked.

I tried to smile. 'I'm okay . . . Where is my baby?'

The nurse gestured with her eyes to my bedside. I glanced across. Next to me was a see-through plastic trolley, and inside it was a little bundled heap of life. I saw tiny hands and feet poking out of the bundle. A fuzz of jet black curls. Eyes closed tight. *My baby.*

'Can I hold her?' I asked.

The nurse shook her head. 'You're too weak. Maybe tomorrow. Anyway, it's not a "her". It's a "him". You have a lovely baby boy.'

She pushed the cot closer. I gazed in rapture at his tiny scrunched-up face. His eyes opened just a fraction, as he blinked in the dim light. For just a moment his gaze met mine and I swear that he smiled. My little baby boy had smiled at me.

'Is he safe?' I whispered. 'They're not going to steal him? I can't watch over him and protect him . . .'

The nurse smiled. 'Don't worry. Look, I'll put a little alarm on him so that if anyone picks him up you'll know, okay?'

The nurse reached into the cot and fastened something around his tiny ankle. I guessed he was safe enough now. I started to sing to him – gently, quietly, a lullaby whispered under my breath, a song that my father and mother had sung to me when I was just a child . . .

⌒ ⌒

It was many days before my baby and I were allowed to go home. Sharif and his friends collected us and drove us back to Southampton. It was high time that we held the naming ceremony. Of course, as he was our first-born son he had to be called Mohammed. I had no boy's clothes for him, so that first day Sharif and I dressed him up like a baby girl.

All of our visitors exclaimed: 'Oh, what a beautiful girl!'

So I told them that 'she' was called Mohammed, and that put them straight! After the naming Sharif and our roommates vacated the flat and went to stay with friends. I was left with a gaggle of Zaghawa women. They cooked for me and washed baby Mohammed and clothed him, while I rested and regained my strength. Every day Sharif would come to visit. This went on for the full forty days, by which time I was pretty much recovered.

For a while Sharif, Mo and I lived the life of a happy family. But at the same time we knew that there was a shadow hanging over us. During this time we were given a little flat to live in, in London. Our new home consisted of a tiny apartment in a Victorian house that had been divided into a dozen similar-sized flats. We had one room with a fold-out bed, and a walk-in kitchen and shower off to one side. It was hopelessly cramped, yet it was *our home*.

Finally my asylum appeal was heard, and I received a letter from the Home Office with the result. I couldn't bear to open it myself, and so I took it to my lawyer. I would need him to read it in any case, because I couldn't understand the complex legal jargon they used. I handed Albert the letter and he opened it with a smile. He knew it was going to be good news. He started to read it out aloud, but as he did so the smile froze on his lips.

He couldn't believe it. He was dumbfounded. My appeal had been turned down. In essence the letter stated that the Zaghawa were not affected by the war in Darfur. It was safe to return me to Khartoum. And while I had spoken out to the Aegis Trust, there was free speech in Sudan so that would not cause me any undue problems. The letter concluded by stating that both Sharif and I had been refused asylum in Great Britain. Once again, we were scheduled for immediate deportation to Sudan.

By the time he had finished reading the letter Albert was stunned. He had a look of total disbelief on his face. As for me, I just felt drained. What was the point in continuing, I wondered. Why go on?

It was Albert's anger that galvanised me into action. We would appeal once more, he said. We would appeal to the highest court in the land. We would go to the House of Lords if necessary, but we were not going to give up.

Albert went about preparing a second appeal, and baby Mo, Sharif and I returned to our little London flat. I was miserable and downhearted. I was also scared. All I wanted was to stay here in peace and safety. I wanted my dignity back, and I wanted to contribute to this society. I was a trained medical doctor, and I knew this country needed doctors. But instead the Home Office forced us to live on handouts, while arguing that my story was a pack of lies.

Each week I had to go to a Reporting Centre to sign for the family, and to be fingerprinted. The Centre was like a prison. There was a row of cells off to one side. It was here that asylum seekers were grabbed by the guards and thrown into the cells, from where they were taken to the airports and flown back to the countries from which they had fled. Being there was so dispiriting, and each time I was terrified that the same was going to happen to little Mo and me.

I was approached by the Aegis Trust for a second time. My first testimony had been very powerful, they told me. Now they were organising a Global Day for Darfur – a worldwide campaign of publicity. No one knew exactly how many had been killed in Darfur, but there were reports citing hundreds of thousands. It was a mind-numbing figure. Whenever I thought about it, I imagined the whole of my homeland bathed in blood and burning in flames. Millions and millions had fled into refugee camps in Tchad, but even these were places of dark suffering. God only knew where my family might be.

The Aegis people asked me if I was prepared to speak out publicly, to the media. I said that I would think about it. I was worried. I had spoken to the press once before, in Sudan, and look where that had got me. Might it get me into trouble again if I did so here in England? I met their press person, David Brown, in a café in London. He told me that the Global Day would focus on violence against women. That was why it was so crucial that I spoke out. The world had to know the truth. He had an interview lined up with the BBC.

I thought about what he had said. I was angry myself now. I was angry that the nightmare in Darfur was ongoing, and I was angry with the British government. Three times they had refused to believe my story – once in person at the Home Office, and twice since then in writing. They were intent on sending me, Sharif and little Mo back to Sudan, and they were doing so in cold, blind ignorance. David was right. The world did need to know.

I understood the power of the BBC. I knew its reach. I remembered my father tuning his little radio into the BBC World Service. I didn't even need to ask myself what he would have wanted me to do in the circumstances. It was obvious. I told David that I would speak to the BBC. In fact, I would speak to any press and any media that would hear me. I didn't give a damn what anyone thought and I didn't give a damn about the shame.

But there was one thing that I wanted to be reassured of. 'If I speak to the press can I be punished? Can they hurt me? Is it safe? I have little Mo to think of . . .'

David smiled. 'This isn't Sudan . . . There's a free press here. No one can do anything to you. You're free to say whatever you want.'

———

The BBC went ahead and filmed an interview with me for *Newsnight,* their flagship news programme. At around the same time I spoke to a journalist from the *Sunday Telegraph* and the *Independent* newspapers. The *Sunday Telegraph* ran a story with this headline: 'Tony Blair admits Darfur is a tragedy. So why is he sending this gang-rape victim back to her attackers?'

Following publication and broadcast of those first stories a tidal wave of publicity just seemed to engulf me. Channel 4 News carried a long report on the abuse of women as a weapon of war. An Arabic news channel put me into one of their live news studios. Al Arabia TV had to run a feature on my story. American TV stations picked up on it, and soon there was a steady stream of journalists and camera crews shuttling in and out of our tiny little flat.

This is what I told the media was happening in Darfur:

Innocent people are dying. There are people with nothing to eat and drink. People living with no homes, on the streets, in the bush. They are lost in the desert, dying of hunger and thirst, dying from war. Why? What have they done? Nothing. People should think about our common humanity. If the same happened to you, would you accept it? If this happened to your family, would you accept it?

Where is the Muslim world? Where is the Arab world? Where are the people of the whole world? How can Muslims kill other Muslims for no reasons? This is something that God forbade. God said, 'Do not take a life without justification and right.' But this is happening with no right, no justification, people killing innocents for no reason.

Darfur is not separate from the world; Sudan is not isolated from the world; but people are standing and watching this happen, those who have it in their power to stop such things. People shouldn't look at this in a political way, because the victims are innocent people. They are dying through no fault of their own. What did they do? They did nothing to deserve this.

I feel like I am one of the survivors, one of those who escaped, and possibly God chose me to send out a message to the rest of the world, to alert the entire world that there are innocent people dying, so that the world might protect them and extend assistance to them.

My face became the face of suffering in Darfur, as newspapers across the world carried full-page advertisements bearing my photograph, and decrying the rape of women in my homeland. It reached the stage where I didn't know any more who or where each journalist was coming from.

Eventually, I could take no more. I told David I would have to call a halt. I was exhausted. And we needed some private space in which to be a family once more. David told me that he understood. In any case, what I had done was more than enough. I had truly broken the silence.

There also had been some problems with the neighbours. There were two Iraqi sisters in a flat at the top of our communal stairway.

They had started accosting the journalists, complaining that they had only one room for the two of them.

'Look! Look! Come! Come!' they would scream. 'Mr BBC, look what your British government gives us – what place is this to live? It is hell! Not even fit for dogs . . .'

'You have a room,' I'd tell them, once the journalists had gone. 'It is somewhere to live. Have some respect. Stop complaining.'

But those Iraqi women never did cease their complaining. They complained to anyone who would listen. Eventually, they were moved to better accommodation. That was how the system seemed to work. If you complained and worked the system, it responded. If you were quiet and respectful, as we were, it was a dead end.

There was a shocking example of this in our building. Across the way from us was a pretty blonde Albanian lady called Zamirah. She had a little baby girl, and she and I used to take Mo and her daughter to a local playgroup. The teachers and the mothers were all very good to us, and it was a lovely place. There were different races and religions at the playgroup, and we all got along just fine. I really loved it there, and so did Mo.

Zamirah was quiet and decent and she never complained about anything. And in contrast to the Iraqi sisters, she never once tried to belittle us because we were black Africans. The sisters were forever trying to do so. But one day Zamirah came back from the Reporting Centre looking as white as a sheet. A car pulled up outside, and she began rushing in and out of the flat, bundling all her worldly possessions into it. I met her at the entrance, and suddenly she was stuffing her daughter's toys into my arms. She looked absolutely finished, and I could see a dark panic in her normally sunny eyes.

'For Mo!' she told me, breathlessly. 'Take them!'

'But what . . .?'

Before I could ask her any more she jumped into the car and was gone, her little girl strapped in behind her. That was the last

I ever saw of them. It was from another of our neighbours, a British woman called Frances, that I heard what had happened. The people at the Reporting Centre had seized Zamirah, so they could deport her. But she had been released so she could fetch her little girl, who she'd left in the care of a friend.

The next time I went to the playgroup the mothers asked after Zamirah and her daughter. I didn't know what to say. We were the only asylum seekers there, and what was I to tell them? That their government had tried to send Zamirah back to the country from which she had fled; that she was terrified; that she had gone into hiding instead? So I just told them that I didn't know what had happened to my friend and her little girl.

The lady who ran the playgroup was a beautiful black woman, called Samantha. She had gorgeous hair that fell to her waist. She befriended me, and she started to visit me at home. Eventually I told her my story, and she listened in floods of tears. She told me that she felt so sorry for me. Why didn't I do some voluntary work, she asked. It would get me out and I would meet people. I told her that I needed to be here to look after my son. I found it so hard to trust people, and I wouldn't let anyone else care for Mo.

Little Mo was so precious to me. Little Mo was my life. It was he who had given me the will to live.

There was one last thing that David urged me to consider doing – as much for myself, as for the cause. James Smith, his boss at the Holocaust Centre, which is home to the Aegis Trust, is himself a fellow medical doctor. He had suggested that I might visit and speak to an audience of doctors and other health professionals about my experiences in Darfur.

I had never spoken publicly before, so I was nervous to do so now – especially if it would mean me talking about the dark horrors that had engulfed me. But I was curious to learn more about the Centre, and the murder of so many innocent millions during the Second World War.

The Nottingham-based Holocaust Centre is Britain's first Holocaust memorial and education centre. I was encouraged by the fact that survivors from the Bosnian and Rwandan genocides had spoken there before me. And because it was fellow doctors that I would be talking to, I felt that they would really identify with my suffering.

One June morning I travelled up there by train. The Holocaust Centre is set within two acres of lovely gardens. After the beauty and tranquillity of those gardens, I was shocked to see the images of the Holocaust that line the walls of the centre's exhibition rooms.

As I gazed at the photos of unspeakable horror and mass murder from the time of the Second World War, I found myself back in the hell that is Darfur. The darkness from which I had fled engulfed me again. I was back inside the suffering of my own people, and my own personal tragedy. I felt the tears start to flow, and I could not stop them.

Yet at the same time I felt a strange kind of contentment and happiness. *Yes*, I told myself, *here at last was a group of people who were investigating and challenging genocide, so that nobody could ever forget the dying of the innocents in my homeland, in Darfur.*

The lecture room was quiet, the audience bathed in darkness. As I stood up to talk to them, I was horribly nervous and I feared that the words would fail to come. But an instant later my voice started speaking, and I began telling the story of my happy childhood growing up in Darfur.

I wanted to convey the ordinariness of it all, the sense in which my own childhood was perhaps so similar to those in the audience. I wanted to communicate the love and laughter of my close-knit family and village tribe, so as to better demonstrate what had been crushed and desecrated when the nightmare descended on Darfur.

I spoke quietly, and with growing confidence, as the words

started to flow. But once I began to relate the horrors that I had witnessed, and those that had befallen me personally, I felt my voice tremble, as if it were going to break. But I strove to hold back the flood of emotion that was threatening to overwhelm me, so that I could go on.

When I finished speaking, silence like an ocean filled that lecture chamber. And then my fellow doctors rose to their feet and applauded me. I knew from the questions that followed that I had touched them deeply. That such things could happen to a fellow doctor – and simply as a result of trying to help the sick and injured in my home country – shocked them to their core.

28

Will to Live

Little Mo was approaching his first birthday, and still we had no news on my asylum claim. I had inquired about working as a doctor or even a nurse, but I'd been told that asylum seekers weren't allowed to work. Sharif and I had tried to look for a bigger flat, but we soon realised that if no one would let me work then we couldn't afford the rent. We were dying to get away, and we couldn't believe how some of the people lived.

In Zaghawa culture we have a saying: 'Your nearest neighbour is better than your far relative.' It means that in your daily lives your neighbours might be more important to you than even your family. But it certainly didn't seem to hold true here. Many of our neighbours were from hell.

The woman next door had nine children, most with different fathers. The whole family seemed to live on benefits. Teenage kids were in and out at all hours, playing loud music, arguing and fighting. One day I came home to find the street cordoned off by the police. It turned out that her children had kidnapped a young boy from the park, and they were holding him hostage inside the house. Theirs was truly a madhouse, and I didn't want to live near such people.

Then there was our neighbour, Frances. If anything, her situation was even more unbelievable. Shortly after we'd moved in I found her slumped on her doormat. I stopped to help, half-carrying her inside. As I did so I could smell the alcohol on her. She must have remembered my help, for she began calling on us.

She was lonely and she wanted someone to talk to, and in our culture we could not refuse hospitality to visitors.

We invited her in and cooked her meals. She unburdened herself of her life story, and I was shocked beyond words. She had a little two-year-old daughter, and it turned out that the girl's father was her son's best friend. Four years back she had been married, with two children and a good job. Then she had fallen in love with her twenty-year-old son's best friend. She started having an affair with him, fell pregnant, and was thrown out and divorced by her husband. He had got custody of the two children, and she had ended up unemployed and homeless. She'd started drinking and been housed here, with the daughter fathered by her son's best friend.

She told me all of this openly, even speaking in front of Sharif. Such behaviour was inconceivable in our culture. It was as if she lived on a different planet to my own. I told her as much. I told her that she had put herself in the fire by her own actions. How could she have done this? Had she lost her mind? She said that it wasn't so unusual in British culture. People might be married but they'd always be having affairs. I didn't know whether to believe her or not.

Frances kept dropping in. We couldn't be unwelcoming, even though half the time she was blind drunk. Part of me was concerned for her and I wanted to help. Each time we would cook her some food and try to cheer her up. Eventually, Sharif fixed a glass spyhole to our door. Whenever she came round and I couldn't face her I just didn't open up. I felt bad doing so – it was wrong in our culture – but I just couldn't keep inviting her into our lives.

One morning Sharif went out to buy some bread for breakfast. Frances had been round the previous night and she had eaten us out of house and home. He was away for ages, and I wondered what might have kept him. I went down to put out the rubbish, and as I did so I caught sight of two policemen just across the street. They were speaking with Sharif. I felt a bolt of panic shoot through me as the nearest took something shiny out of his pocket. An instant later he had handcuffed himself to my husband.

Oh my God! What was happening? Where were they taking Sharif? *Where were they taking him?*

I dashed across the road. 'What's happening? What're you doing?'

The policeman stared at me for a second. 'Sorry, love, but we've been told to take him . . . Who're you, anyway?'

'He's my husband . . . But why are you taking him? What for?'

The other policeman pulled out a notebook and pen. 'First off, love, we'll need your full name and date of birth.'

I told him. He made a radio call to check that I was who I said I was. Then they explained that they were taking Sharif to the police station. They had spoken with the Home Office, and my husband was slated for immediate deportation to Sudan.

'Look, I know this is tough on you, love,' the policeman added. 'But it isn't easy for us either. We're just doing our job.'

A car pulled alongside and Sharif was bundled in. The policeman scribbled down the address of the police station and handed it to me.

'Bring any personal effects,' the policeman told me. 'Anything he might want – a change of clothes, that sort of thing.'

As the car pulled away Sharif was gazing out of the window at me. I realised that I hadn't even been given the chance to say goodbye.

I felt the claws of fear tearing at my heart. They had taken Sharif. *They had taken him!* Surely that was it now? What on earth was I to do? Who could help him now? I thought of Samantha, the nursery-school teacher. Surely she would help. I tried calling her, but there was no reply. I felt mounting panic. I was alone on the street, I'd left little Mo in the flat, and Sharif was being sent back to Sudan. *What was I to do?*

All of a sudden I thought of David, the man from the Aegis Trust. I called his mobile. It rang and rang and for a moment I thought he wasn't going to answer. At the sound of his voice I burst into tears.

'They've taken Sharif!' I wailed. 'They've taken him. They're sending him back . . .'

'Who's taken him?' David asked. 'And why?'

'The police. They took him just now. I don't know why. But they're going to deport him . . .'

'All right, look, d'you know the address where they're holding him?'

I gave David the name of the police station.

'Okay, this is what we'll do. First, call your asylum lawyer and ask if there's anything he can do to stay the deportation. Okay?'

'Yes, I'll try.'

'I'm going to call some press. If I can get them to you, are you happy to go to the police station with them?'

'Of course. Anything. We have to stop them.'

'Right, I'll call you back as soon as I know any more.'

The phone went dead. I rushed upstairs to comfort little Mo. I'd heard him crying from the street, and I thanked God that he didn't know what was happening to his father. Mo was the spitting image of his dad, and he and Sharif were so close. Sharif was very liberated for a Zaghawa man. He would carry little Mo everywhere in his arms, like a proud father. Normally Zaghawa men would leave all that 'baby stuff' to the mother.

Almost immediately David came back on the phone. He hadn't been able to raise the BBC, but he'd spoken to Channel 4 News. They had a car on its way to me, complete with a camera crew and a reporter. He couldn't guarantee it, but he hoped that media pressure might force the Home Office to stay Sharif's deportation.

I rushed about, getting Mo and myself ready. I was angry now, and I sensed Grandma Sumah's fiery spirit rising within me. I recognised the Channel 4 team from the previous interview. We headed for the police station, where the cameraman set up his equipment on the street – the camera looking directly into the station doorway. The reporter readied herself for action. Together, we walked in with the camera rolling. I caught sight of Sharif sitting in a side room. I pointed him out to the reporter.

She marched up to the desk and announced who she was. She had a microphone clipped to her collar, so the sound could be recorded by the camera outside. She demanded to speak to Sharif; and she asked to interview a police spokesperson who might explain to her why they were about to deport a man to a country where his life was in danger.

'They're refugees from the war in Darfur,' she said. 'I presume you do know what's happening in Darfur? Several hundred thousand killed, mostly women and children. Millions of refugees . . . Not exactly the nicest of places to send someone back to . . .'

The police spokesperson said that they were only acting on instructions. He showed us a fax from the Home Office. It ordered Sharif to go to the Reporting Centre, from where they would deport him. Strictly speaking Sharif wasn't under arrest, he said, so they had no problem with him doing an interview. He was allowed out onto the street, where he spoke to the reporter for several minutes about the fearful prospect of being sent back to Sudan. Then I spoke about the trauma and pain of having our family torn apart.

Eventually, the police told us that Sharif was free to make his own way to the Reporting Centre. The Channel 4 crew needed to rush back to the studio, in order to get the story on air that evening. It was an outrage what they were doing to us, the reporter said, and the story was bound to have a big impact. As for Sharif, he knew what he had to do now. He had no choice but to disappear. He said a hurried goodbye to me there on the street, hugged little Mo tightly, and then he was gone, shouldering his way into the crowd.

I spoke with David later that day. It turned out that there had been mass arrests all across the country. Darfuris were being held in dozens of locations, pending their deportation to Sudan. Even more worrying was the legal background to all of this. The House of Lords was about to hear a case arguing that it wasn't safe to return Darfuris to Khartoum. The Home Office were expected to lose, and so it now looked as if they were trying to deport as many of us as they possibly could, before they lost that hearing.

The only reason that Sharif had managed to escape was because I had a profile in the media, and that gave us a little bit of power. Even so, they hadn't stopped hunting for him. A week later they came for him again. I was woken at six in the morning by a hammering on the door. I opened up to find a mixture of policemen in uniforms and plain clothes. The plain-clothes officers showed me their ID. They were peering around me into the room, and I knew that they were searching for Sharif.

'What do you want?' I asked.

'Who's here with you?' one of them countered.

'There's my son. That's all.'

I opened the door wide so they could see into the room. A policewoman in uniform took a couple of steps inside. She caught sight of little Mo fast asleep on the bed. Mo must have felt her eyes on him, for he woke up and started wailing.

'I'm sorry,' the policewoman said. 'The baby ... D'you mind if I check the other rooms?'

I shrugged. 'There are no other rooms. But go ahead.'

She poked her head around the corner of the walk-in kitchen and shower. As she did so, the plain-clothes officers started knocking on the doors of the other flats. I heard them asking if 'Mustaffa' was there. I didn't know if they'd simply got Sharif's name wrong, or if they were trying to be clever or something. I didn't really care.

'Do you know where your husband is?' the policewoman asked.

I shook my head. 'No, I don't. And his name is Sharif. *Sharif.* Not Mustaffa.'

'You've no idea where he might be?'

'I last saw him when he was told to go to the Reporting Centre. Since that day I haven't seen him.'

'And you don't know where he is now?'

'I don't. I would like to know. Sharif is my husband, and the father of my baby.'

They left, the policewoman apologising again for disturbing me. I knew that she was just doing her job. She'd tried to be nice to me, and to treat me with respect. The police here were a joy, in comparison to the rapists and murderers that I had faced in Sudan.

The following morning I went on GMTV. I talked about the way in which my people were being sent back to Sudan to face arrest, torture and worse. I knew what would happen to them at the hands of the authorities, for look what had been done to me.

Sharif remained in hiding. I spoke to David regularly, and he told me that the situation was worsening. In some cases whole families were being seized and threatened with deportation. Some had been deported already. David had tracked two Darfuri men to Khartoum, where they had been arrested and tortured. David had managed to get them out of Sudan, to a place where it was safe to record their horrific stories, and see the proof of the scars of torture on their bodies – stories that he had fed into the international media. Yet still the Home Office was trying to deport people.

I was angry, and my anger just wouldn't go away. Sharif was angry, and getting angrier by the day. I spoke to him on his mobile phone. He told me that he was reaching the stage where he *wanted* to be deported. He hated this country and what it was doing to us, to him. I told him that he couldn't leave without Mo and me. Either we would all go and face the horror, or we would all stay. But he wasn't going back there alone.

For two months Sharif remained in hiding, and then the House of Lords issued its judgement. The Home Office had lost, the Lords ruling that Khartoum was not a safe place to return Darfuri asylum seekers. The deportations had to cease. I called Sharif. I gave him the news. For now at least he was safe. He could return to us. He could come back to me and little Mo. For now at least we could be a family again.

I sat Mo on my lap and jiggled him up and down. I sang a little song for him. It was what my parents had sung to me when I was still a child.

> *Come here my love,*
> *I have a song for you.*
> *Come here my love,*
> *I have a dream for you . . .*

Epilogue

Every night after I finished working on this book, I would go to bed in my one-roomed flat in London and see in my dreams all the people who had died. I saw the fields of dead children. The rape victims. The burned villages. The slaughter. I saw the dead of my family, my loved ones.

During my darkest moments I concluded that for those who had died, life had perhaps dealt them the better hand – for the living have to live with the memories and the trauma every day, for the rest of their lives. The survivors live every day with the dark and empty holes where much-loved fathers, brothers, mothers and children used to be.

For me, the scars run deep and will take many a year to heal.

One day as I was working on the writing, a police helicopter started to circle overhead, again and again and again. It was obviously tracking a joy-rider, or something similar. With the repeated thud-thud-thud of the rotor blades, I started to become increasingly fraught.

I covered my ears with my hands and curled up in the chair. I became increasingly panicked. 'It's inside my head . . . Inside my head . . . Deep inside my head . . .' I kept repeating.

I was back in the hell of the day when the helicopter gunships attacked my village, followed by the murderous Janjaweed militia.

For the wider victims of the Darfur conflict it will take lifetimes for the trauma to heal. That's if it ever will.

It is now almost six years since the conflict in Darfur began. Some 400,000 people have died in the conflict in Darfur, and over two and a half million have been forced into vast, chaotic refugee camps – which in themselves are places of hopelessness and suffering.

Time after time, the world has been alerted to the slaughter and the rape and the horror.

The word 'genocide' has been used, and the phrase 'never again' has been repeatedly heard on the lips of world leaders. But what has actually been done to stop the slaughter?

No one should underestimate the ongoing severity of the situation in Darfur. The following are quotes from highly authoritative sources from 2007 and early 2008, concerning the ongoing crisis in Darfur:

United Nations Humanitarian Coordinator for Sudan, Manuel Aranda da Silva, said this about Darfur: 'The situation is worse than it has ever been . . . The violence and the threat to humanitarian workers continues unabated.'

United Nations World Food Programme spokesperson, Simon Crittle, reported that: 'The humanitarian situation in Darfur remains absolutely critical. At any time we could face a catastrophe if the security situation gets worse than it is already.'

A spokesperson for Médecins Sans Frontières (Doctors Without Borders/MSF), which has more than two thousand staff on the ground in Darfur, stated that: 'It is very difficult for aid workers to move outside the camps, which means it is hard to do exploratory missions to areas where there is need. The situation is very bad and is not getting better.'

Aid agency Danish Church Aid concluded that: 'We continue to work in Darfur despite the worsening security situation . . .

The situation in Sudan's Western Darfur province is worsening by the day.'

British aid agency Oxfam spokesperson, Alun Macdonald, declared that Darfur 'is certainly the most dangerous that it has been . . . Every place we work has had a security incident in the last three months. If it gets much worse we would certainly have to consider if we can stay at all.'

Matthew Conway, the UN's Chad spokesperson for the Office of the High Commissioner for Refugees, stated of the humanitarian crisis: 'The scale is mind-boggling. Complete desolation and destruction. And the stench, my God, the stench.' Commenting on the ethnically targeted violence, Conway concluded: 'We are seeing elements that closely resemble what we saw in Rwanda in the genocide of 1994.'

UN Undersecretary for Humanitarian Affairs, Jan Egeland, gave a briefing to the United Nations Security Council, declaring: 'Our entire humanitarian operation in Darfur – the only lifeline for more than three million people – is presently at risk. We need immediate action on the political front to avoid a humanitarian catastrophe with massive loss of life . . . In short, we may end up with a man-made catastrophe of an unprecedented scale in Darfur.'

The action that has been taken on the political level is to mandate a United Nations peacekeeping force for the Darfur region. The UN/African Union Hybrid Mission in Darfur (UNAMID) mandates some 26,000 troops to go in on the ground in Darfur, to stop the conflict.

In theory, UNAMID went into action in December 2007, but its implementation has been less than easy. In practice the force remains chronically undermanned, badly resourced and with little of the military hardware (i.e. helicopters) required to deploy in such a remote and challenging region.

So compromised is UNAMID that the UN's own Undersecretary

for Peacekeeping Operations, Jean-Marie Guehenno, talked of the mission failing even before it was begun.

'Do we move ahead with the deployment of a force that will not make a difference?' Guehenno asked. '[A force] that will not have the capacity to defend itself and that carries the risk of humiliation of the Security Council and the United Nations, and tragic failure for the people of Darfur?'

At the start of 2008, when the UNAMID peacekeepers were supposed to be on the ground in force, Jean-Marie Guehenno stressed that insecurity in Darfur had reached unprecedented levels.

While the peacekeepers fail to take hold on the ground, the humanitarian crisis has continued unabated. In 2007, some 300,000 newly displaced people flooded into already chronically over-crowded refugee camps, bringing the total to 2.6 million internally displaced persons (IDPs) and refugees.

In December 2007, the UN issued a stark report warning of the effect the delay to the UNAMID peacekeepers going in is having on the ground. 'As a result people in Darfur are beginning to lose hope, and that may be another factor taking a toll on their health ... These people have been in these camps for years now, and the energy that was around a few years ago and the hopes that this situation might soon be over and people could go home – all that's gone now.'

Who is responsible for this failure to act to stop the Darfur crisis? On one level, it is the international community that has failed to muster an effective and robust peacekeeping force – one armed and manned and mandated to stop a brutal, genocidal conflict.

On another level it is the Khartoum government – the National Islamic Front (which has recently re-branded itself the National Congress Party) – that does everything in its power to frustrate international efforts to halt the 'genocide by attrition' that is ongoing in Darfur. This includes repeatedly flouting UN Security Council resolutions designed to bring about an end to the killing.

In January 2008, in just one incident alone, the armed forces of the Sudan government deliberately attacked a UNAMID transport convoy. This attack was designed to shock and intimidate the barely nascent peacekeeping force, while signalling to the world community that Khartoum would continue to act with impunity in Darfur.

Khartoum's obstruction of the peacekeeping mission is its way of most publicly defying the efforts of the international community to bring about an end to the suffering. How is it able to defy world opinion, repeatedly flout UN Security Council resolutions, and fly in the face of a robust stance taken by the United States, in particular, on Darfur?

The answer here is largely China. China's unquestioning support for the Sudanese regime – disregarding its long record of brutality and horrific excess – takes powerful economic, military and diplomatic form.

China has repeatedly abstained from or blocked or significantly weakened a series of United Nations Security Council resolutions on Darfur, and each time to the advantage of the Khartoum regime.

China has effectively empowered Khartoum to defy the international community at its will. Why has China done so? The answer is oil. China is a net importer of oil, with an increasing thirst for energy. Its greatest single overseas supplier is Sudan, which pumps some 500,000 barrels per day of oil. China is also the largest single investor in Sudan today.

China's cosy relationship with Khartoum is even more sinister. Much of the petro-dollar that China pays to Sudan for oil is returned to China in arms purchases. During the period of Sudan's growing oil production, China has become the regime's leading arms supplier – providing the tanks, artillery and aircraft that have been used to wreak such devastation in Darfur.

Despite a United Nations arms embargo on Darfur, the UN Panel of Experts on Darfur has repeatedly found that Khartoum completely ignores that embargo. Human rights group Amnesty International has reported that among those weapons shipped into Darfur are arms and military supplies of Chinese manufacture.

So confident is Khartoum of its ability to defy the international community that it has – in effect – laughed in the face of the United Nations and the International Criminal Court (ICC) in The Hague. In March 2005, the United Nations referred the case of war crimes in Darfur for investigation by the ICC.

In the spring of 2007, the ICC issued its first indictments, charging a Janjaweed militia leader, Ali Kushyb, and a political official, Ahmed Haroun, with a broad range of crimes against humanity. Khartoum has not only refused to extradite both men to face charges, but has treated the ICC indictment with shocking contempt, and promoted Haroun.

The ICC's Chief Prosecutor, Luis Moreno-Ocampo, has repeatedly called for Haroun to be handed over for trial. 'When will be a better time to arrest Haroun? How many more women, girls have to be raped? How many more persons have to be killed? . . . What is at stake is, simply, the life and death of 2.5 million people.'

This year, 2008, is the sixtieth anniversary of the original Genocide Convention, the long-fought-for international agreement whereby genocide was outlawed as a crime against humanity, and where countries of the world signed up to an agreement to stamp it out, once and for all.

This is the key phrase of the Convention: 'The Contracting Parties confirm that genocide, whether committed in time of peace or time of war, is a crime under international law which they undertake to prevent and punish.'

The fate of the people of Darfur now rests upon the success of the UNAMID peacekeeping mission, and its ability to enable the aid agencies to continue feeding and caring for several million internally displaced people and refugees.

In Darfur, it is high time that that phrase 'prevent and punish' was made a reality.

~

As of the date of writing this book, I have not been able to find my family, or make contact with them. I will keep searching.

Halima Bashir
London, February 2008

In May 2008 Halima won her case and was granted asylum/refugee status in the UK, along with her family.

GLOSSARY

Arabic–English

acidah – maize mash

angrheb – a funeral bed

bataniyah – bed cover

bhirish – a white burial shroud

damirgha – durum wheat porridge

Fakir – Muslim holy man and healer

fustan – dress like girl's school uniform

halal – allowed

haram – forbidden

haribah – fire

hijab – an Islamic totem prepared by a Fakir, to be worn

immah – turban

khawaja – white man

kissra – sorghum pancakes

mehia – an Islamic totem prepared by a Fakir, to be drunk

muslaiyah – Muslim prayer rug

nephirh – state of national emergency

shahid – martyred

Zaghawa–English

aba – father

abu – grandma

agadi – Zaghawa gold necklace

agadim – possibly mythical wolf-like creature
Ahrao – the Arab enemy
Arab hagareen – 'the Arabs treat us like animals'
baa – a house
beeri – traditional Zaghawa woman's hairstyle
birgi – plant used for medicine
eya – mother
fangasso – sweet fried doughnuts
foul – bean stew
garagaribah – spatula for making sorghum pancakes
gini – a hamlet
goro – sorghum beer
gory – stockade for livestock
gubhor – locusts
gumbhor – traditional Fur woman's hairstyle
herdih – horses
hiry carda – cowboy
hjar – leopard
jahoub kadai – scarecrow
kawal – dark savoury powder made from fermented plant
keyoh adum jaghi gogo keyh – 'let's play the moon-bone game'
koii – a measure of drinking water
libah – goat's milk pudding, made from colostrum
molletah – salad made from leafy plant
mousarran – dried animal intestines
nasarra – foreigners
orwa – firewood
pirgi – a medicinal tree
sinya nee – the time when someone knows they are about to die
tagro – a container made from a gourd
taihree – circumcision woman
tibrih – gold, the money-saver
zit karkar – hair oil

The Aegis Trust

The Aegis Trust, founded in 2000, is the leading NGO working to prevent genocide worldwide. Based at The Holocaust Centre, which opened in 1995, Aegis coordinates the UK All-Party Parliamentary Group for Genocide Prevention and is responsible for the Kigali Memorial Centre in Rwanda, which commemorates the 1994 genocide and plays a vital role in educating a new generation about the dangers of ethnic division.

Since 2004, Aegis has been at the forefront of the campaign to end the Darfur crisis. It successfully campaigned for referral of Darfur to the International Criminal Court, has helped to organise the global 'Day for Darfur' demonstrations, and continues to work for an end to the removal of Darfuri survivors – such as Halima – from the UK to Khartoum as failed asylum seekers. Last year, it rescued two Darfuris from Khartoum who had been tortured after being sent back from the UK.

Aegis is responsible for 'Fund for Darfur', an initiative launched in December 2007 to provide support in the region to Darfuri survivors of systematic rape, torture and mass atrocities, and to assist destitute survivors outside Darfur in places such as the UK.

For more information: visit www.fund4darfur.org

To find out more about the Aegis Trust and how you can offer your support or get involved: visit www.aegistrust.org

Waging Peace

In early 2007 a Waging Peace researcher was carrying out inter-
views with refugees who had crossed the border from Sudan
into neighbouring Chad. While she was doing so some of the
women encouraged her to speak to the children. After talking
to them about what they wanted to do when they grew up she
gave them crayons and paper and asked them to draw their
most vivid memories.

While some of the children drew pictures of their schools and
villages before the attack, most depicted the destruction of their
homes, the murders of their family and neighbours and the fleeing
of survivors.

What they drew contradicted all the Sudanese government denials
of involvement as tanks, planes and helicopters bearing Sudanese
flags rampage through villages and towns in many of the 500
drawings Waging Peace collected. Some of the children were
as young as six when Janjaweed militias and government troops
stormed into their villages, destroying homes and killing and
raping family members.

The pictures were brought back to London, where they featured
on the front page of the *Independent* newspaper, as well as a
number of European publications. The pictures have since been
presented to the International Criminal Court by Waging Peace,
where they will be used as contextual evidence, helping jurors

in any future cases understand the devastation that the Darfur conflict has brought to hundreds and thousands of children.

This is just one element of Waging Peace's work; the organisation continues to conduct research on the ground, lobby international agencies and inform the public about the conflict. It is funded through donations so can only survive on the generosity of others who are dedicated as it is to ending the genocide in Darfur.

If you would like to donate or know more about Waging Peace please visit www.wagingpeace.info/